HEART OF STONE

HEART
OF
STONE
THE UNAUTHORIZED
LIFE OF MICK JAGGER

LAURA JACKSON

BLAKE

To my very special husband David

Published in Great Britain in 1998 by
Blake Publishing Ltd
3 Bramber Court
2 Bramber Road
London W14 9PB

The Publishers would like to make it clear that at no point
did Ms Jackson speak with Marsha Hunt, and that the information
regarding Ms Hunt was taken from her autobiography.

A CIP catalogue for this book is available from the British Library

ISBN 1 85782 213 7

Designed by Hammond Hammond
Typeset by BCP
Printed and bound in Great Britain by
Creative Print and Design (Wales), Ebbw Vale, Gwent

3 5 7 9 10 8 6 4 2

CONTENTS

Acknowledgements   vi

1. DARTFORD DAYS   1
2. STEPPING STONE   11
3. JAGGER'S JEALOUSIES   23
4. READY, STEADY, SEX!   33
5. HIGH TIMES AND GOOD GRASS   53
6. DRUGS AND DEVIATION   73
7. RIFTS AND RIVALRY   89
8. DEATH KNELL OF THE SIXTIES   105
9. HEART OF STONE   121
10. DUCKING 'N' DIVING   139
11. BAWDY LANGUAGE   153
12. TROUBLE AND STRIFE   171
13. COSTLY AFFAIRS   189
14. SEXUAL INDISCRETIONS   199
15. ROUGH RIDE   213
16. UNDER PRESSURE   227
17. MARRIAGE OF CONVENIENCE   239
18. PLAYING AWAY   249
19. ROUÉ OF ROCK   257

Index   273

ACKNOWLEDGEMENTS

Grateful appreciation to all those people whom I interviewed for their time and trouble, as well as their honesty. My thanks for all contributions to: Richard H Allen; Ian Anderson; Pat Andrews; Eileen Atkins; Bachir el Attar; Ginger Baker; Chris Barber OBE; Virginia, The Lady Bath; The Marquess of Bath; Dave Berry; Allan Clarke; Lady Chryssie Lytton Cobbold; Ray Davies; Gary Glitter; Rolf Harris; Werner Herzog; David Jacobs; B.B. King; Amanda Lear; Michael Lindsay-Hogg; John Mansfield; Gerry Marsden; Phil May; Malcolm McLaren; Stanley Meadows; Harold Pendleton; Janie Perrin; Mary Peters CBE; Mark Rankin; Noel Redding; Lord William Rees-Mogg; Lord Rossmore; Robert Stigwood; Dick Taylor; Robert Woods; Mary Whitehouse CBE; Vicki Wickham.

Also for their help: British Film Institute; Dartford Grammar School (Mr D. J. Patterson); Dartford Library (P.M. Stevens); Sherman Derby; Elgin Library staff; European Institute for the Media (Achim Kaemmerer); Al Garthwaite; Bernice Gibson; H.P. Bookfinders; Russell Leadbetter; National Film Archive, Paris; National VALA (John C. Beyer); John Oliver; RTL2, Munich; Col Sir John Ruggles-Brise; Unique Pictures, Elgin. Special thanks to David for his invaluable research and unwavering support as always every step of the way; also to publisher John Blake; Executive Editor, Adam Parfitt; and Production Editor, Charlotte Helyar for all their help.

1

DARTFORD DAYS

JUST AFTER NOON on 18 August 1997, months of speculation about whether or not the Rolling Stones were about to undertake a major world tour came to an end when Mick Jagger, at the wheel of a flashy 1955 red Cadillac convertible, ferried himself, Keith Richards, Charlie Watts and Ron Wood across New York's Brooklyn Bridge to announce the tour to waiting press assembled on the waterfront. Sprinting into the journalists' midst, Jagger himself voiced the first inevitable question: 'Could this be the last time?' Realistically, of course, it could be. A slick, professional and spectacularly triumphant finale to bring the curtain down on an astounding and colourful career. But nothing can be taken for granted with the Rolling Stones. Nor with Jagger, not since he first began back in 1962 to front a raw rhythm and blues band with attitude.

Jagger's life has been one of licentious upheaval, of sex, drugs and rock 'n' roll. He started out and still remains the focus of intense media attention in his long and raucous professional career. His fortune by 1997 was said to be around £120 million. Yet, in good old rock-music tradition it was all a far cry from his modest beginnings.

Michael Philip Jagger was born during World War Two in south-east England at Livingstone Hospital in Dartford, Kent, on 26 July 1943. He was by all accounts a baby quite happy to lie smilingly in his cot and in no hurry to walk. His mother, Eva, had worked as a hairdresser and later sold make-up for Avon cosmetics, but her main preoccupation in life was her home. Neighbours were said to be struck by her social pretensions. His father Basil, known as Joe, was a physical education teacher at a local school and as fanatical about fitness as his wife was about cleaning. College educated, he would write a book on basketball, and eventually secure a place on the British Sports Council.

Home was 3 Brentlands House, Brent Lane, but his parents soon moved to the less down market West Dartford and 39 Denver Road, where Jagger's brother, Christopher Edward, was born on 19 December 1947. Jagger had just started Maypole infants school by then, and maybe the disruption caused by the arrival of the new baby made him the aggressive boy that his teachers there recalled. It was Chris Jagger's lot to be forever in his older brother's shadow; from an early age he also endured the usual physical rough and tumble common between brothers, the jockeying for position. That is not to say that discipline at home was slack. Joe was a strict father, and, when justified, would hit his boys. Whatever Jagger got up to behind his parents' backs, on the face of it he made sure he seldom disobeyed either of them.

Jagger was born with a head of red hair, which mellowed to a mousy brown, and his looks were saved from ordinariness by his outsize lips, which, when he smiles, almost crack his face in two. Over time his nature became controlling, anchored by a cold detachment, which may be rooted in his upbringing. Once a star Jagger remained acutely conscious of his mother's aspirations, yet he would bluntly describe her as 'very working class' and his father as 'bourgeois', maintaining that he fell somewhere vaguely, and by implication dissatisfyingly, in between.

His daily routine was, by contrast, very clearly defined. The back yard at Denver Road served as the family's private gym, and, starting them young, Joe drilled his sons in various fitness regimes. A fit body equalled an agile brain he insisted, and it began to show.

Jagger's early aggression mellowed into an overall restlessness. He now scarcely walked when he could sprint and ran around generally making an effort, so much so that by the time he left Maypole he had changed from a difficult pupil to one of their favourites.

In the second week of January 1951 Jagger enrolled at Wentworth County Primary school, only a short walk from his home. Here his sunny disposition would win him friends, among them one Keith Richard. He too was born in Livingstone hospital, one week before Christmas 1943. At the age of seven, both boys were of slight build, Richard with a mop of black hair and prominent ears.

While the Jaggers considered themselves middle class the Richards were strictly working class, his father Bert Richards being employed at a local lightbulb factory. With his father and mother, Doris, Richard lived at 33 Chastilian Road.

Reflecting on this early period Jagger later remarked, 'We weren't great friends then, but we knew each other.' It wasn't a wrench when three years later they were separated by the Jaggers moving house again. The Richards family were themselves relocated to a soulless housing scheme in a rough part of town. In contrast the Jaggers moved to leafy middle-class Wilmington and a three-bedroom detached, whitewashed house complete with fruit trees, extensive garden and a driveway.

Joe was on the central council of physical recreation and launched the Kent County Basketball League. He felt completely at home there, commuting to work in London in the company of his neighbours, mostly professional people, and Eva was in her element in the provincial gentility of London's south-eastern commuter belt. In accordance with their new status, their annual holiday destinations grew ever more exotic. Previously they had basked in southern Spain, but in 1954, Jagger had his first glimpse of the glamour of the French Riviera and St Tropez.

Jagger returned from France with a cheap acoustic guitar round his neck. He liked it apparently because he thought it made him look cool. But, as his brother later vouched, 'Mike had no interest in music. He didn't take piano lessons or anything like that.'

So far Jagger had not proved to be especially bookish either, but as the 11-plus selection exams approached he applied himself to ensure he passed. With his parents only too happy to encourage him, his efforts paid off. He also passed the entrance exam for Dartford Grammar School and started there in mid-September, clad in its strictly enforced uniform – navy blazer, charcoal trousers, tie and cap.

For the first three years there Jagger was a model pupil. Teachers remember him as willing to learn, and Jagger later maintained that until he was 15 he did nothing but study. As at primary school, so at Dartford Grammar he showed no signs of being disruptive, verging on being a teacher's pet, something that rendered him unpopular among some of his peers. Among his friends though was classmate Dick Taylor.

'I lived in Bexleyheath,' says Taylor, 'which was very much the suburbs of London, built up in the thirties and with long stretches of back yards. Mick on the other hand lived in Wilmington, a village just outside, but which was a world away. It always seemed very American, white middle-class suburbia, where the houses were quite roomy. I was 11 when I first met him, and we went right through school together. He was quite sporty, into basketball and stuff. He wasn't much interested in music until like the rest of us he got into jazz and rock 'n' roll a few years later.

'Dartford Grammar wanted to be straitlaced, but it was a losing battle. They always dinned into us that it was Britain's first grammar school to have its own army and RAF cadet corps, and I think they would have wanted to reach greater heights. Some of the teachers had actually fought in the war, which had opened up their minds a bit, and there was one particular biology teacher who was as much a Ted as the boys. He was absolutely terrific, and we could all relate to him. But the headmaster was a horrible little man. He was short so we called him Lofty. Boy, had he a glint in his eye. He could fix anybody from a great distance in a crowded assembly with his beady stare. An ex-teacher told me later that we'd been the smartest class they had, but quite vicious to one another.'

Jagger had no such reputation, but rather one of being a good mimic. He enjoyed practising on his elders, which one of his teachers found insufferable. It was perhaps an early sign of Jagger's later trademark lack of respect for authority.

As a teenager Jagger did not strike up particular friendships. After school he hardly went out and invited no one home. Yet he wanted to be popular. Or, more to the point, he wanted to stand out.

His chance came with his father's consultancy on an ATV series, *Seeing Sport*, designed to encourage youngsters to take up various sporting activities. Jagger appeared on the show demonstrating how to paddle a canoe or scale a rockface. To be on the telly was prestigious, and Jagger loved the attention it drew. He later confessed, 'I was a star already. I was thinking, Never mind the bloody canoe, how does my hair look!' Effortlessly then he had achieved minor celebrity. And he took delight in it – a natural showman.

As his adolescence progressed, Jagger joined the basketball team and was appointed captain. But he had no interest in holding school office or in being a team player, or indeed in music. He failed to make selection for the choir. What he was keen on was being high profile, on being visible. A reputation as someone with an eye for the girls and a rebellious nature were ways to achieve this.

As a teenager Jagger was never conventionally handsome. But he had something. And in time-honoured adolescent tradition he bragged to his mates about his considerable hands-on experience with girls. As an adult he claimed to have had his 'first screw' at the age of 12 with not one but two girls, in a potting shed. He'd later earn a reputation for having a bad memory, as in fact it would be several more years before he lost his virginity. Not something any young man would ever have admitted to in his teens.

As for rebellion, these tales, though rooted in reality, have become embellished over time, as his ex-form master, Richard Allen recalls.

'Mick of course has become Dartford Grammar's most famous living old boy, but he was not in my recollection particularly distinguished in any way at school and certainly not known as a rebel.'

It would seem that he began to indulge in minor infractions like skiving off the weekly cross-country run, chancing a choke on the odd cigarette or squeezing his whippet-like frame into tighter trousers than the regulation school uniform. He did grow bolder at pushing his luck at trying the headmaster's patience by displaying a faint but discernible contempt. Yet, shrewdly, he never crossed the line nor landed himself in any real trouble, neither at school nor at home, where he still obeyed his parents without question.

'His dad expected him to do daily workouts, weight lifting,' Dick Taylor recalls. 'Mick would immediately jump to it. There were times when he and I were leaving the house, and Joe would call him back to do press-ups, and he'd drop everything and get down and do them on the spot. That alone was unusual but it wasn't until he was about 19 and still obeying his parents to the letter when the rest of the country's younger generation was breaking away, that I thought it was really strange. I have a clear memory later on of Mick, myself and Brian [Jones], at his parents' house for a meal when we had formed the Rollin' Stones and us all having to say grace first. That was the kind of home it was.'

But outside those four walls there was a brave new world. By the late fifties the music scene was energized by the emergence of rock 'n' roll. It had a verve and vitality that couldn't help but get through to Jagger. It was in the air, he would see it on TV, on *Cool for Cats*, *6.5 Special* and *Oh Boy*. But although Bill Haley and Elvis Presley intrigued him, one of the strongest attractions for Jagger was the American lifestyle itself. Jagger was impressed by its spirit of opportunity, and for a while he affected a bad American accent declaring that for him 'the States is where it's at'. The influence of the United States was vast at the time and new and refreshing. Jagger equated success in music with the attainment of the things he desired most in life. Although he would soon be involved in his first band, his primary objective remained making money from what he liked doing. Music could be a vehicle to what he wanted, which in common with lots of adolescent kids, was to own a big car.

Despite the razzmatazz of rock 'n' roll Jagger's tastes settled on the music that originated from the Mississippi Delta. Black blues had been around for ever but were now reaching out to a wider audience to ignite the rock 'n' roll revolution. Jagger was interested initially in Big Bill Broonzy and Muddy Waters. But his first love was the raucous and outrageous Little Richard. It was a passion Dick Taylor shared.

'Well, it was the era of luminous socks, wasn't it?' he says. 'The rock 'n' roll fashions had really infiltrated, but the artists who inspired us – Little Richard, Chuck Berry and Jerry Lee Lewis – had a pretty amazing effect on us all round. Although it's important to say that a lot of jazz and blues had already been around for a while in Britain so we weren't totally ignorant. Muddy Waters and Broonzy had been taken over here by Chris Barber, but it was so hard at our age to get to see them live. You could import the new records if you could afford to. You could also pick up the odd album outside Soho record shops if you knew where to look but it was difficult to really satisfy our need at the time.'

To counter this Taylor started a band, which Jagger joined as singer.

'Mick and I had already spent a lot of time together,' he says, 'and along with some other guys shared an interest at least in listening to the same type of music. There was a bunch of us to start with, but, gradually, we thinned out until there were just four. Mick and Alan Etherington had known each other since primary school, and Bob Beckwith and I had likewise been friends for years. We started hanging out then, going to each other's houses to play records, but we ended up mainly at my mum's house. We were only at Mick's place a couple of times.'

The reason for this was that Joe considered his son's new interest a waste of time. Fats Domino and Chuck Berry records sounded like jungle music to him, and he often said so. But Jagger dug in his heels for once with his father, and with Taylor on drums, Etherington playing maracas and Beckwith on guitar, he had his first taste of fronting a band.

'We gelled. It wasn't a band I started with great things in mind,' Taylor recalls. 'We didn't even give ourselves a name at first, because we never played in front of anybody except my long-suffering mum. We really played for the sake of it and had no thought of appearing in public, I suppose because we never thought we were ready.'

Emboldened even by this covert frontline position Jagger considered stepping up his tilting at school authority. But he was best at creating the illusion of being a rebel, without really taking a stand. In any case he looked the part, which was half the battle, and probably as far as he could sensibly go with the somewhat repressive regime at home. Teachers now called him moody, and he perfected a sullen look, curling his thick lips into a perpetual sneer.

Outside school this disdainful mask could sometimes slip. Like on an evening when he was 15. Jagger and Taylor saw Buddy Holly and the Crickets at the Woolwich Odeon Theatre, where Taylor recalls how his friend closely studied Holly's movements. Likewise when Jagger watched the new bands on TV it was for ideas on how to act on stage. At home though he felt he got scant encouragement. His parents believed they were indulgent of him, but Jagger remembers it differently.

'My father was bloody awful,' he said years later. 'He was such a disciplinarian. He was a school teacher. I mean they're not known for their libertarianism. I wanted to be a musician. It was so obvious, and he just didn't want me to be.'

He was throwing himself with enthusiasm into the band's endless rehearsals.

'He jumped about a lot,' Taylor says, 'and was a good enough singer. He'd always been a great mimic and would listen to these Chuck Berry records, then try to pull off the overall sound. I'm sure he made up a lot of the words to "La Bamba", but the way he did it, it sounded all right to us. I can't say that any of us thought, Wow! What a talent! We were just grateful that he didn't make you wince!

'I had a small drum kit and played bloody awful, but it's because there was always such competition in bands to play guitar. Mick though was never interested in learning to play an instrument.' But he wanted to be a flamboyant front man. And he was right that he had a talent for showmanship. Or, at this stage, showing off.

Jagger was still interested in being seen as a young lady-killer. Though he was a bit skinny-looking, he was bold, brash and determined. He had by now got himself a girlfriend, a couple of years younger than him. What she apparently remembers vividly was Jagger's interest in make-up at that time. He enjoyed as much as she did experimenting with his mother's cosmetics. Maybe it was an outlet for his theatricality for which he had shown some talent. Or preparation for performing out front with the band. He still practised with them and had begun importing blues records direct from Chess Records in Chicago.

In the summer of 1959 Jagger gained passes in 7 O-Levels to enter the sixth form, his sights set on 3 A Levels, which he achieved. When Jagger turned 18, he got a place at the prestigious London School of Economics, part of London University, supported partially by a local-authority grant. His headmaster Hudson grudgingly predicted, 'He should be successful in his subjects although he is unlikely to do brilliantly in any of them.'

Jagger enjoyed the prestige of pursuing an economics degree at the LSE. It was one of the best university colleges in the UK. His grant was not large, however, so it made sense to continue living at home and commute into central London by train. After a couple of casual jobs as a Christmas postman and a porter at Bexley Mental Hospital, in late September 1961 he began what would become a daily routine for the next year or so. Breakfasting at home, he cycled to Dartford station for the train to London's Charing Cross, from where he made his way to the LSE. Within two weeks, though, he had bumped into an old acquaintance in jeans and denim jacket with upturned collar on Dartford station platform. It was a meeting that would put paid to his academic studies and set his life on a different course.

2

STEPPING STONE

*I*N THE INTERVENING years life had treated Keith Richard differently from Jagger. In the rough neighbourhood to which his family had moved he was seen as effeminate by the other kids. He had had to learn how to look after himself the hard way. Having failed the 11-plus he enrolled at Dartford Technical School but left without a diploma to enter Sidcup Art College. Until his voice broke at 12 he had sung in a church choir, and he has claimed that his dismissal from it turned him into a yob.

Subsequently his grandfather had introduced him to the guitar, and he had learnt the basics by ear. He listened to John Lee Hooker, Muddy Waters and Chuck Berry, and it was the Berry album under Jagger's arm that drew him into conversation with the man who had once been a childhood friend.

That meeting has been well documented and has gained the status of legend, but at the time there was little portentous about it. Dick Taylor already knew Keith Richard from Sidcup Art College.

'By this time Keith always wore the same thing – skintight jeans, denim jacket and a gaudy purple shirt, and he didn't seem to give a shit. He used to play Elvis records a lot and loved rock 'n' roll. He gave off an air of being a bit of a lad, but actually underneath it he was all right. At college we all used to congregate in the cloakroom to talk about music, and I didn't know it at that time, but Keith knew about the band Mick and I were in and had badly wanted to join us, but he'd been too shy to mention it. He was hoping to be asked.'

Of the meeting between Jagger and Richard that mid-October morning Dick says:

'It's such a hairy-moulded story now when really there wasn't much to it. Keith mentioned it to me in passing later that day, which got us talking about the band. I told him to come along and hear us which he did and next thing, he was in. Simple as that. In those days and certainly with a band like ours, which wasn't a serious deal, guys dropped in and out of line-ups all the time. Anyway with Keith on board we continued as before, listening and studying music, playing for our own amusement and to no one in particular.'

Jagger's first few weeks at the LSE had marked him out as a loner to the extent that a natural reticence was perhaps unfairly interpreted as standoffishness. But he soon loosened up, especially when he realized that he had the perfect chance here to vamp up his image. He amended his laddish account of how he lost his virginity by saying that it was while working as a hospital porter with a nymphomaniac nurse, standing up in a broom cupboard.

Revelling in his reputation and deriving increased self-confidence from it, he was spending more nights in London, staying in friends' flats instead of returning to Dartford. He had bad skin problems and a waiflike build, but it did not deter him from creating his image as a sexual athlete. Subtlety had never been his style, and now at every opportunity he put on a show of having a one-track mind.

At parties, he would single out the most attractive girl, wrap her in his arms and be frank about his urge to take her to bed, describing the delights in store for her. He enjoyed the wind-up and the reaction he provoked, even if the woman turned him down. Mostly it was just a case of messing about and of finding out who he was and what he wanted.

Jagger's LSE tutors saw the change in him from eager student to Teddy Boy with attitude. He'd been ambivalent about the course from an early stage, but it became clear to them that he was struggling with aspects of it. They advised a shift in direction, but the one he eventually took was probably not what his college tutors had envisaged.

Jagger's waning interest in the LSE may have had a lot to do with his friendship with Keith Richard and the influence they had on one another. Whereas they had not been very close as children, a firm bond was forged as 18 year olds. But there was a gap between them in circumstances and character. Jagger apparently preferred shrewdly to play by the rules if it got him what he wanted, while Richard had no respect for authority and no professional ambition whatsoever. Perhaps it was that anarchic attitude that Jagger admired – that and the buzz he got from knowing that Richard looked up to him.

Their common interest in Chuck Berry and more particularly in rhythm and blues cemented their friendship further. But Jagger wasn't sure that the band in which he sang was going to go anywhere. And blues bands rarely made any money, which was important to Jagger. The music held a strong attraction, but Jagger and the other enthusiasts with whom he hung out began to believe they were the only people in Britain to feel that way. But they were wrong, as they'd soon find out, courtesy of the man considered to be the father of British blues, Alexis Korner, a Turkish-Greek of Austrian descent.

In early 1962 trad jazz still dominated the British music scene, but a blues revival was beckoning. Trombone player Chris Barber, who led one of Britain's biggest jazz bands, had brought Muddy Waters over to perform in the UK in 1958 and had subsequently introduced a blues segment into his repertoire. For this, guitarist Korner and harmonica player Cyril Davis were enlisted to play electric R&B, fronted by vocalist Ottilie Paterson. Their sets proved a huge success, particularly at London's Marquee Club.

'In the mid-fifties Alexis had been playing folk clubs, and they wouldn't let him use an amplifier,' Chris Barber recalls. 'In 1959 he played with Muddy, and it was after that that he and I were responsible for getting the blues going in Britain. Alexis was very keen, but he wanted to play blues all night, and, as brass players, the rest of us said no. So he started his own club.'

Korner also formed Blues Incorporated, a revolutionary step as the first white blues band. This drew young R&B fanatics who felt threatened by the hostile reaction to their music from staunch traddies. Korner led a curious line-up. Besides the 15-stone harmonica player, there was Andy Hoogenboom, soon replaced by Jack Bruce, eventually bass guitarist with Cream. Tenor sax was handled with aloof detachment by Dick Heckstall Smith, and Dave Stevens played piano. The drummer was a dour young man called Charlie Watts. Korner advertised the emergence of his new blues club, located in west London's Ealing, in the *New Musical Express*. The action would take place in a small room beneath a teashop, and the first date was 17 March 1962.

That one ad sparked a migration of R&B enthusiasts from all over Britain. Dick Taylor remembers they were no exception.

'As soon as we saw it we had to go. Mick had newly passed his driving test and so he borrowed his dad's car and we all headed to London.

'Ealing club was a small hole in the ground opposite the Ealing Broadway tube station. It backed on to the railway, and you could hear the trains through the bedlam of the music. There was a bar at one end, the stage at the other. It wasn't always crammed to the ceiling, but there was always a great atmosphere. The place just reverberated to the blues, and it seemed pretty damned good stuff to us.'

The following two Saturdays saw Jagger descend the steep stone steps into the alley that led to the club, where he mixed with other future luminaries like Eric Clapton and Jeff Beck.

'We were overawed at first, but then we got cocky, thinking, Aw, we could do this! They're not so hot,' says Taylor. 'It only featured blues purists, and we were into Chuck Berry and Bo Diddley, and we began to feel the acts weren't into the super hip stuff like us.'

But before they had the chance to get too blasé they were knocked out by a young musician who'd been coming to the club since it opened, but to whom they had not been introduced.

Brian Jones had been friends with Alexis Korner for months and had frequently slept on his kitchen floor before moving to London permanently. He had been sitting in with Blues Inc fairly regularly. But it was 7 April that saw his first guest appearance, accompanied by his friend Paul Pond, an Oxford English undergraduate, better known today as Paul Jones, one-time front man with Manfred Mann. Immaculately dressed and playing a new Gibson Brian had selected the Elmore James classic 'Dust My Blues', on which to play breathtaking bar slide guitar.

Jones was the first slide guitarist in Britain, and as Jagger, Richard and Taylor walked in they could only stand and stare at the precision with which this serious-looking 20 year old created the inimitable Delta whine. Jagger, as Taylor recalls, was impressed. 'He just gaped and breathed, "Oh! Now he's *good!*"'

Well used to studying performers on TV and stage, analysing their gestures, memorizing their movements, Jagger found Jones a master of it. But what he most saw in Jones was a primitive and powerful sensuality. There was something mesmerizing about him, and Jagger liked that quality. It was what he wanted to achieve as a singer. He knew he could never match the intensity of Jones' guitar-work, but he appreciated his ability to manipulate a crowd.

That night Jones had used the stage name Elmo Lewis – half the name of his hero Elmore James and half his own name, Lewis Brian Hopkin-Jones.

'Brian was riveting,' recalls Dick Taylor. 'Both he and Paul were wearing shades, and Brian would occasionally turn his back on the audience while he was playing. He was dead calm.' In fact he wasn't. Jones had hidden his nervousness, and though exhilarated by his performance was only too glad to step off stage. As soon as he did, he was ambushed by Jagger et al, and they all moved to a corner table to talk blues for the rest of the night. After that they met often at the Ealing club.

'We were into R&B,' recalls Taylor, 'Muddy Waters and Robert Johnson, whom Brian was into in a heavy way, but the stuff we wanted to play was a little less classic blues.' It was a feeling shared by another of their friends, Richard's fellow student at Sidcup Art College, Phil May, later lead singer with the Pretty Things.

'I knew Keith first because he jammed with Dick Taylor and me in the college cloakrooms,' May says. 'My first connection with Mick, whom I met through Dick, was when he loaned me a batch of notebooks packed with lyrics of all these R&B songs. We'd go to any gigs we could in our area, but it was a pretty hard thing to do. To hear R&B you had to drag the streets. You put a *lot* of work into finding out where they were to be played and more often than not by the time you heard the rumour, you'd missed the gig and some geezer would come up to you raving about a blindingly great guy on harmonica the other night.

'It became a bit like trainspotting – enthusiasts had a network through which you'd try to get the word around. However, we didn't have the snobbery about R&B that was rife in London where there was very much a dividing line with the purists. That's why later on the Pretty Things and the Rolling Stones got slagged off. We started with the roots, but we speeded it up. It meant more to us that way. In London you got guys whose every breath and harmonica line was perfectly imitated, and we thought such precision was pointless. Keith particularly was more rock 'n' roll than R&B.'

Jagger's flexibility had more to do with keeping his options open. Blues Inc currently had no regular vocalist, and it was a feature of each Saturday night that anyone eager to perform could get up and sing with them. Soon after he'd watched Jones perform Jagger made his own début with backing from Charlie Watts and Cyril Davis, Richard and Taylor. He gave a nervy rendition of Chuck Berry's 'Around and Around'. 'I think it was more rocky than Alexis was used to,' Taylor recalls. 'He would've preferred that we'd played something more bluesy.'

Be that as it may, when word spread that Korner was looking for a band to deputize for Blues Inc at Ealing, Jagger was interested.

'We wanted the job,' explains Taylor, 'so we decided to record ourselves. We did it at my mum's house in the back dining room. That was when it dawned on us, Bloody hell! We better call ourselves something, and it's only then we came up with Little Boy Blue and the Blues Boys. We took the tape to Alexis at the club.' Taylor is the first to admit the tape was not up to much, and so he, for one, was not surprised when nothing came of it.

Korner later quipped, 'For a kid in a cardigan he moved quite excessively.' But Jagger's début was not his only performance at Ealing. Blues Inc invited him to perform occasionally. They were not prepared though, to tolerate Keith Richard. To certain experienced musicians he lacked ability and style. But it wasn't long before Jagger decided he enjoyed the backing of a tight, cohesive sound, and when in May Korner offered him the job as stand-in for

Long John Baldry with Blues Inc, he rapidly moved on. It didn't go unnoticed or unremarked on by the Blues Boys, and although both Richard and Taylor could see why Jagger had taken the opportunity, they somewhat resented his departure.

In time Jagger's talent as a stage performer would provide a blueprint for rock's future front men, but in these early days he took a lot of getting used to. The rather fey wrist movements for example, and Richard, watching sourly from the audience, later called him embarrassing. Jagger struck poses, steepling his fingertips on his bony hips, bending forward and pouting his fleshy lips. This was provocative in the roughhouse atmosphere of the club. Vocally he imitated Chicago bluesmen, forging an emotional bond with a music that he was discovering via Alexis Korner.

Jagger, Richard and Taylor all turned up at the Bricklayers Arms in Berwick Street in response to an advert Brian Jones had placed in Soho's club information sheet *Jazz News*. He was auditioning a new band in a pub backroom that he'd hired for a few shillings an hour. Jones already had two on board – Ian Stewart, known as Stu, a Scotsman who played boogie piano, and guitarist Geoff Bradford. Others had come and gone. According to Dick Taylor, Jones asked Jagger to join after hearing him sing – then to discover that he came as a package deal. Jagger insisted that he would only join as singer if Richard came in as guitarist.

Jones had no objection but Geoff Bradford did. He was openly hostile to Richard, a feeling largely based on Richard's worship of Chuck Berry. There were tensions, but when push came to shove Bradford was out.

The band was still incomplete – more of an idea than a reality. It had no name, no drummer and no bookings, but for now Jones booked the Bricklayers' back room for rehearsals three times a week. Sessions Jagger only sporadically attended and it showed when Jones cadged them a spot at Ealing as Ginger Baker, arguably rock's greatest drummer, recalls.

'I'd just met Brian at the club. He'd just got together with Mick Jagger, and they were going to play the interval. Alexis asked Jack Bruce, Johnny Parker and myself if we could help them out. I didn't like Jagger, but we agreed to play. It was really quite amusing. Jack and I got into some pretty complicated time patterns with the evil intent of throwing Jagger and it worked! Then to my surprise Brian went over and stood beside Mick and shouted, 'One, two, three, four,' showing Mick where the beat was! I always respected him for that.'

Jagger's first priority, though, remained Blues Inc. The crowds at Ealing were steadily growing and he had a commitment to the band that sometimes conflicted with the demands of Jones' rehearsals. By mid-1962 he was spreading himself thin. There were the two bands and the LSE, and although at college he had passed his part one exams, his interest in his studies was waning.

Not so Jones' approach to rehearsals, as Dick Taylor confirms: 'Jones was a hard taskmaster. Mick like the rest of us had to knuckle down and work.' But while Jones remained convinced his band had a future Jagger was not so sure.

In a seemingly satellite development, however, significant ground had been broken for R&B when Korner was offered a regular Thursday night slot at the Marquee. It was seen as proof that R&B was slackening jazz's grip on popular entertainment.

'Myself and Harold Pendleton ran the Marquee, and we'd asked Alexis if he would like his own night there,' says Chris Barber. 'He said yes, so we made it a regular Thursday stint.'

This arrangement had been in place for several months when, at the end of the first week of July 1962, Blues Inc appeared on the BBC Light Programme *Jazz Club*. Jagger saw it as some vindication that he'd been right to favour this band. It was proving successful and he was excited at the prospect of a platform on national radio. But his joy was shortlived when he was told that he could not be part of the line-up. The BBC fee stretched to paying for six people and Jagger ranked seventh. As reserve vocalist he was the obvious one to drop.

All was not lost, though, as Jones saw the break he'd been waiting for and moved in to secure the vacant Marquee spot for his band. He'd been having difficulty in finding a permanent drummer, though by then it was Mick Avory, later of the Kinks. The nameless six-piece could hardly face a Marquee audience thus, however, and so Jones decided on the Rollin' Stones, in honour of a favourite Muddy Waters song.

On 12 July, for a £20 fee, the Rollin' Stones made their Marquee Club début, playing to their first audience together. Jagger sang, Jones played lead guitar and harmonica, Keith Richard coped with rhythm guitar, while Dick Taylor and Mick Avory anchored the sound with bass and drums respectively. Ian Stewart was on piano. If Jagger's thoughts lay with what was happening across town at the BBC it didn't show, although he was nervous as he sang his way through a dozen numbers. Accounts conflict as to how this first fee-paying performance was received. Some recall them getting a rough ride. And Pendleton is said to have regretted having hired them when he heard the boos. But Taylor maintained that they went down well enough.

'The crowd was reasonably positive,' he says. 'We felt very overawed. So many big names had played there, and we all, including Mick, were fully aware that we weren't in the same league. I do remember that earlier during practice, a cleaner stopped to listen to us only to remark, "That lot will never get anywhere. What a bleeding racket!" Korner disagreed and booked them again at both the Marquee and Ealing.

Regular work helped get the band into its stride, and they began to attract ever bigger crowds. A few personnel changes also began to evolve. Mick Avory, who didn't get on with Brian and whom Richard dismissed as terrible, left to be replaced by Tony Chapman. His tenure was brief. He left before the year was out. Steve Harris, who had occasionally sat in, filled the spot a couple of times, before Carlo Little, the latest in this succession of drummers, appeared on the scene. Meanwhile, that autumn, Dick Taylor would leave to study at the Royal College of Art (going on later to form the Pretty Things with Phil May). He was temporarily replaced by Ricky Fensen.

All this upheaval had little effect on Jagger. Career-wise he remained open-minded, but he wanted to earn a living. He considered politics, but he later admitted that it seemed too much like hard work, and, incredibly, it was even harder to achieve in this field than it was in music.

At 19 Jagger had no regular girlfriend, though he liked to impress his friends with his tales of how he was having fun with some newer richer acquaintances outside the band. Sometimes he turned up late at a friend's flat not able to get home to Dartford after a party. It was one such occasion that he made a move on

Brian Jones' current girlfriend.

When Jagger had first met Jones, he had been fascinated to discover that in addition to a child who had been adopted Jones had a second son, this time with his steady girlfriend from hometown Cheltenham, Pat Andrews. Brian preferred to keep his past private and his personal life separate but that had proved impossible when Pat had followed him to London with the infant. It'd been difficult at first but now all three shared a flat in Powis Square, North Kensington, and Pat had long since met the other Rollin' Stones. In the early hours of one morning she and Brian were woken by banging on their flat door.

'Brian got up and answered the door. It was Mick, and he was very drunk. He tried to tell us he'd just come from a big Rothschild party and that he couldn't get home so he'd walked to our flat, hoping to crash with us. Brian was annoyed at being disturbed, and Mick was staggering about so he pushed him on to the settee and we went back to bed. Of course he couldn't drop off to sleep again which annoyed him even more. When it came time to rise, I was seeing to the baby and Brian in a foul mood seemed to do everything he could to delay going off to work. It dawned on me he wasn't keen to leave with Mick, who was still hungover, in the flat. Maybe it's because he knew he couldn't be trusted in like circumstances or maybe he knew he couldn't trust Mick, but eventually he had to go. It'd only been about three hours since Mick had arrived and the drink hadn't fully worn off so I made him coffee and sat at the far end of the settee while he drank it. Grinning he suddenly swung up close, threw his arm around me and made a pass. I wasn't interested. Brian was a very jealous man, but it wasn't just that. I loved him, had never been unfaithful to him, and I certainly wasn't about to start with Mick.'

As autumn wore on the axis in Jagger's life changed. He left the parental home to live in London. Brian Jones was moving into a flat at 102 Edith Grove, Chelsea, with Keith Richard and Jagger was keen to join them. When he moved in he discovered that life in the two-room apartment, at the unfashionable end of the King's Road, was not what he was used to. He was compulsively neat and the grime and chaos of the cold flat was anathema to him. But he liked his bit of rough. His walk on the wild side. Even his middle-class accent became more streetwise.

Sometimes, when roughing it proved too uncomfortable, Jagger would return to Dartford for a while. He was not prepared to suffer too much for his street credibility. He enjoyed his creature comforts. But what he was unaware of, and would not have been at all comfortable with, was that Brian Jones was thinking of replacing him as singer with the Rollin' Stones.

3

JAGGER'S JEALOUSIES

JAGGER HIMSELF WAS still not persuaded that he would make it with the Rollin' Stones. 'A musician comes into this business for one of two reasons,' Alexis Korner maintained. 'There are compulsive players who have *got* to play. If they make money, great, but they've *got* to play. Then there are people who think, "Ah! This is how I'm going to make it." Mick is the latter.' Perhaps this was part of the reason why Jones – something of a purist – was not sure that Jagger brought the right kind of energy into his band.

In late October 1962 Jagger had his first experience of a recording studio, when the band cut three tracks in the primitive conditions of Curly Clayton Sound Studio, north London. But the tape was rejected by EMI. There had also been more unsettling personnel upheavals, which, by early in the new year, had meant the arrival of two new band members, one of whom at least was a familiar face.

To fill the vacancy left by Dick Taylor, Brian Jones had advertised in the music press for a bass player, and in November their on-off drummer, Tony Chapman, introduced a friend to the band. His name was William George Perks, but he was known as Bill Wyman, another ex-grammar school boy, who had served his two years' National Service in the RAF. Married with a son, Wyman worked as a technician in Streatham, south London. He had been playing in the Cliftons, a semi-professional outfit, where he had met Chapman, but he was disillusioned with them.

Wyman wasn't much impressed either with the Stones. A stylish 26 year old, he felt a lot older than them, and didn't appreciate the long-haired scruffiness of Jagger, Jones and Richard. Ian Stewart had a regulation short back and sides and appeared to Wyman the only normal one among them. Nevertheless he went to an audition at their latest rehearsal venue, the Wetherby Arms, a pub near to Edith Grove. He was invited to join virtually on the spot, although he remains convinced that his arsenal of musical equipment was the deciding factor.

Within a couple of months Wyman was followed by Charlie Watts. Jones had been after the drummer for a while, but Watts was as stubborn as he looked. Raised in London's Islington, and a graduate of Harrow Art School, by this time he had left Blues Inc because he hadn't wanted to become a professional musician. He was playing with Blues by Five, which he was already considering leaving. Ginger Baker had replaced him in Korner's band and had urged Jones to persist in his pursuit of Watts for the Stones. This was something that had now paid off despite the fact that Watts saw it as a backwards step. Nevertheless, 'I liked their spirit,' he confessed, although at the time his friends thought him mad.

They would have been somewhat justified had they had the chance to observe aspects of Jagger's behaviour outside the band. When he wasn't at the LSE, staying late at the library or playing football for the university second XI, he would wander the flat in a negligée. His camp period, as it became known, lasted some time, during which Jagger reverted to his love of make-up. He also painted his fingernails and put on the stockings and stilettos that had been left behind by Brian's ex, crowning his image with a hairnet. Jagger may have been exploring the bisexual aspects of his personality, but it's more likely he enjoyed the shock effect his appearance had on people and wanted to work on it before trying it out on stage.

It certainly provoked a reaction from Richard, who thought he looked like a classic King's Road queen and teased him mercilessly with an amused Brian Jones. There was no evidence to support any idea of his emergent bisexuality. Although gay men existed among their friends, it is said that when Jagger was once woken to the feel of a tongue exploring his ear, his reaction was to throw the man out.

Richard and Jones had become close by spending time together at Edith Grove while Jagger studied. Theirs was a working relationship. They had been developing a unique dual guitar style. Jones motivated Richard, steering him away from his natural sloth into making a commitment to something. As a result, a bond formed between them that to Jagger seemed stronger than the one he felt he had with Richard. Trios are always problematic, and he began to feel the odd man out in this one. Yet he continued to resist taking the step that would have helped matters by wavering about throwing his professional lot in with the band. Later Wyman assessed his new friends at that time, with Richard at constant risk of having no direction at all, Jones single-minded about his music, and Jagger's talk of becoming a lawyer.

Jagger couldn't decide whether or not to turn professional. He talked it over with Alexis Korner who recalled that he was full of 'what ifs?' What if the Rollin' Stones failed? What if it wasn't worth the risk? What if he passed up a chance to aim for a sound profession? Korner suggested he had nothing to lose by staying with the band for a few more months.

Stones' gigs were now at a range of clubs in and around London, and while the fees were usually not high, it was all good experience. Even the disastrous December gig at the Piccadilly Club where they had met Giorgio Gomelsky, a colourful character, who would become important to them.

At the Ricky Tick in Windsor they had begun to attract what proved to be a passionate following. Brian Jones had met Linda Lawrence, who became his new love, and this club, housed in a dilapidated once fine mansion, would also bring Jagger into contact with his first serious girlfriend. In the meantime he had met Cleo Sylvestre, a 16-year-old schoolgirl.

Sylvestre loved R&B and frequented the Marquee for

performances by Blues Inc and the Rollin' Stones. She had dreams of becoming a singer, and from her first meeting with Jagger she believed they were on the same wavelength. She found Mick shy, and as she later put it, 'no heart throb', but they began dating. 'None of my friends thought he was a great catch,' she confessed. But she clearly did. She became devoted to him and turned up at all his gigs without fail.

Jagger wrote Sylvestre love notes to coax her into bed. 'Darling, I want to share my life with you. I don't just want to sleep with you' was one among them that expresses the strength of his determination. Over the 18 months they dated he even once proposed, and Sylvestre was a little unnerved by this. He'd come on too strong for her, and she became scared to meet him. 'All I wanted was a kiss and cuddle,' she lamented in that age-old female fashion. 'He wanted sex.'

While Jagger juggled with his frustrations, Jones had been making connections that would give him something to sing about. Jones' manically assertive personality had been ramming the message home that the Stones stood for a harsh, new and vibrant brand of R&B. And it was this that had been drawing the crowds in the clubs. At the Marquee the Stones now attracted crowds five times as big as Blues Inc.

'It didn't last though,' Chris Barber recalls. 'Cyril Davis sacked them because he didn't think they were authentic enough. I personally liked the Stones and still like listening to Jagger, but to me he never succeeds in sounding anything but a take-off of Muddy Waters, which is no bad thing!

'I don't know whether they were told that it was Harold [Pendleton] who had wanted them out, but Keith Richard blames him to this day for them getting the push. I honestly never could understand the fuss. They were only a support band, which were never treated well anyway. It was like that in those days. In fact I defy the Stones to say that in their early days they treated their support bands very well!'

Harold Pendleton confirms being stuck with the blame. 'Because I went with the main band to the pub during the break and returned when the interval band was finished I never actually saw the Stones perform at the Marquee but one night I was leaving with a friend and I saw this band loading up their gear. I shouted, "Goodnight, lads!" They shouted back, "Fuck off!" My mate explained that Cyril hadn't liked them and had given them the sack.'

Despite this setback the Stones were now appearing regularly at many of the outer London boroughs of Putney, Sutton, Richmond and Ealing. Entry was 4s (20p), and their loyal army of fans pursued them everywhere, packing into small venues and jumping queues to get in. The band had their own casual, some said scruffy, style. They couldn't afford to buy stage clothes. This, and in those days the unusual sight of them lighting up a cigarette or downing a pint between numbers, added to their appeal.

Jagger could see the anticipation on the faces of the audience. There was a tangible power to be drawn from them, and he longed to exploit it. This was something that Jones did automatically, with his peculiarly menacing energy forming just a part of a magnetic stage presence that Jagger found hard to match. His guitar work agitated the claustrophobic club atmospheres. Other musicians recognized it.

'Brian invited me and Jack [Bruce] to the first gig the Stones played at the Cy Laurie Club in Windmill Street,' recalls Ginger Baker. 'Mick was just standing stationary at the microphone singing, but Brian was leaping all about the stage, playing lying on his back and even jumping into the crowd while he was playing. It was Brian, not Mick, who was the showman in the band.' Other musicians agreed.

Ray Davies, later of the Kinks, says, 'Brian was one of the most compelling musicians ever on stage.'

And Alexis went further, 'Brian had more edge to him than any of the others. The whole nasty image of the Stones started with Brian, not Mick. He went out to needle people. You'd see him dancing forward with a tambourine slapping it in your face and sticking his tongue out at you in a nasty way. Then he'd move back before you actually took a punch at him.' Whether or not Jagger felt upstaged he could not have been unhappy at the efforts Jones was making, badgering anybody who could help the band. It began to look as if the Stones might just take them where they all wanted to go.

At the end of January there was the first recording session with the new line-up at IBC Studios, Portland Place, with engineer Glyn

Johns. But the tape of the five tracks they'd cut lay around, having been, Johns believes, sent out to all the wrong people by the studio owners. Yet it has to be said that there was a distinct crudeness to the group harmonies, with Jagger at times almost shouting rather than singing. An ability to be heard, however, proved essential at their new regular venue, the Crawdaddy.

So called after the Bo Diddley song 'Do the Crawdaddy', their gig there was on Sunday nights in the back room of the Station Hotel, Kew Road, Richmond. The Crawdaddy went on to become a springboard for many musicians and was the brainchild of the flamboyant 29-year-old Russian *émigré*, Giorgio Gomelsky, whom the Stones had previously met at the Piccadilly Club. He was an exhausting and colourful personality, as his friend Chris Barber recalls.

'Giorgio liked to consider himself a kind of Rasputin, and in a way he was a bit like that. He was the sort of man who when I saw him coming, I'd take cover. He always had a harebrained scheme going that he wanted to involve either myself or Alexis Korner in, and he would be full of great plans, which would all end up a complete waste of time, but he was great at creating opportunities for young bands.

'He was the first to attempt to introduce sitar playing into a band's repertoire here, long before the Beatles. I remember him banging on at the Yardbirds about this, and he let them hear the sitar. Jeff Beck said, "Yeah, but 'ere, I can do that on my guitar!"

'Giorgio was ahead of his time. He loved putting people together. There was a group called Steam Packet, which was Brian Auger, Julie Driscoll and Long John Baldry. He did a lot of things like that. He matched Steve Winwood from the Spencer Davis Group with a guy from a band called Deep Feeling who was Dave Mason. He didn't put the Stones together of course.'

Fate had a hand in the Stones' regular residency at the Crawdaddy when February's atrocious weather had prevented the Dave Hunt Group, featuring Ray Davies, from playing their gig. The Stones stepped in, and within weeks their growing number of fans had followed them to their new haunt, in an invasion of miniskirts and cuban-heels.

It was all a long way from their first appearance there when Brian Jones had glumly pointed out to the irrepressible Gomelsky that there had been more people on stage than off. But Giorgio had promised them then that they were still on the brink of something big. His confidence in this had something to do with the relationship between the Stones and their audience, as Phil May recalls.

'It was all strangely arresting. At first the Stones sat on stools, but then they'd get up, and the music would get more rocky. It was a club thing, a kind of cloaked reverence which carried out into the audience so much so that to go leaping about like demented apes would have been sacrilege and through it all this pub backroom just gave off this amazing vibe.

'After not too long the audience began to change. Instead of folk in duffle coats coming to stand and listen, determined to catch you out with the wrong lyric here or the wrong key there, which often happened, people came to be turned on by it. An urgency injected the gigs, and it became very much a physical thing. R&B gigs were as physical as you could get.'

Everything moved fast for the Stones from this point on. Brian Jones had been writing to the BBC and other media outlets in an attempt to gain exposure for the band. At the Crawdaddy he harassed Gomelsky continually to get him to use his contacts in the music business for them. Gomelsky was successful in this. On 13 April 1963 the Rollin' Stones had their first newspaper coverage when they featured in a one-page article about the club in the *Richmond and Twickenham Times*. Gomelsky then booked them into R.G. Jones studios in Morden, London, to record music for a short film of his, though it was never released. And he had managed to get the Beatles, whose first chart single 'Love Me Do' the previous October had reached the Top 20, and who were on course for stardom, to call by the club to watch the Stones. The two bands ended up back at Edith Grove that night.

Jones considered formalizing their arrangement with Gomelsky with a contract, and certainly the Russian saw himself as the Stones' de facto manager. Jagger, though, was said not to like him. In his opinion Gomelsky was strictly small time. But it also riled him that with all the exposure they were getting via Gomelsky's efforts, Jones was seen as the Stones' leader and natural spokesman. The rivalry between Jagger and Jones, which had been brewing for some time, began to show more and more as the two jockeyed for position.

When Peter Jones from *Record Mirror* called at the club to meet the band he was left with two distinct impressions. First, having conducted most of his interview with Jones he identified him as the one in charge. But he hadn't failed to notice that it wasn't for the want of Jones impressing the fact upon him. And second, he noticed that Jagger had not only bridled at this but also was quick to dismiss Gomelsky's significance in their lives.

'Mick went out of his way to tell me that Giorgio was *not* their manager,' he maintained.

Regardless of the band's surfacing internal politics, it was Peter Jones' enthusiasm for their music that provided the link that would bring the Stones the attention they needed at the Station Hotel. It came from the brash 19-year-old Andrew Loog Oldham, and from Eric Easton. In some respects Oldham dreamt of big things without necessarily having the means to achieve them and always had an eye for the main chance. After a spell of doing odd jobs he had worked his way into Brian Epstein's company NEMS as a fledgling publicist, although he was never assigned to Epstein's flagship band, the Beatles. He didn't last long there, and it had been at the offices of *Record Mirror* that he'd overheard talk of an unknown blues band on the cusp of stardom.

Oldham immediately saw an opportunity but lacked the resources to go it alone. He needed a partner, which is where Easton came in as an established London-based agent, who had until now handled only middle-of-the-road artists. Easton was unprepossessing and quiet and seemed an ill-match for the shaggy-haired band with the aggressive reputation. Nevertheless he agreed to go along that Sunday, 28 April 1963.

The Rolling Stones – the g had recently been added – were performing that night in the absence of Giorgio Gomelsky who'd been called away by a death in the family. Sensitive to the generally subdued air about the club, they had not put on their best performance for the two strangers watching them. Nevertheless they were impressed.

After the show Easton homed in on Jones and talked to him intently for some time. Oldham had also headed for Jones, but he found him too intimidating and backed off, turning his attention instead to the others. Feeling that he needed to assert himself, Oldham returned to the table in time to hear Easton stipulate that

Jagger be dropped in favour of someone who could sing better. Jones had no objection, but Oldham insisted that Jagger should stay. And so it was left.

Oldham was flash, but when it came to it he knew little about the music business or record producing, and Brian Jones, who lived and breathed his music, had no respect for him. Jagger, on the other hand, according to Oldham, really liked the fact that he was younger, thrusting and more arrogant. He felt this would benefit the band. This difference in approval would prove to be a powerful weapon in Jagger's later ascendancy in the band.

At this early stage, though, Jagger was happy to keep a low profile, drinking coffee in a nearby West End café while Jones alone met Eric Easton the day after the Richmond gig. At Easton's London office in Argyll Street he signed an exclusive management contract on behalf of the Rolling Stones. And Jagger was not involved in a couple of band changes that arose as a direct consequence. There was the decision that Keith Richard should drop the 's' from his original surname, Richards, to give him a sharper image. Then the need to tell Gomelsky that the Stones were formally under new management. And the dismissal of Ian Stewart from the band. The last was the result of Oldham's belief that the piano player was too conventional to be a Stone.

Now the Stones caught the attention of Dick Rowe, head of Decca's A&R department. He'd driven hundreds of miles to see them at the Crawdaddy after he had received a letter from Gomelsky, magnanimously still promoting them, and a recommendation from George Harrison. Having turned down the Beatles for Decca, he was determined not to miss out again and fast made contact with Eric Easton. With Brian Jones ensuring the return of the tape that they'd recorded at IBC, the path was clear on 3 May for the Stones to agree to a two-year contract with Decca Records. Signing a recording deal with a major record label was, and still is, the Holy Grail for all bands. Jagger and the band floated on a cloud of euphoria for a while.

But Jagger also had reason to be pleased with himself on a personal front. He had met someone who would become his first serious girlfriend. Their relationship would develop into one of the most problematic and headline-making of the decade.

Chrissie Shrimpton was just one of many girls who frequented the London clubs, enjoying the music and the hysteria of places like the Ricky Tick whenever the Stones played there.

'The Stones had built a tremendous following there and were already hot,' club owner John Mansfield recalls. 'Brian played all the harmonica solos – in fact, all the solos full stop. He and Mick by now were slap out front together; their mikes at pole position as it were.'

Months before, as Jagger and Jones were competing for prominence, for a dare during the gig Shrimpton had managed to climb up into the fish nets that looped from the ceiling. She had crawled over the heads of the crowd towards the stage, but she got into trouble when the nets snapped under her weight, and she fell out. She was saved from injury by Brian Jones, who broke her fall. But she already had eyes only for Jagger, whom she'd previously seen with Blues Inc at Ealing.

It was spring 1963, Chrissie Shrimpton was 17 years old and enjoying her reflected glory as the younger sister of fashion model Jean Shrimpton, then dating the young David Bailey. She was a lively girl, glamorous and well connected, two factors that probably played their part in bringing her to Jagger's attention. At the Windsor club she bet a friend ten shillings (50p) that she could get the singer to kiss her.

Just like Sylvestre, Shrimpton was drawn to Jagger, without knowing precisely why. She clearly found him attractive and charismatic, and he was in a band on the rise, which gave him some power. And there was his talent and undoubted sex appeal. Set against this, though, he still suffered from acne, and she noticed that he was shorter than he appeared on stage. And what surprised her too was his giggle, the femininity of his mannerisms. Yet that first connection led to the beginning of what became a passionate, turbulent relationship. They were both very young, but maybe each recognized something useful in the other. For Jagger her connections with the Bailey set. For Shrimpton his role as singer in a rising rock 'n' roll band. Shrimpton would defend her new man from criticism by some of her friends who found him too odd looking to be attractive. She knew better. And she was right.

4

READY, STEADY, SEX!

JAGGER AND SHRIMPTON were soon an item. He invited her to see the band at Richmond a couple of days after that Ricky Tick gig. She was pleased to go, but when he chose to read too much into her eagerness she was quick to put him right. After the Stones had performed one of the usual electric shows at the Crawdaddy in late April, Andrew Oldham walked out of the hotel during the interval for some fresh air. There he found Jagger and Shrimpton involved in a huge row in a nearby alley, less than 48 hours after they had first met.

It was a bitter exchange, which, according to Oldham, revolved around Jagger's expectations of sex. It grew more and more heated until Shrimpton suddenly slapped Jagger hard across the face. He left abruptly and rejoined the others. It would not be long before Shrimpton's resistance wore down, and they became lovers. It was a passionate relationship, but marked by physical altercations between them.

On a daily basis things were calmer. Shrimpton took the train to London where she attended secretarial college and Jagger was still at the LSE. They would meet after class to walk in the parks. Jagger was reluctant to introduce her to the bachelor squalor in which he was living at Edith Grove and gradually they began to discover more about each other. She had spent a happy childhood in Lane End, a village near High Wycombe, before the family had moved to Rose Hill Farm in Burnham. The convent-educated girl had been, in her sister's words, 'truly naughty and rebellious at school'. Jean, three years her senior, who became one of the most photographed women of the century, later confessed to having envied Chrissie's spirit. These wayward ways had not yet extended to allowing Jagger to sleep with her at her parents' home, as he often pressed her to. When early one morning Mrs Shrimpton entered her daughter's bedroom to find Jagger asleep there, Shrimpton was not with him. She had spent the night in her older sister's room.

Despite her volatile temperament the romance blossomed. Within weeks Jagger had fallen in love. In fact, for a man who had promoted himself as a footloose ladykiller he was remarkably free with his proposals of marriage. Just months before, he had proposed to Cleo Sylvestre. Now in the first flush of this new fling he urged Shrimpton to wed him. Sensibly she suggested they wait.

On 7 June 1963 the Stones' first single 'Come On', a Chuck Berry number backed by Willie Dixon's 'I Wanna Be Loved' was released in Britain. It had been recorded initially at Olympic Studios in Barnes a month before. After a brush with legendary US producer Phil Spector, Oldham had ideas of being a producer, despite his lack of experience. Decca had then insisted on a recut at their own West Hampstead studios. It was a number barely two minutes long for which none of the band much cared. Jagger later dismissed it as 'real shit', but it was an exciting step at the time when he was able to show off advance copies to his family and friends.

Having resisted months of pressure from Jones and Richard to leave the LSE he had recently given in, although, erring on the side of caution, he maintained he was merely taking a year off. It was a decision Jagger did not regret when the release of this single coincided with the Stones' début national TV appearance on the top ABC show *Thank Your Lucky Stars*. It was recorded in Birmingham and was the one time the Stones allowed themselves to be persuaded by Oldham into wearing identical clothes. This lip service to conventionality, however, was not enough, and their brief TV appearance drew a flood of complaints to the station switchboard about their attitude and appearance.

'Come On' reached number 21 in the UK charts, and one reviewer dubbed them a bluesy but commercial band destined for limited chart success. But regular TV spots and more gigs lay ahead. These would not be at the Crawdaddy, though. Their residency there came to an abrupt end when the brewery, alerted by a feature in *Record Mirror* about the club's rowdy reputation, closed it down. Eric Easton quickly replaced it by Thursday night stints at the Scene Club in Piccadilly's Ham Yard.

Ambitions of all sorts began opening up Jagger's mind. He had adored being on telly and dreamt of a Top 10 hit next time, maybe a tour, and reviving his old love of the States he coveted the idea of the Stones conquering America. His sartorial style by autumn 1963 was a crew-neck sweater and tight, drainpipe trousers. He had also begun to let his hair grow longer. His self-absorption intensified by the day, and as Shrimpton affirms, he could hardly be dragged away from studying his image in the mirror.

Oldham and Easton were keen to exploit the furore the Stones' TV début had provoked, and the hype to market the Stones on the basis of raw sex appeal began. Jagger wanted that focus to fix specifically on him, and he spent hours posing, pouting at himself, trying hard to smoulder. His girlfriend had to take a back seat and came to resent this specific aspect of the Stones' success. Fame was also to boost Jagger's ego – a development in itself guaranteed to destabilize their already rocky relationship.

Jagger was visiting Burnham regularly now for late night sex in Shrimpton's bedroom, which was made less risky by the pill. He would slip away before morning to avoid parental detection. It was better there than in the filth of Edith Grove, but although the relationship was important to him, he was not indifferent to other attractions closer at hand.

The suspicion that Jagger might be two-timing her was not a product of Shrimpton's imagination. Up to his old tricks, he was still writing to Sylvestre, sweetly rebuking her for not having turned up as promised to watch him at some club and at the same time reporting that in her absence he had fallen out with Shrimpton again, and again made up. In another he revealed the sexual frisson he'd got from both girls' presence at a gig. He called himself in one letter a 'bad boy' and warned that he might well be round in person that night.

'I wasn't jealous,' cooed Sylvestre, acknowledging that he had a different relationship with her than the sexual one he had with Shrimpton. The same could not be said of Chrissie Shrimpton.

Envy of a different kind gnawed away at Jagger himself. Now that the Stones looked like becoming an item he wanted the spotlight on himself and was putting ever more effort into achieving this. But the fact remained that Brian Jones continued to eclipse him, with an infuriatingly natural ease. Throughout the summer the band were busy with daily recording sessions with Decca and almost nightly gigs. Jagger had developed a stage act that involved a series of disjointedly athletic movements, in which his arms and head spasmodically twitched and his legs seemed in danger of knotting. It had evolved from the Crawdaddy days, he told the press, when the crowd had to dance that way because of the crush. It was a good foil for Jones's intriguing stillness. But Jones had a natural authority that was hard to beat.

In those early days of the sixties musicians and the media were feeling their way forward as entertainer Rolf Harris recalls.

'About this time I was the compère for a trial TV programme [featuring popular music] made at a church hall in Sydenham by the BBC. It was to feature the Rolling Stones, but the powers that be at the Beeb took one look and said "Forget it!" I was a dreadful compère, didn't understand any of their music and gave nothing to the show in the way of up-to-date style or any feeling of the youth of the day. I was probably the main reason they did nothing further with it, but about a month later *Ready, Steady, Go!* hit the airwaves with an almost identical format, and everyone knows how successful that was.'

Ready, Steady, Go! would become highly influential on the 60s' music and social scene, a focus for the beat boom. Made by Associated-Rediffusion with hosts Keith Fordyce, Michael Aldred and Cathy McGowan, its slogan was 'The Weekend Starts Here'. It was a lively show in a tiny studio crammed with excited youngsters to give it a clublike atmosphere, aired early on Friday evenings. Vicki Wickham started as secretary at *RSG* before rising to programme assistant, editor then producer and it was when she and Cathy McGowan visited a Twickenham club that they first met the Stones.

'They were playing at Eel Pie Island,' says Vicki Wickham 'and the place was hot and packed. Cathy and I had gone specifically to see what they were like and found them thrilling to watch, especially Brian Jones. He was the cutest thing we'd ever seen! I mean, the other four were all OK, but Brian was absolutely stunning, and it was him Cathy and I wanted to talk to. Giorgio Gomelsky was there, and we sat with him and Brian for the whole night. Basically we said, "Look, we have this show, do you want to come on it?" Brain said yes, and that's how it all started.

'The band were all eclipsed by Jones. You had to see this guy, be around him in person, to really grasp what I mean. Cathy was enormously taken with him. And Brian was also very obviously the leader. He took the decisions, got involved with everything; he was making it happen for them where it counted. It was only later, when the Stones appeared on *RSG* regularly that I noticed Mick.' It was this kind of reaction that was making Mick uneasy as frontman.

On 28 August the Stones made their first appearance on *RSG*. It was live with all the anxiety this entails. 'We were the only show doing this kind of thing,' says Wickham, 'and the studio was one from which children's programmes were being made. We had limited equipment and great problems handling live shows. Of course the Stones turned up at the very moment they went on air. It was chaos a lot of the time, and we never felt that we got it right, but it was a lot of fun. I think its spontaneity was what made it so big.

'I remember sitting in the canteen after that first show with Mick and Brian. It was just after their first single, and they were both saying how great it would be if they could have a hit record in America.'

It was becoming rare for Jagger and Jones to agree on anything. For this and a few other reasons, their flatshare at Edith Grove was about to end. Although in September they attended recording sessions at Kingsway Studios, Holborn, they were about to live their lives more separately, a fact that came to have far-reaching consequences.

Brian Jones had been conducting a typically complicated love life but now settled matters by agreeing to move in temporarily with the family of Linda Lawrence, the woman he had been dating after their meeting at the Ricky Tick. Soon after his move to Windsor the lease expired at Edith Grove forcing Jagger and Richard to find somewhere new. They moved into a flat at 33 Mapesbury Road, Kilburn. It couldn't help but be an improvement in their living conditions, but what was clear was that with Jones more distant his bond with Richard would weaken. When Andrew Oldham, who had always got on better with Jagger than Jones, moved in too, from this point on there would be a pronounced shift in the balance of power within the group.

The Jagger/Richard/Oldham partnership has often been described as an unholy alliance, and it was at Mapesbury Road that Oldham encouraged Jagger and Richard to start writing their own material. This would segregate them further from the other three band members. Here too they became absorbed with how they could best gain more control in the band and turn the spotlight more on Jagger as lead singer. Jagger also re-established his formerly close friendship with Richard, although he possibly also realized that Oldham was the one to keep in with. At the same time he needed to find time for his girlfriend. Chrissie Shrimpton, now working at Decca, had also moved in to the two-bedroomed West Hampstead flat. Jagger and Shrimpton shared one room, Richard and Oldham the other. Some doubts emerged on whether Jagger and Oldham were 100 per cent heterosexual. Shrimpton is said to have remained convinced that Jagger was heterosexual. When asked by Oldham's girlfriend Sheila Klein about the sleeping arrangements at the new flat, and specifically about whether their respective boyfriends shared a bed, Shrimpton is said to have assured Klein emphatically that only she, Chrissie, slept with Jagger. Oldham, too, is said to have taken pains to reassure Shrimpton that his relationship with Jagger was purely professional.

Professionally speaking the Stones were entering a vital phase of their career in the last quarter of the year, starting with their first major tour of Britain, which began on 29 September 1963. Eric Easton had secured them the 30-date round trip as support band to the American duo the Everly Brothers, which also featured Bo Diddley. It opened at London's New Victoria Cinema.

The tour would be punctuated by significant moments. First they were thrilled to be billed alongside their cult R&B hero, whose appreciation of Jones' musical ability led directly to the Stones backing him at his next BBC radio *Saturday Club* date. Their début appearance there was on 26 October, after which they were asked back to do a lead spot in their own right. Then days later came the release of their second single.

Oldham was still urging Jagger to try his hand at songwriting, an endeavour that had not yet borne fruit. He was worried that there was no follow-up to their first single. A chance meeting with John Lennon and Paul McCartney, then pop's current hottest songwriting team, had resulted in a new song from them for his band. It was 'I Wanna Be Your Man', which the Stones recorded at Kingsway Studios. Jones' belligerent slide guitar gave the short number Chicago blues authenticity, and its B-side was a solid twelve-bar blues instrumental 'Stoned', credited to all five Rolling Stones. The single, which would reach number 12 in the charts, was released on 1 November, two days before the tour's end. It made such an impact that the audience at the final show began chanting, 'We want the Stones.'

By the end of the year the difference was plain to see. Club dates were wild, their live performances rated highly by the likes of *NME*, and they had started to feature in the music polls. The gathering momentum attracted journalists for interviews, which invariably were handled by Jones. Jagger didn't yet have the confidence to take on the media. He still needed Jones to control things and deal with the press. But he wasn't comfortable with it.

Keith Altham, then writing for one of the growing number of teen magazines, would later become a Stones publicist. He confirmed how Jagger often kept himself in the background, watching Jones carefully on these occasions, clearly waiting his moment. Altham once said that 'Mick was particularly adroit at playing the guttersnipe,' and believed that even this early on Jagger saw himself as separate from the band. But Jagger knew the band's interests were in his interest, and it pleased him to see the band's photograph splashed across a magazine cover.

By 1964 the Stones' profile was building fast. With it Jagger was changing, revealing aspects of his personality that made it difficult for Shrimpton, or indeed for any close relationship. Oldham's idea that the five young men should be seen as emotionally unattached was hardly unique as a marketing ploy, but his rule that none of them should be linked to any specific woman was new to the Stones. Wyman, with his nickname 'The Ghost', because of his pale gaunt complexion, already had a family, who seemed to have no desire to court attention, Watts was quietly dating Shirley Ann Shephard and Jones was living with his lover, though this had become more complicated with her pregnancy. Richard kept a low profile where women were concerned, but Jagger, their front man, was linked with the high-profile and strong-minded Shrimpton.

From Jagger's very public behaviour over the years it might be argued that it has never seemed to be in his nature to form an emotional tie to a woman, even a wife, that was strong enough to endanger or compromise his plans. He was always ambitious and single-minded about his career. Any sacrifice could and would be made. This was already in place at the start when he told Andrew Oldham that he considered a serious girlfriend as nothing more than excess baggage to a rock star. In some ways he was right – and just being painfully honest and direct about it. It might have been music to Oldham's ears, but Jagger soon found that putting this attitude into practice came at a price.

In private Jagger may have declared his love for Shrimpton, but his public behaviour did not back this up. When, like the other girlfriends, she was banned from the recording studio she came to the conclusion, 'Mick really doesn't respect women.'

But Jagger spelt out to her exactly what he expected now. His public image was critical, and under no circumstances could they be seen in public acting in any fashion that might reveal the true nature of their relationship. Not unnaturally it was extremely hurtful to Shrimpton and caused immense trouble between them. If he spotted fans waiting for him it was not uncommon for Jagger to ask Shrimpton to vanish for a while. He would let go of her hand and cross the street while he signed autographs. One evening outside their Mapesbury Road flat she found it all too hard to bear, and once inside the flat she lashed out at him, kicking and slapping him.

The experience was harrowing for Jagger, but it was an indication of how crushed Shrimpton felt. And Jagger didn't always double up and back off. Sometimes, it is said, he hit back. Justifying their mutual volatility Shrimpton maintained, 'We were very passionate.'

Jagger tried to help by repeating that once he was more established he would announce their love to the world. She was, after all, the first girl he'd taken home to meet his parents, a move he hoped she'd take as confirmation of his seriousness. But any respite in hostilities between them proved temporary. Public scenes over the coming years included rows in restaurants and an escalation in physical violence that often resulted in them hurting each other.

Life was scarcely more tranquil in the band. Oldham's desire for Jagger to write songs had paid off when, in December, the American solo artist Gene Pitney recorded the first Jagger/Richard composition 'That Girl Belongs to Yesterday'. This gave all three a taste for success.

December also revealed the fact that Brian Jones had made a separate, secret deal with Easton to be paid £5 more than the others in recognition of his leadership of the band. The other Stones found this unpalatable. It was a trigger to their efforts to oust him, at least as a first-division Stone, and a concerted effort to do so followed by Richard, Jagger and Oldham. Brian Jones was strong in many ways, but he had his weaknesses, and the rest of the band knew what they were and how to exploit them. Although Jones was hardly a victim, Bill Wyman later said that the constant jibes from Jagger and Richard were, in his opinion, often spiteful and hurtful. This was compounded, according to the bass player, by their manager's favouring of Jagger, and his desire to relegate Jones below Richard. When it came to the song writing, Wyman also confirmed that only Jagger and Richard were given a real opportunity to write, when it was clear that writing, more than the music, was important to Brian Jones. The creation of such a two-tier system inevitably had unwelcome repercussions.

From New Year's Day 1964 life hardly stood still. The Stones joined the Dave Clark Five, Cliff Richard, the Hollies and the Swinging Blue Jeans in a converted church hall in Manchester to record the pilot edition of BBC TV's new pop-music show *Top of the Pops*. It was common for trouble to arise between London bands and those from other parts of the UK, as Gerry Marsden of Liverpool's Gerry and the Pacemakers recalls, 'The Stones were a great blues band and provided inspiration for many others, but they were Cockneys, and we were Scouse, and never the twain shall meet, in peace anyway. It's a bit like the Scots and the Sassenachs. There was a big north–south divide between them and the Merseyside bands.'

Before transmission that evening a scuffle broke out between some of the Stones and Merseyside's Swinging Blue Jeans, which quickly escalated into a full-scale brawl, with studio staff running for help. Jagger didn't get involved this time, but was less fortunate later on tour when he reacted badly to the regular abuse the band now received. A taunt of 'queer' in response to their long hair provoked him to respond, for which he received a punch on the nose. It knocked him out. And Richard fared no better when he sprang to Jagger's defence.

Feelings towards the band were no less hostile when their second UK tour commenced. It would last throughout January and had come about courtesy of Australian entrepreneur Robert Stigwood, film and TV producer and founder of RSO Records.

'I first met the Stones at Eel Pie Island in Twickenham,' Stigwood recalls, 'and thought they were a great bunch of guys. It was basically on the strength of that that I gave them second billing on this tour.'

It was billed as GROUP SCENE 1964 with headliners the Ronettes, a three-piece black American, all-girl group from the Spector stable. Although the lead singer, ex go-go dancer Ronnie Bennett was engaged to Spector, Jagger, emboldened with drink, made an unsuccessful play for her. Jagger stoked his ego with tales that he was having an affair with Bennett's sister, Estelle, although according to Dave Berry, who with his backing band, the Cruisers, was on the support bill, it was all talk. Days into the tour Jagger's old flame Cleo Sylvestre realized her ambition to make a record when her Oldham-produced single 'To Know Him Is to Love Him' was released; a sentiment Shrimpton was unlikely to endorse if she were to get wind of the stories about Estelle Bennett.

The tour itself exceeded expectations, and the press, already jaded with Beatlemania, were keen to report on it. The Stones and their music, rawer, rougher, raunchier than any UK band before, had an effect on the audience that made good copy. But the band did not have it all their own way, as Dave Berry recalls.

'The Stones generally went down better than everyone else, sure, but I remember that several reviews made the Swinging Blue Jeans the star band. They closed the first half and went down a storm. There were even a few occasions, and I've got the clippings to prove it, that *they* were considered the top act.'

Jagger's performing style remained gauche and clumsy, yet oddly appealing, though the eye was still drawn to Jones. But Jagger's indisputable charisma served him well when in breaks from Regent Studios and working on their first album, he enjoyed socializing with the Shrimpton–Bailey set. He partied with top photographers, designers and film makers, moving among the new sixties' supposedly classless aristocracy.

Press reaction to the recent tour had produced the headline CAN ROLLING STONES CRUSH THE BEATLES? but others dismissed them as 'pop weirdies', whose greatest ability was to scowl at the audience. Jagger didn't always stop at glowering. When playing Greenwich Town Hall the previous November, to one heckler's cry of 'Git yer 'air cut!' Jagger had quickly retaliated, 'What, and look like you?'

After the release of another Jagger/Richard composition, 'Will You Be My Lover Tonight/It Should Be You', recorded by the obscure artist George Bean, in early February the Stones set off on a third UK tour. During this their third single came out, the Buddy Holly number 'Not Fade Away'. For this they had a little help from their friends. Allan Clarke, lead singer of the Hollies recalls.

'Denmark Street in London was *the* place for music then. Graham Nash and I just happened to be passing by the recording studio and got dragged in. Gene Pitney was already there with the Stones laying down the track so we got stuck in with the oohs, aahs, tambourine and maracas. We didn't realize it was going to be a single, but that sort of thing happened a lot in those days. There was no competitiveness, and bands often hung out together.'

Brian Jones was the Stone Clarke saw most of, though he sometimes mixed with the rest of the band at the popular Ad Lib, a club above Soho's Prince Charles cinema.

'It was a fantastic place,' Clarke says. 'I'd go in already out of my mind and come out worse, but it was great. They had a crazy chef who, whenever the record "Woolly Bully" came on, would come dancing out of the kitchen with steaming pans of whatever was cooking at the time in each hand.'

Backed by 'Little By Little', 'Not Fade Away' gave the Stones their biggest hit so far when it reached number 3.

TV appearances were frequent now, but in between, Jagger managed to take a holiday with Shrimpton in Paris. He had enjoyed the headline that had appeared mid-March WOULD YOU LET YOUR SISTER GO WITH A ROLLING STONE? But as far as Shrimpton was concerned this sort of exposure only spelt trouble.

At Oldham's insistence Jagger and Richard were writing more and more. The rather mindlessly titled 'Shang A Doo Lang' he used to launch his new discovery Adrienne Posta, a dizzy teenage blonde. It was at Posta's 16th birthday party at the end of March, which doubled as promotion for the single, that Jagger first met Marianne Faithfull. Like Shrimpton, Faithfull was convent-educated. Just 17, she had long blonde hair, a waifish build and delicate features. She was there with her fiancé, Cambridge undergraduate John Dunbar, but both Oldham and Jagger picked her out for different reasons. Oldham wanted to sign her as a singer, while Jagger was sexually attracted to her. The fact that she was clearly attached to Dunbar only made it more of a challenge.

Faithfull's entrance had come at a bad moment for Shrimpton. Jagger had recently proposed for a second time, and she had accepted. But since then he had been backpedalling furiously. It couldn't have been easy for Shrimpton to hear him tell journalists he had no intention ever of marrying. The tension between them, which was beginning to wear Jagger down, spiralled because of it. It had spilled out in a public row at the party that night, where they eventually restricted themselves to icy glares.

Jagger was aware that Shrimpton was watching him when he approached Faithfull to introduce himself. When he didn't seem to be having the effect on her that he had wanted, he accidentally on purpose made his mark by pouring his champagne down the front of her dress. This did little to increase his appeal to her, and there was no progress in the relationship then. Later in the year, though, she would record the Jagger/Richard song, 'As Tears Go By'.

On 16 April the Stones released their début album, which included 'Tell Me', the first Stones Jagger/Richard composition. In just over a week the album went straight to number 1 in the UK charts. Its release had followed a gig at the Mad Mod Ball at the Empire Pool, Wembley, where fans had rioted in a way that would become all too familiar.

'To have boys as enthusiastic as the girls was an odd thing,' recalls Phil May. 'You'd have this packed theatre, where the first third of the crowd would be blokes who emanated a dangerous atmosphere while chicks were collapsing in the crush. For the Pretty Things and the Stones there was a dual sexuality coming across, and it was no more a conscious thing by myself than it was with Mick, but it was turning blokes on. It came from the music. Almost everything in R&B lyrics like "Squeeze my lemons" and so on, was sexual, so in practically everything you were singing about then, there was screwing going on in the song, and Mick, like me, in the way he interpreted this, fed into the overall vibe.

'Jagger wasn't the best front man that's ever been, but the Stones' sound was exciting, it put British music into sexual overdrive and with the boys brawling at the front, it was like walking a tightrope. He knew if he fell off it could be dangerous. Fights blew up all the time, equipment was wrenched off the stage and the bouncers always had a hard time coping but it's all part of the buzz.'

According to May the friction that later evolved between the Pretty Things and the Stones was a media invention.

'At fan grass root level,' he says, 'an element had crept in that you had to make a choice. Us or them. The more lunatic fringe opted for us and the cooler dudes went for the Stones. You couldn't like us both supposedly among the hard core, and the newspapers perpetuated this.'

The second-best exposure to TV was live performance, and the next month the Stones were off on another UK tour. By now the 'dirty' tag had really taken hold. Their untamed look was a huge talking-point, and they were regularly refused entry into restaurants and turned out of bars and cafés. At one point when he saw that their long hair was eliciting so much fuss Jagger played devil's advocate, in a revival of old instincts.

'It doesn't represent anything special to us,' he maintained, intentionally disingenuous because in the sixties the length of a man's hair was a clear statement of rebellion. At one rural school, pupils had been suspended for having 'Mick Jagger hair'. Jagger courted this personal controversy. It upped his profile as a rebel. Now he dismissed the hostile questioning about the band's stage image by saying, 'They don't have to come and look at us then.'

Their début album broke all the rules of marketing. It had no title and no band name on the front of its sleeve. In America it was given a title and released as *England's Newest Hit Makers: The Rolling Stones* by London Records, who launched an advertising campaign to hype their tour that was about to start there.

The UK tour was winding down, and it had been an exhausting battle to be heard every night above the noise of the audience enthusiasm. There was no respite, though, and after studio sessions at Regent Sound, Jagger prepared to fly with the others to America at the start of June. It was a trip about which they all felt nervous – and with good reason.

'Tell Me' had been released as a single in the States, backed by 'I Just Wanna Make Love to You'. It had reached number 24, but in middle America the band flopped. Humiliatingly, on one occasion, a performing monkey got an encore, and they didn't. Despite the highlight of recording at Chicago's famous Chess Studios in June, their patchy reception and the bad press on national TV from unflattering remarks made by entertainer Dean Martin, had affected Jagger. He lashed out at Eric Easton about it over the transatlantic telephone line.

And, battered by the experience, he was barely back on British soil when he was dourly predicting, 'I give the Rolling Stones about another two years.' Ever the survivor, he added that he was banking all his song royalties for the future. All this pessimism, despite a *Record Mirror* poll that had voted the Stones Best British Vocal Band and Jagger the Most Popular Individual Group Member.

Jagger had been greeted at the airport by Chrissie Shrimpton, fresh from her new job at Radio Caroline. She also accompanied him when the Stones were taken by armoured van to the BBC's White City studios to tape the weekly TV programme *Juke Box Jury*, hosted by David Jacobs.

'It was one of the only two times that we had five panellists. The other occasion was when we had a group on called the Ponytails,' recalls Jacobs.

'At camera rehearsal they were very disruptive indeed, as we had fully expected them to be, but then Brian Jones grew very impatient with them and shouted, "Quiet, everybody. This is Mr Jacobs' show, and you're not going to spoil it for him. So behave!"

'Miraculously they all did exactly as they'd been told, and the show then went off beautifully. The place was mobbed with fans, but they were very well behaved.'

This controversial edition of *Juke Box Jury*, during which the band voted every new release a miss, was aired on the day the Stones hit the coveted number 1 slot in the UK singles chart on 4 July with 'It's All Over Now'. It was recorded at Chess Studios and raced up the charts to displace the Animals' distinctive 'House of the Rising Sun'. Jagger's recent holiday in Ibiza with Shrimpton on the face of it seemed to have done little for his earlier pessimism for his response to the single's success was not over positive.

'I don't care a damn if our new record has reached number one. What's it matter anyway?' he said. Probably all part of an attempt at cool, a disenchantment with establishment acknowledgement. Or maybe it was because the immediate result from their recent US tour had been no real money. Only the benefit of increased international exposure with which to sell more records.

At the beginning of July Jagger had attended the management meeting at which the Rolling Stones became a limited company. Business matters would later come to obsess Jagger. He soon had to switch hats to performer again, though, as a new UK tour loomed. There would be the usual accompanying riots and arrests. Costs of repairs to concert halls were now running high, and their reputation got worse, or better, depending on the outlook. The missiles hurled on stage became more varied, and they all risked serious injury. But it got the adrenalin pumping, and was better than being ignored.

Since the summer the Stones had become newsworthy enough to be regularly pursued by TV camera crews. The media were there again when at the start of August they played at Longleat House in Warminster, the Wiltshire family seat of the Marquess of Bath.

'Longleat was the first stately home to open to the public,' the present Marquess recalls, 'and we were also the first to put on rock concerts. We had asked ourselves what would bring in the tourists. My parents kept reading all about these pop groups and how they were drawing big crowds, and so my father thought it would be a good idea to invite them to perform here.

'Among the first to come were the Bachelors, Billy J Kramer, Freddie and the Dreamers and the Shadows. The only problems I recall revolved around bad luck with rain. My father was always rather put out at the lack of dependability of the British climate. This was in the days before insurance was taken out for these events of course. I was abroad when the Stones played here but I heard plenty about it afterwards.'

The Marquess's mother, Lady Virginia, was on hand with her husband to greet the Stones on their arrival. Fond of music, they were curious and eager to meet this notorious band. Jagger, fresh from the new aristocracy, was keen to meet the old aristocracy.

'They came here first for lunch. I remember all of them very clearly. I thought Mick Jagger was attractive with his lovely big mouth, and he was very charming and polite.

'Because such a crowd had turned up I drove them the back way to where they were to be playing. My husband and I were absolutely amazed at the number of fans. It was a tremendous day.'

It had become customary for female fans to faint at Stones' concerts. Even policewomen on duty to control the crowds had been known to pass out. This Longleat gig proved no exception, although not all of them were genuine cases, as the Marquess recalls.

'Barriers had been erected at the steps which led up to the front door, and fans were trying to find a way to cross them when they saw one young girl who had fainted being stretchered over the railings and carried inside to the Great Hall where the Stones were. All of a sudden great masses of girls began fainting and ending up in the house where, I must say, they were remarkably quick at recovering!'

The non-stop gigging continued into November, by which time the band had returned to the States for a second time. Armoured cars were now the only safe way for the Stones to travel. Police dog handlers were a regular fixture at venues, and arrests and casualties escalated. The band's bad-lad reputation had led to their exclusion from certain airlines and hotels not prepared to test out the rumours of wrecked rooms and terrorized guests.

The Stones' success was frenetic, and Jagger loved it. The increasingly colourful journalism, that focused on the sexual dynamics of the band, the criticism of arousing the audience to mass orgasm. At the time he had this to say:

'I get a strange feeling on stage. I feel all this energy coming from the audience. What I'm doing is a sexual thing.'

He maintained that a kind of social hypocrisy existed in that the Stones' overtly sexual approach was unacceptable because it came from men. That women had been acceptably doing this kind of act in clubs for years without adverse comment. Anyway he was just doing what came naturally.

'I do a strip tease. I take my jacket off, and I loosen my shirt, but I don't stand in front of a mirror and practise how to be sexy.'

Fame meant that the Stones were safer moving house once too many fans got to know where they lived. Jagger, Shrimpton and Richard had relocated to Hampstead – 10a Holly Hill to be precise. Oldham remained at Mapesbury Road, soon to marry Sheila Klein. But Oldham's own marriage made no difference to his insistence that 'the boys' remain eligible.

By now Charlie Watts and his fiancée Shirley Ann Shephard were keen to get married. Along with Shrimpton, Shephard had recently managed to persuade the manager to let her join the band in Paris, but it had been a grudging concession. Jagger, like most young rock stars whose fame went straight to their groin, was by now indulging in the favours of groupies. Not surprisingly he was in full agreement with Andrew Oldham.

'You'll get in our way,' he truthfully warned Shrimpton. And in fact life on the road was not best suited to partners. If she was there to check up on him or just keep his attention, she was on a road to nowhere. Struggling to keep the relationship on her terms Shrimpton's response was to snap her heels together and raise her arm in a Nazi salute.

When Shrimpton was party to Watts and Shephard's secret marriage in mid-October, she and Jagger had one of their most celebrated fall-outs. Angry at her subterfuge, that she might have helped to jeopardize the Stones' whole sex-machine image, Jagger became rough with his lover and apparently grabbed her so hard that he supposedly left big purple bruises on her arms. But he could not hold her off for long, and she fought back, gouging the flesh of his cheek with her rings.

Though all very spectacular, it all ended predictably enough in bed. Unless Jagger hadn't the nerve to end his relationship with Chrissie, it must be assumed that he derived some thrill from its combative nature. His protestations of true love had to be measured, however, against his susceptibility to casual sex on tour. Especially in America, where their second tour was tremendously exciting and a far cry from their first one.

In California at the end of October they headlined twice on the TAMI show at the Civic Auditorium in Santa Monica. Marvin Gaye, the Beach Boys and Smokey Robinson and the Miracles were among the other acts. But Jagger took most notice of James Brown, nicknamed the Godfather of Soul. In his dressing-room he practised what he'd admired of Brown's stage act and would later incorporate it into his own.

On 13 November the Stones were playing at the Hara Arena in Dayton, Ohio, and 'Little Red Rooster', their latest single, had just been released. The Willie Dixon number had been recorded in Chicago and was backed by 'Off the Hook.' Jones had missed the Dayton gig, having been admitted overnight to hospital suffering from a virus that had given him a dangerously high temperature. His influence, however, was stamped all over the new single as it is his slide guitar work that makes the number. The following week the Stones performed it on *Ready, Steady, Go!* and watched it go straight to the top.

Jagger had returned from America more than ever determined to take his prime place as front man and edge out any contenders for the title, particularly Jones. One of his best means of doing this was via his songwriting. He and Richard had had some more compositions recorded by other artists, including 'As Tears Go By', which had reached number 9 in August. Jagger's desire to be the brightest and the best led him to seek the limelight at every turn. This was echoed in his hectic social life, where he frequented clubs like the Ad Lib, Bag O' Nails and Scotch of St James, Piccadilly. Here in addition to musicians he met more of the new aristocracy, including the influential London art dealer Robert Fraser and

Chelsea antiques dealer Christopher Gibbs. Still the talk among the likes of John Lennon was of Jones' stunning slide guitar, and it made Jagger introspective.

The power play between Jagger and Jones persisted, increasing in intensity. But however much the two men fought for supremacy within the Stones, with all the by now well-documented tales of tit for tat, the band itself came to epitomize the Swinging Sixties.

5

HIGH TIMES AND GOOD GRASS

*T*HE DRUG-TAKING that would by turns alleviate and aggravate the jealousy and paranoia within and around the Stones began in earnest in 1965. Jagger had started off with the occasional joint months before, but by spring he was a heavy dope smoker. He would later graduate to harder stuff, although he never became an addict.

At first he tried to hide his indulgence from Shrimpton, not least because he had been clear that he did not want any involvement in this illegal activity. Shrimpton went along with it until the day she mentioned at the Stones' office that the reason she never touched drugs was because her boyfriend didn't. Spluttering into his coffee, someone disabused her. Jagger, he said, had just left the building that afternoon stoned out of his brain, apparently a not unusual occurrence. After the inevitable row that night Shrimpton and Jagger began smoking grass on a regular basis at home, which helped promote some much needed harmony.

Home was a place Jagger would see little of in the coming 12 months. But female company was not something that he or the rest of the Stones missed with life on the road, as Olympic pentathlon gold medallist Mary Peters recalls when she met them during their short tour of Ireland.

'I had just won the Sports Personality of the Year Award after the Tokyo Olympics and had been invited to have my photo taken with the Rolling Stones, but they weren't interested in the occasion. There were crowds of girls mobbing their dressing-room door and even more packing the street outside screaming for the band, and they were only interested in soaking up all the adulation. I felt like a broom in the corner of the room.'

Following recording sessions at Regent Sound studios, 15 January saw the release of their second album, *Rolling Stones No. 2*, which went to number 1 while they battled through a riotous tour of Australia, New Zealand, Singapore and finally Hong Kong in mid-February.

In the intervening time the Mighty Avengers had released 'Blue Turns to Grey', a single written by Jagger and Richard. Most of their new material was being recorded by other artists. It was time for them to record one of their own compositions. This came with 'The Last Time', their third consecutive number 1. Backed by 'Play With Fire' it was released on 26 February and performed that same night on *Ready, Steady, Go!* The song's success marked the creative domination that would scotch any songwriting ambitions of either Jones or Wyman. This resulted in great resentment, certainly from Jones.

Jagger's continually evolving stage style was still unrefined. He would jerk his head and swivel sideways from the waist, his legs shuffling uncoordinatedly, his arms rotating as he gazed into the camera in a kind of rebellious anti-crooner posturing. Of all their TV appearances the band were arguably most at home on *Ready, Steady, Go!* as Vicki Wickham recalls.

'The Stones almost became our in-house band, and they got to be very big, very fast. Mick loved the show, particularly because we often featured black acts, which meant he could borrow moves from them. For instance he watched Ike and Tina Turner closely and in time got a lot of steps from them.

'The audience reaction was phenomenal. After each show, girls would send the Stones all kinds of gifts.'

Such an atmosphere meant it wasn't hard to generate a buzz in the studio crowd before the show started, which made the job of the programme's warm-up man easier. He was Paul Raven, who later found fame as Gary Glitter.

'He was out of work at the time,' recalls Wickham, 'and a mutual friend asked me if there was a job for him. So he joined us to tell the kids who was coming on, crack jokes and generally get them going, and he was fab at it.'

Vicki Wickham was aware of the band's undercurrents, which were more than a healthy spirit of competition. 'By this time Andrew Oldham was on the scene,' she recalls, 'and it was obvious that there was a gradual shift going on. Along with Andrew, Mick began insistently to home in on me to talk about the show. Likewise he would make it his point to get to the director Michael Lindsay-Hogg first. It was a smart move. It forced people to pay attention to him. It worked with me because previously I hadn't noticed him at all.'

Clearly Jagger believed he now had the confidence to push his way to the fore.

'He became terrific to work with,' says Wickham, 'and knew exactly what he wanted personally.'

Wickham was not alone in noticing Jagger's determination to shine in the band. 'I had watched the Stones at the Glad Rag Ball at the Empire Pool, Wembley, late 1964,' Michael Lindsay-Hogg recalls, 'and was struck then by the charisma exuding from Mick who was really only a boy at the time. But the first time I met him was when the Stones came to perform "The Last Time". I was kind of ignorant then. I liked rock 'n' roll, but I came from America, and I had to have it all written down at first, what their names were and who did what in the band. But to me Mick was always kind of like a prince.'

This was more the reaction Jagger had been striving to achieve.

'Everyone was aware that *he* was aware of his own presence and talent,' says Lindsay-Hogg. 'I'd met stars before, and although he was young, he was different from other rock 'n' rollers.'

Jagger's absorption with himself made it hard for the director to do his job that first night.

'I was real keen to shoot "The Last Time" well, but during filming Mick foiled every shot by gazing deep into the monitor, studying how he looked, focusing entirely on his own appearance. I guess at the time it was an unusual style but it sure didn't help me at all.'

Lindsay-Hogg sensed another dimension to Jagger's narcissism.

'There were problems in the band,' he says. 'There was definitely rancour between Brian on the one hand and Mick and Keith on the other, because Jones had started the band, and he was the most glamorous Stone with all the sex appeal, and they wanted to change that.'

The third person crucial to their success in this, Andrew Oldham, made his own mark on Lindsay-Hogg.

'Andrew', he recalls, 'wore dandy clothes and had unusual sleek wraparound sunglasses, but he was very quick to be aggressive. His attitude was attack rather than sit back, and his first instinct was to go for you. I noticed he was quick to grasp if someone was attaching themselves to the band and would immediately figure out how that could affect or advance him.

'Oldham always made a point of telling people that his chauffeur carried a gun. Jeez, the boy looked 16, it was hardly likely. He had a limo with tinted windows and was the first person I knew with one. It was in that car that I first smoked a joint. We were on our way to rehearse with the Stones, and I was in the back with Andrew. He was playing a Brian Wilson tape of new songs he'd been sent, and he pressed the button for the screen to go down and asked, "Eddie? The box please!" This silver box was handed back full of these perfectly rolled joints. It was a funny baptism.'

Whilst performing 'The Last Time' on *RSG* fans pulled Jagger off stage. He suffered only a sprained ankle, but enjoyed some tongue-in-cheek embroidery of the incident: 'A mass of girls smothered me,' he said. 'I was stamped on by scores of stiletto heels!'

Personal safety became a serious concern throughout the two-week UK tour, which, supported by the Hollies and Dave Berry, began at the Regal, Edmonton.

'In those days it was still the old style variety shows,' Berry recalls. 'Johnny Ball was our compère who'd come away with the funnies then introduce the next act. You couldn't wear make-up on stage on a Sunday. It'd something to do with it being illegal to hold a theatrical event on the Sabbath. Pop concerts were classed as different, and so got round that rule, but if you wore make-up that made it a theatrical performance.

'There was an act on the bill called the Checkmates who were a Barron Knights-type turn, and one Sunday in Manchester they came on wearing make-up so the theatre manager brought the curtain down on the rest of the night. We were all totally bemused but they stuck to their guns.

'It was a fortnight of absolute bedlam though, every night booked into a different hotel, and they weren't the same kind as today. It was all railway-station hotels, which were guarded by po-faced grumpy night porters, with whom you'd to fight to get a drink after hours. We usually managed though and had many an all-night session.'

Alcohol probably contributed to an incident that furthered the Stones' bad-boy reputation. It took place on 18 March at the end of the tour, after their final gig at the Romford ABC Theatre. It was at the Francis Service Station, Stratford, in London's East End, that a refusal by the manager to let the band use the toilet led to Jagger, Jones and Wyman urinating against a side wall. It was midnight, and only one other male customer was present to verify the tales of the foul language that accompanied their abusive behaviour. Dave Berry was travelling with them.

'When we stopped at the filling station the manager got really agitated as soon as he saw who the band were,' he recalls. 'The Stones were out to create a little bit of hell and enjoyed winding the guy up by dancing about the forecourt.

'And of course there was the usual bonus of having a journalist with them. That went on all the time. A *Daily Express* guy would want something for the paper, and you'd make it happen, go to a hotel knowing you'd be chucked out with the journo on hand to witness it, which means the next day you get coverage, and he gets a story for his paper.'

The *quid pro quo* this time got out of hand when what was no more than excessive high spirits became inflated into a national outrage by press coverage. It resulted in their arrest.

Throughout spring the Stones went on a European tour, which ended mid-April in Paris. And Vicki Wickham recalls the Stones' performance at the Olympia Theatre.

'Cathy [McGowan] and I had flown over specially. It was jammed, and you couldn't hear a note. We joined them later in the police riot wagon that was their getaway vehicle that night. It was so peculiar. We all headed for something to eat and pulled up outside a high-class French restaurant in this grim-looking armour-plated van.'

The previous year when Wickham and McGowan had been in Montreux, Switzerland, with the Stones Wickham recalls that Jagger often disappeared.

'He did that a lot, would just go off with no explanation.' In Paris, though, he stayed put.

On his return to London Jagger had just days to spend with Chrissie Shrimpton before embarking on their third US/Canadian tour. But even this short time together was eaten into by plans for the band to be photographed by an exciting new photographer, Gered Mankowitz. He had been surprised to be invited to shoot the Stones and awaited their arrival at his Mason's Yard studio with enthusiasm, only to be given the inevitable runaround. The band were extremely late. Then they took hours to settle down. His brief was mean and moody, but it was hard to achieve as the Stones played up like a bunch of kids.

Jagger's giggling Mankowitz had expected, but not the fact that he didn't find him easy to capture on film.

'Mick didn't stand out at all,' he said. 'It was Brian who was striking in the pictures. He sort of leapt out at you.'

Viewing the results, Oldham was not a happy man. If prominence wouldn't happen naturally, Oldham had to ensure that it was manufactured. When the official programme for the tour, about to commence at the Maurice Richard Arena in Montreal on 23 April, was produced, Jagger suggested he should be called 'Mick the Magic Jagger'.

The tour was certainly magic in that it was a huge success. Along the way they recorded *Shindig* with Jack Good. And also guested on the *Ed Sullivan Show*, where their first appearance on the prestigious CBS network TV show six months earlier had resulted in so many complaints that Sullivan had vowed they'd not be back. But with 'The Last Time' in *Billboard's* Top 10, the ban wasn't justified.

At live gigs crowds were going crazy, and the action was hot off stage too. Throughout the six weeks, despite the promises of fidelity Jagger had made back home, he found it hard to resist the women who threw themselves at him night after night. The hotel corridors that connected the rock stars' suites saw naked giggling groupies with champagne bottles running from room to room, spreading their favours, and anything else, around. Jagger's long-distance protestations of missing his girl back home partly pacified her, but Shrimpton must have known that the writing was on the wall.

Any pending domestic discord was preceded by what happened the night after their final gig at New York's Academy of Music. Jagger was careful with money, and it seems the same was true of drugs. At their last party of the US tour he left with Richard for his hotel room for some peace and quiet in which to get stoned and relax. The easy availability of drugs around the Stones normally precluded any trouble, but things turned nasty when a handful of guests found their supply had run out. Heading for Jagger's room and finding the door locked they began battering on it with their fists. And then their feet. When Jagger opened it, he just told them to get lost. He'd had enough for one day. The tour was over, and he wanted some privacy. Or maybe to hold on to his stash. Whichever, he was deprived of both when he was jammed against the wall of his room and mugged for his stash.

Next day Jagger left with Richard to explore the vastness of the Arizona desert. By now in their early twenties the bond between them had been strengthened by their joint career within a career. Writing songs for the Stones and other artists gave them status and leverage within the band, and a bigger share of the royalties. It also increased their share of power within the Stones. Their marked closeness had long been remarked upon, as Michael Lindsay-Hogg concurs: 'Mick and Keith were very much linked all the way through. If you think of two fingers tightly entwined, then that was them.'

For the past few years they had also lived together, even after Chrissie Shrimpton had become a regular part of Jagger's life. But that now came to an abrupt end. Maybe Shrimpton and Jagger wanted some space to try to build up their relationship. In any case back in London he and Shrimpton rented a centrally located basement flat at 13A Bryanston Mews East, near Marble Arch. Richard remained behind at Holly Hill. The interior decorator, later fashion designer, Thea Porter advised on the substantial renovations they undertook to their new home. But if Jagger thought the house move would outwit the fans, he was proved wrong.

In their perpetual battle in the popularity stakes the Stones topped the Beatles in the US polls and would soon do the same in Britain. The rivalry between fans at street level was so pronounced it often turned ugly, especially among the girls. One day Jagger returned to his new home to find Shrimpton in a street fight with a teenage Beatles fan who'd taken exception to remarks made by Shrimpton about near neighbour Ringo Starr. Jagger pulled Chrissie free and moved the other girl on and out of the way. When the press got hold of the story that Jagger had 'assaulted' a 15 year old girl by kicking her, he was asked to comment on the incident. If they thought he'd deny it, they were mistaken.

'I got really annoyed. Sure I kicked her,' admitted Mick. 'She was laying into my girl and using filthy language.'

In further mitigation he pointed out that as he had been wearing lightweight plimsolls he could not have injured her.

'In fact,' he complained, 'I got the worst of it, because she gave me a few hard clouts.'

Such public embarrassments were all part of a high-profile lifestyle, which included consorting with the British aristocracy, of which Jagger had become an honorary member. That summer Jagger was invited to the 16th birthday party of Lady Victoria Ormsby-Gore. Announced on entry as 'Mr Michael Jagger and Miss Christine Shrimpton' he turned heads with his elegant Edwardian-style suit. Also present was the Queen's controversial sister HRH Princess Margaret, with whom Jagger would later become good friends. He spent some of that night at her table. Feeling abandoned, Shrimpton grew angry as she watched him ingratiate himself. His off/on Cockney accent was replaced by a lisping slur, and he was undoubtedly impressed by the Princess as well as by her cleavage in the low-cut gown. Shrimpton finally walked out, and Jagger went after her. But it would be the last time he put her feelings before his social ambitions.

That complications would develop between Jagger and Shrimpton was inevitable. They were young and immature. Jagger was part of a hugely successful band, Shrimpton, known mostly because of her famous sister and infamous lover, perhaps felt a lack of her own identity. Although not to underrate her abilities, her work writing regular columns for fanzines was often gained through her status as Jagger's girlfriend. Now even that seemed in limbo.

While Jagger was best man at David Bailey's marriage to Catherine Deneuve that August, press talk said that Jagger would be next. That he'd make Shrimpton his wife. But Jagger stressed that he had no plans to wed.

But now his was more than a façade of confirmed bachelordom. Jagger was indeed drifting away from Shrimpton. His life had changed and his public persona along with it. He had moved on and outgrown his old life, including his girlfriend. He was a star, and he wanted someone whose status appeared more equal to his own, a more glamorous high-profile woman in her own right. He had actress Julie Christie in his sights. But only because Marianne Faithfull seemed lost to him.

Jagger had remained infatuated with Faithfull, the more so perhaps because she would have none of him. And in May, pregnant, she had married John Dunbar. Jagger was aggrieved that she could prefer the Cambridge natural-science student to him. But he could do nothing about it. It seems likely that Shrimpton was unaware of how much he wanted Faithfull. So although the band's success continued unabated, so too did the tension between them.

It was a tense time for Jagger with unexpected hazards of live performance to make it more so. When the Stones had played *RSG* live at Wembley, the show went horribly wrong, as Vicki Wickham recalls.

'We had these huge risers on wheels, and what none of us stopped to think of was security. Well, the kids saw a chance to get at the boys and began jumping on to these risers, and eventually they swamped the Stones. Without exaggeration they were almost ripped to shreds. It was all so new to us, and we were incredibly naive about many things, but I can tell you it was not a good moment in our careers.'

They survived the ordeal to take on Scottish and Scandinavian tours, which ended in June, in time for the court summonses for the Francis Service Station incident. Despite Jagger's image as a bad lad his rap sheet showed nothing worse than a couple of minor motoring offences. On 22 July 1965 at West Ham Magistrates Court they were fined just £5 each and condemned by the magistrate for their arrogance.

That same month there was a moment of light relief on *RSG* when the Stones did a send-up of the hot new American duo Sonny and Cher's hit single 'I Got You Babe'.

'It was an idea myself and Michael came up with because we thought it would be a laugh,' Wickham recalls. 'Looking back on it I'm amazed now that they did it, but they were a fun band.'

Miming to the number, Brian Jones and Cathy McGowan were Sonny and Cher, with the other Stones and Andrew Oldham joining in for the chorus. Oldham was paired with Jagger and had to read his lyrics from a note in his hand. But he got easily into the spirit of things. According to Wickham, although Oldham was always outrageous and willing to experiment with the Stones' image and performance, he was hard to know.

'He was always into a box of pills,' she explains, 'and depending on what colour and type they were, this decided what kind of conversation you could have with him. I was witnessing for the first time what the world of drugs looked like. He was very flash.'

Flash was beginning to outgrow its usefulness when in late August the Stones hit the charts with what is still their most famous number, '(I Can't Get No) Satisfaction'. The single, backed by 'The Spider and the Fly', had already been released in America, where it claimed the number 1 slot, as it did in Britain. It had a surprising history. Legend has it that its distinctive riff had come to Richard as he was on the edge of sleep one night in a hotel room on tour. And that Jagger had instantly recognized it as the beginnings of a great song to which he rushed to put the lyrics. But then Richard later admitted, 'If I had had my way 'Satisfaction' would never have been released.'

By now Richard was living each day on a diet of amphetamines and cocaine. It would have been unwise to be guided by anyone's judgement in those circumstances, so a vote was suggested at which Jagger sided with his co-writer not to go with the song. Fortunately the others decided to overrule their unusual crisis of confidence. When it became a hit Jagger's relief allowed him to forget that he had ever entertained any doubts, preferring his recollection of events. 'I had to fight like crazy against Keith to put it out,' he said.

But there was another twist to the story. It remains unsubstantiated, but nevertheless some among their musical contemporaries say that 'Satisfaction's impressive, agitating riff had been thought up by Brian Jones. Noel Redding, bass player with the

Jimi Hendrix Experience, is adamant.

'It is said it was Brian who thought up the riff, played it to them. Then the lads said, "Yeah, right – thanks," and took it.'

By autumn 1965 it was certainly a pivotal time for Brian in the band and in various ways for others too – including Andrew Oldham.

'It was a pulsating time dominated by the Beatles, Stones, Kinks and the Who,' Michael Lindsay-Hogg recalls. 'I had been in the room with Andrew when he phoned the Stones to tell them they'd just gone top in America and boy, was Jagger caught up in the heady euphoria. To him they'd come from playing in a Richmond hotel to being hot stuff in the States, and he had the feeling really that pretty much anything was theirs.' He was right.

The success of 'Satisfaction' gave Jagger even more self-assurance, sometimes making him insufferable. Much of this he fortunately exhausted with his simulated sex on stage. The once gawky front man had begun to find his feet. At rowdy press conferences he enjoyed the wind-up of the media and the public. He was sexually more satisfied, he said, but not so financially. None of the Stones felt that their personal fortune looked as healthy as it should.

Acutely aware of their discontent, Oldham brought in one Allen Klein, an accountant from New Jersey. Klein handled a variety of clients, including soul singer Sam Cooke. The previous year Klein had pursued, but been denied, the chance to manage the Beatles. He courted the Stones with promises of lucrative deals.

Jagger later said that Oldham had sold Klein to them as a gangster-type figure. Days after 'Satisfaction' was released he met the band at London's Hilton Hotel, and soon after was signed up as their co-manager. A new agent, Tito Burns who handled Bob Dylan, was also brought on board, and Oldham was politely relieved of his fiscal responsibilities. It was Eric Easton who got the rawest deal. Quite simply it had been decided that he was dispensable, and Oldham was delegated the job of axing him.

Strung out on a variety of substances Oldham later blamed his drug intake for his own subsequent loss of grip on the Stones. Had he not been 'too fucked up to notice', he claimed, he would never have let them slip through his fingers. But his ambition was to be rich and famous. His talent was for hype. He had already achieved fame vicariously through the Stones, but, like them, he was not mega-rich. Klein promised that, and a lot more besides. He was a shrewd operator who hadn't taken long to identify their Achilles heel.

To back the new single the Stones returned to the road, this time with a September tour that was marred by the violence among the fans. So much so that police had to use fire hoses for control. The trouble on the tour started at the Dublin Adelphi Theatre gig. Wyman found himself beaten back against the piano. Jones fought off three at a time. Richard fled as soon as Jagger was knocked down. And Charlie Watts played on regardless. In Germany street riots in Dusseldorf caused hoteliers to cancel their reservations. And in Berlin Jagger turned up the heat by goose-stepping on stage at the Waldbühne Halle. To avoid injury when trying to leave the building that night the band had to escape using the underground passageways that were part of Hitler's wartime campaign centre.

If some thought the Stones had gone crazy, the title of their new album was very apt. *Out of our Heads* was released on 24 September 1965, to coincide with a 22-date UK tour, at the end of which their eighth British single, 'Get Off of My Cloud', was released in late October. The chaos that followed the Stones around the UK paled against the mayhem of their Canadian/American tour. It opened at the Forum, Montreal, moving on to New York the following day. By the time they reached The Gardens in Boston, Massachusetts, on 5 November 'Cloud' was simultaneously number 1 on both sides of the Atlantic.

Appropriately it was Guy Fawkes night when all hell broke loose. The fans outside the venues clambered over the cars in which the band were travelling. In one city a car roof threatened to cave in under their combined weight. Desperate girls who clung to bumpers had their fingers ripped off. Many were trampled in the crush. Jagger could only gape impotently as blood from injured fans spattered the windscreen of his car. But when his limo was conveyed by private elevator to the penthouse level of one hotel he took it as a sign that he was at last a superstar.

The delirium caused by the behaviour on stage crossed into insanity. Later analysing this, Germaine Greer spoke of the prevailing sense that there was revolutionary power in pleasure, strong enough to tear walls down.

'It was no ordinary hysteria,' she said. 'Because it was actually quite specifically genital.'

Male exhibitionism that was sexually potent enough for girls to wet the theatre seats. Jagger responded to this by strutting the stage. The girls became frenetic, bombarding them with a hail of bras and pants. Notes pinned to the underwear gave names and phone numbers, messages and tip-offs of parents being away for the weekend. With the exception of Charlie Watts who, as ever, remained faithful to his wife, the Stones outdid themselves this trip. According to Wyman's log he had nine times more women than Jagger.

As Jagger sang 'Satisfaction', thousands of miles away Chrissie Shrimpton had none at all from her relationship with him, and had, it is said, started to broadcast the fact. Her errant lover had given her a £20 weekly allowance while he was away on tour. But, by late 1965, it is said that she could be found in any one of London's trendiest nightclubs complaining about his absence all year and his steady indifference to sex, presumably with her. Although it takes effort to sustain an active and imaginative sex life within a long-term relationship, Shrimpton would not be Jagger's only steady girlfriend to remark on his increasing coldness over time, as if illicit, uncommitted sex were the only exciting kind. And sex had more to do with power than love.

In America Jagger was spending time with singer Patti LaBelle, who, along with her group, the Bluebells, was supporting the Stones. But even unaware of this fact Shrimpton was exhausted by the suspicions that gnawed away at her. And so she began dating P. J. Proby, the Texan singer with the dramatic voice and trademark beribboned ponytail, loose white shirt and velvet trousers. He had been banned from TV appearances after his skintight trousers split on stage. But her interest in the star with the hit record 'Hold Me' was no more than an attempt to bring Jagger into line. It was a ploy that worked.

Jagger had been having sex with a different stranger every night, but when he heard that Shrimpton was seeing another man he quickly reached her by phone. He broke down and promised not to look at other women if she would break it off with Proby.

'Whenever he'd stray,' said Shrimpton, 'I'd just go out with somebody else, and Mick would be back like a shot. He would never let the woman be the one to call things off. Mick *has* to be the one in control, giving the orders, calling the shots.'

Shrimpton flew to Los Angeles to join him at his hotel as the 5 December gig at the Sports Arena brought the tour to an end. After which they headed to Jamaica on holiday.

Relations with his girlfriend might have improved over the holiday, but it would be a temporary reprieve. Although she didn't care to know it, in Jagger's mind she was probably already on the way out.

The year 1966 had begun with the Stones' appearance on a special *RSG* show, 'The New Year Starts Here'. It would prove just as hectic as the last 12 months. The globetrotting, the intense recording sessions and record releases promotion that started with '19th Nervous Breakdown' on 4 February.

By this time Shrimpton suspected that Jagger had progressed from grass to LSD. She based this on his increasingly odd behaviour when at times he appeared to be hallucinating. But any strangeness, according to Jagger, stemmed from Shrimpton herself. It is said she believed that the Stones' latest hit had been written about her. This he dismissed as neurotic. But her suspicions, if anything, seemed confirmed when his lyrics in subsequent songs became more misogynistic, although it was clear that some of the women he met in those days showed little respect for themselves and threw themselves at his feet. Perhaps Shrimpton should not have taken it so personally.

But it wasn't only Shrimpton who was feeling the squeeze. Brian Jones had endured a rollercoaster year in the band and was in the throes of another. The resentment he believed to be targeted towards him hadn't helped his confidence. His health wasn't good either, leading him to miss gigs, which in turn had stoked more resentment. His friend singer Phil May had kept an eye on things.

'Jagger and Richard together were quite a force,' he explains, 'and this was one of the things that flipped Jones out. Two's company, three's a crowd, and all that. Mick and Keith closely guarded what they believed was their chemistry, and when it came to songwriting made sure that Brian never got a look in, which led to a lot of animosity. And I know he was bitter. His postbag was every bit as big as Mick's, but he was between a rock and a hard place in that band, and when for a time Brian lived in the same building as myself and Dick Taylor in Chester Street, that only made matters worse.

'Mick had quite an elusiveness about him, became rather elitist and wouldn't hang out much with guys from other groups, but Brian did. He and I would go out about 4 a.m. to Covent Garden for a drink and a bacon sarny and stay out for hours. We were on so much stuff anyway that we couldn't contemplate even trying to shut our eyes till after 7 a.m. One morning we arrived home to our building both well gone and the porter said, "Good morning, Brian. Good morning, Mick." And, blimey, did Jones get worked up, running after the man saying, "Yes, I'm Brian. But this isn't Mick! This is Phil May. He's from another band." He was really paranoid about it for some reason.'

Another dimension added to the tension. In Germany the previous autumn Brian Jones had met and was now dating Anita Pallenberg, the fashion model of whose entrance into the Stones' circle Jagger had been wary. She was on assignment in Munich when she'd gatecrashed backstage. Blonde and multilingual she had a strong face, though not classically attractive. According to her, Jagger, whom she later dismissed as a crude lippy guy, deemed her such a threat that he had ordered Shrimpton to stay away from her. For Jones it added a force to his life that would later turn against him, but initially had positive effects that Jagger is said to have disliked.

Jagger also disliked the fact that he was under constant risk of injury on tour. Whilst playing the Salle Vallier, Marseilles, a chair flung at him from the audience resulted in eight stitches around an eye. By the time the European tour ended in Copenhagen early April the fans were so fearless they were beating up the police. Jagger's fear for his own safety allied him squarely with the law. 'I kept out of it as much as possible. I don't like seeing police being thumped,' he remarked.

That spring Jagger was restless again, this time moving out of Bryanston Court into 52 Harley House, an apartment block near Regent's Park. This was just days before *Aftermath* was released. The album's original title, vetoed by Decca, had been *Could You Walk On the Water?*. All the tracks were Jagger/Richard compositions and said to showcase Jagger's ambivalent attitude to the female sex. It was hailed as a triumph for them, and for Jones' genius as a multi-instrumentalist.

A month later the number 1 hit 'Paint It Black' followed. Its strength lay in the sitar playing that dominates it. Jones' innovative work on the Hindu instrument completely transformed what had begun life as a lightweight number. It took his standing among his peers to an all-time high. It was all good for the band, but fuelled its internal rivalries. Something not helped by what happened later during the new single's performance on *RSG*. Director Michael Lindsay-Hogg recalls.

'I came up with the idea for Mick to think of himself as Lucifer, and for dramatic effect at the end of each verse he should throw up his hands and another light would go out. Unfortunately near the end of the song kids trampled on a cable, which broke the vocal link, and you couldn't hear his singing. It was live, but we always recorded it and gave them a playback afterwards, and when Mick discovered what had happened he and Keith were seriously pissed off. I explained that it didn't matter because the mesmeric quality of the sitar was what was really going on in the song anyway. But it didn't help.'

Soon after this Jagger, worn down by the internal machinations within the Stones and feeling the strain of his turbulent relationship, collapsed at home from nervous exhaustion. A Harley Street doctor pronounced him unfit for work, but he managed to appear the next night on a TV show called *A Whole Scene Going*.

Just a couple of weeks later he had to be fit enough to join the band for yet another US tour. It began on 24 June 1966 and was problematic from the start. First the UK press reported that the Stones were to sue some top hotels for refusing them accommodation. Then, within hours of their first sell-out gig at the Manning Bowl in Lynn, Massachusetts, their equipment was stolen. When it all ended, Jagger recuperated in Mexico. On his return to England in late August he was involved in a car crash. Neither he nor Chrissie was hurt, but the damage to his Aston Martin DB6 was extensive.

Controversy continued with the release on 23 September of 'Have You Seen Your Mother, Baby, Standing In The Shadow?'. The album it preceded by a couple of months, *Big Hits (High Tide And Green Grass)*, would go on to be hailed as the sixties' best greatest hits compilation, but the single's sleeve had a colour shot of the band in drag.

They had known photographer Jerry Schatzberg for years, and when Oldham came up with what was an outrageous suggestion for its time, he rounded up the Stones in all their finery in a New York back street off Third Avenue. For the shoot Jagger was made up like a Negress, and his grin at being swathed in furs and bonnet supports his later assertion that he loved dressing in women's clothes. Cross-dressing would become a feature of Jagger parties, which, according to him, is all something to do with being an Englishman.

With their new single stalling at number 5, the lowest UK chart position for two years, the Stones opened a two-week UK tour at the Royal Albert Hall, supported by Ike and Tina Turner. 'River Deep, Mountain High' was already a hit, and Jagger carefully watched Tina Turner throughout her performance. Her stagecraft was worth studying. But it was P. P. Arnold, a member of their backing group, The Ikettes, who Jagger fell for, though not with any known success.

Shrimpton's days as Jagger's girlfriend were numbered. He was too young and the glory had gone to his head too much to tolerate a romantic liaison that caused him so much trouble. He would say, tongue in cheek, that 'All women are groupies,' but it was true that sex was easy to come by for him. And commitment, for everyone, is harder. He has himself admitted that it is anathema to him.

For a surprisingly long period then, whilst never sexually faithful, he had nevertheless sustained a relationship with Shrimpton. But it was different now. With Anita Pallenberg around, the brunette seemed dowdy by comparison. And, according to friends, privately he would point out that he didn't find Shrimpton attractive enough any more.

He'd had his eye for some time on his own blonde acquisition, but so far, although not true to her husband, she had still eluded him, apparently turned off by his uncouthness. Marianne Faithfull had been around the Stones long enough to have seen Jagger often under some influence and considered him on those occasions to be a 'lousy drunk'. Yet, as the tour tailed off in early October, all that was about to change.

By autumn 1966 Faithfull's marriage to John Dunbar had been

failing for some time. Legend has it that she tried sex with Brian Jones and Keith Richard with intentions of moving on to Jagger. But, according to her, she and Jones, whilst both on drugs one night, were only at the foreplay stage when unflatteringly, Jones passed out on her.

It was a different story with Richard. Him, she did sleep with, and by this time her head was already full of romantic notions. She maintains this night of passion remained a secret for decades, only later admitting that it was a wonderful night of sex, apparently the best of her life. Unfortunately the earth hadn't similarly moved for Richard. What she imagined to be just the beginning, he made clear the next day was the end. Worse, the one-night stand meant so little to him that he encouraged her to have sex with Jagger, who had been wanting her for years.

When she accompanied Jones and Richard to the Bristol hotel in which the band were staying when they played the Colston Hall, it was with no burning desire to bed Jagger. After years of lusting after her, he seems to have been equally slow to make a move. It could have been because she was extremely stoned, but it was sunrise before they fell into bed.

'We'd been circling each other that long,' said Faithfull, 'but I still didn't know what I really wanted to do.' She described herself as having been deeply moved by his kindness. But for all that she left soon after with her son Nicholas for Italy.

Jagger's ego, indeed many men's, would have made it hard to believe that she could spend the night with him and not want to come back for more. But Faithfull's own admissions speak instead of the logical way she looked at the advantages for her of pursuing a relationship with him. En route to Italy she had stopped in Paris, where a message awaited her from John Dunbar. He wanted her back, but she tossed the letter away. It was too much fun being unattached, and frankly, she admits to her promiscuity. In the French capital, days after sleeping with Jagger, she had sex with the male model boyfriend of her travelling companion. This devastated her friend and meant nothing to Faithfull.

Once in Positano Jagger plagued her with long-distance phone calls, desperate for her to let him join her there. He laboured under the illusion that she was the vulnerable child-troubadour of Oldham's original creation when, in fact, she was in some ways not so unlike himself. Flattered though she was to find his stack of messages, it was not enough to prevent her from continuing to think through her situation. Her husband she viewed as unworldly. Someone who made little money. She was supporting her son herself, something she never cared for. In some ways Jagger was her meal ticket, and by becoming his girlfriend she would no longer need to work. But there was a snag. Her heart hankered after Keith Richard, and she rang manager Allen Klein to discuss her dilemma. Klein supposedly warned Faithfull that it would destroy Mick if she didn't let him into her life. Although an obvious ploy and gross exaggeration, it pleased Marianne to believe it.

'But the whole time I was with Mick I was in love with Keith,' she later mourned. Her decision then to allow Jagger in was a calculated one. She saw him as most likely to provide her materially with what she wanted. She clearly wanted him. But not to the extent that her heart should rule her head. And so it all began.

This was scant comfort to Chrissie Shrimpton, when over the coming weeks her lover dated Faithfull behind her back. The end came when she waited for Jagger to join her at the airport on 15 December. They had planned the holiday in Jamaica for over a month, but he didn't turn up. Anxiously she rang the Stones' office, pleading to speak to Jagger. But he was Christmas shopping in London with Faithfull.

The vicious end game that followed peaked with a painful showdown between them three days later at Harley House, which finally ended their relationship. Later that Sunday night Shrimpton was reported to have been admitted to the Greenway Nursing Home, Hampstead, after an attempt at suicide by overdosing on sleeping pills.

She survived. But if it had been a cry for help it fell on deaf ears. A characteristic that would often surface is Jagger's ability to remain apparently distant from a person's suffering, even in the case of someone he once professed to love. The Stones' office immediately closed down her line of credit. On Christmas Eve her belongings were removed from Harley House. When the hospital bill for her treatment was sent to Jagger he returned it, refusing to pay. Shrimpton later maintained that his treatment of her was not so much personal as indicative of a basic animosity she believes he feels towards women in general.

'The fact is,' she revealed, 'Mick doesn't like women. He never has.' She would not be the last woman to think that. But it seems they found him hard to resist.

6

DRUGS AND DEVIATION

WITH FAITHFULL JAGGER quickly moved on. She too appeared untroubled by Shrimpton's suicide bid. Referring directly to it, she once admitted: 'I can't pretend that I was sympathetic to her plight. On the contrary, I was feeling pleased with myself.' It was an honest but nevertheless harsh response of one human being towards another.

In mid-January 1967 the Stones' new single, 'Let's Spend the Night Together', was released, followed by the album *Between the Buttons*. It was immediately after this that Jagger and Faithfull's affair went public. She was appearing in the Italian Song Festival in San Remo, and when he flew into Cannes to meet her, the press were on hand. To escape their attentions they hired a boat and took to sea for a week, where in the best romantic tradition a tempest blew up to endanger their lives. Jagger behaved well and kept his head, able to comfort Faithfull and her child. So much so that Jagger managed to sow some genuine emotion in Faithfull for him.

Once on shore they held their first joint press interview, she looking at him adoringly. 'After that I was never away from him,' she said.

She was also hardly away from drugs. At their rented house in Positano they both dropped acid. But whereas Jagger's intake was relatively controlled, she particularly smoked a lot of hash. Feeling too out of it one night at a local nightclub she tried to buy some mild uppers. The pills she got were a form of travel-sickness tablets, of which Jagger took one and Faithfull swallowed several. She slipped the remaining pills in her pocket and promptly forgot about them.

On their return to England Jagger wanted Faithfull to move in to his Marylebone Road apartment. But she didn't feel right stepping so fast into Shrimpton's shoes. She must have had some feelings for what had happened to her. She had no qualms, however, about sifting through the few personal belongings left behind, possibly curious to get a fix on the woman who had once figured so strongly in Jagger's life. Caving in to Jagger's pressure in the end she moved in with him, while Nicholas and his nanny remained at her Lennox Gardens flat.

Now that the bumpy ride with Shrimpton was over Jagger was looking for a less draining relationship. Notwithstanding his need to have a glamorous woman on his arm, he also liked to know that she was safe at home. It hadn't escaped his notice that by retaining her own place, Faithfull was showing that she wasn't entirely committed. Years later he'd find a woman's independence, especially financial, attractive, but soon after Faithfull's arrival they rowed about her determination to lead her own life. And as Shrimpton had done before, Faithfull walked out on him, leaving Jagger back in the old routine. He had to make a big effort to coax her home.

Initially Jagger revelled in his new romance, but in time he would feel the effects of Faithfull's drug use. He contented himself with grass, acid and the occasional amphetamine, despite encouragement from his lover to be more adventurous. In private he was exploring himself, in inimitable sixties' fashion. He loved dressing up in Faithfull's clothes. He liked dropping acid with her too, their intimacy sometimes gatecrashed by other people. At such times the drug would take Jagger into a world of his own, where he would dance feverishly for Faithfull, his body coiled like a corkscrew. Thoroughly out of it, Faithfull would watch his performance enraptured by it. He was her very own Dionysus. According to her, though, he also had other fantasies.

When Jagger and Shrimpton had moved house Keith Richard had not remained alone at Holly Hill for long. In autumn 1966 he had moved in with Brian Jones at his Courtfield Road flat. At the time this had pleased Jones, who felt he had an ally at last in the Stones. In reality Richard only had designs on Jones' lover Anita Pallenberg. When by the year's end Jones realized this, the atmosphere had darkened enough to drive Richard out.

It was inevitable he would move back in with Jagger. By this time, like Bill Wyman and Charlie Watts, Richard had bought a country house. His was Redlands in West Wittering on the Sussex coast, but he preferred the buzz of London, and had never been happy too far from Jagger. Likewise Jagger missed Richard's company. When he told Faithfull that Richard was coming to stay at Harley House, he said it would make their songwriting easier.

Considering her own feelings for the guitarist Faithfull was edgy about the new arrangement. She was worried that Jagger would find out about their one-night stand. Then something happened to make her wonder if she shouldn't tell him after all.

The couple were in bed as Jagger teased Faithfull to guess what his pleasure would be that night. She was listing everything from sexy underwear to kinky S&M, when he supposedly made a suggestion that surprised her. Richard was on the other side of the wall in the next bedroom, and, according to Faithfull, Jagger began to shout out his fantasy that Richard might join them. He'd like to lick every inch of the guitarist's body, he said. And, Faithful claims he added, 'Then I'd suck his cock.'

Whether this was a real wish or just a big wind-up, Faithfull was thrown by it. Possibly she felt jealous that his fantasy had not centred on her and confused by her own feelings for Richard. But it was then that she wondered whether or not to admit to her night with Richard. If she had it might just have brought the strange sexual brew to the boil. She later believed that Jagger might have thought more of her if she had.

Relationships were the last thing on Jagger's mind after reading the newspapers one morning early in February. The *News of the World* were running a series of exposés of the debauched lifestyles of the rich and famous, and in its pages Jagger found himself reported as admitting he had taken LSD. And that he had been seen consuming and distributing the amphetamine Benzedrine at Blaise's nightclub in Kensington. The article claimed that Jagger had told the reporter that he had to take bennies to stay awake.

He was furious. But Faithfull only laughed. The truth was that the journalist had mistaken Brian Jones for Jagger, an extraordinary error by 1967. But the confusion only thickened when, later in the day, West Coast America woke up to a Los Angeles radio DJ announcing that in London Mick Jagger had died. In a variation of the old 'Rumours of my death have been grossly exaggerated,' Jagger, still angry, took the opportunity to set the record straight when appearing with the Stones on the *Eamonn Andrews Show* that night. Furthermore he intended to sue the newspaper. Two days later his lawyers issued the requisite libel writ.

His righteous indignation seemed odd considering that he did take drugs, although the public perception of drug taking in the mid-sixties was not a winning formula for success. It could have been damaging to his career, much as it could be in the 1990s. But it was unclear what exactly upset him. Was it the fact the *News of the World* exposé, in which other rock stars were accused of drug taking, might demystify and downgrade the bad-lad Stones image? Or was it because it was publicity they themselves had not orchestrated? Something he never liked. Or merely the fact that he had been mistaken for Brian Jones? In the immediate aftermath Jagger is also said to have suspected it was part of a set-up by government agencies.

All this being so, Jagger made a less than intelligent decision, just days later, to join a party of people at Redlands and try out a new drug. Robert Fraser had rung to tell him about David Schneiderman, a young American, who would deliver to them an assortment of narcotics. When the Stones' recording session ended at Olympic Studios, late on Saturday 11 February, Jagger and Marianne left for Sussex to join Christopher Gibbs, photographer Michael Cooper, Fraser, a mate of Richard's Nicky Kramer and Schneiderman, affectionately known as 'Acid King David'. Brian Jones and Anita Pallenberg had intended to go too but never made it, unlike Beatle George Harrison and his wife.

They partied until dawn, when the Harrisons left, and everyone else fell asleep. Schneiderman woke him and the others a few hours later with tea and White Lightning, a drug similar to LSD. Jagger usually had a good reaction to acid, but it only appeared to send him to sleep again. When he woke at noon he was still tripping and was fed a different equally premium drug. To stir the lethargy they all went out for a drive in the country and a walk on the beach, before returning to Redlands tired and dirty from playing in the sand. Faithfull, wet through, went for a bath, leaving Jagger lying in a light stupor, gently coming down from the day-long trip.

Less than an hour later he lay curled up at Faithfull's feet. She was reclining on a sofa wrapped in an enormous fur rug whilst her clothes dried. At 8 p.m. Schneiderman alerted Richard to someone knocking on the front door. Assuming it to be auto-graph hunters he swung it open to confront instead a squad of grim-faced police officers with a search warrant. The confusion that ensued would later produce some mythic stories. Not least the cops' discovery of Faithfull, spreadeagled on the sofa, with Jagger's head buried between her bare thighs, eating a Mars bar wedged up her vagina. Faithfull later dismissed the tale as total fabrication. But what *was* true was that they were well and truly busted.

The house smelt of hashish and incense. Isolated into small groups Jagger watched anxiously as his lover was led away for searching by a WPC. His nervousness was not so much about what might happen to her, more what her unguarded tongue might say. When four pills were found in a pocket of his jacket slung over a chair in an upstairs bedroom, Jagger instantly said they were his. These were in fact the tablets left over from Positano. Understandably his motive was firstly damage limitation, as he feared that under pressure Faithfull could inadvertently make matters worse. In any case it was a small risk. They were only travel sickness tablets, legal in Italy.

Accounts vary as to whether a diligent search was carried out, or whether it was a cursory effort, a mere going through the motions once Jagger had been found in possession of pills. The police, however, went about bagging and tagging various items until they came to Robert Fraser, on whom they found 24 jacks of heroin. He lied that it was medication for diabetes, and the police accepted this. Only as a formality was one confiscated for testing.

But the strangest occurrence involved Schneiderman. The briefcase in which he was carrying his drug supplies was the single most damning piece of evidence in the house. The individual packages inside it, wrapped in silver foil, identified only by coded initials even looked suspicious. Yet detectives, there on a tip-off that a wild drugs party was in full swing, accepted the explanation that it was photographic film, that could not be unwrapped for risk of exposure. They promptly handed back the case.

At the time there was huge relief, but later in the cold light of day, they didn't have far to look to focus their suspicions about what might have happened. No one, it seemed, knew anything about Schneiderman. Not his real name, not his nationality, nor how he had sprung from nowhere in the previous fortnight to move so freely in exalted music circles. The man with the briefcase full of pills he denied himself walked out of Redlands and their lives that night for ever.

Starting to sober up that night Jagger was still concerned about the potential risk posed by Faithfull, whom to his dismay he saw was enjoying herself hugely. Someone had provocatively put on a Dylan record at full blast, and she was out to have some fun. She recalls it as a great moment when she let the rug slip, tantalizingly enjoying the reaction this drew from the dozen or so policemen present. In contrast Jagger was displeased with her. Feeling her behaviour inappropriate he grew increasingly tense.

He was no less so when there was no mention of the bust in next day's newspapers, something he found hard to accept as good news since it fuelled suspicions that something odd was going on. Claims later surfaced that a covert attempt had been made to bribe the police to take no further action. That criminal associates of gangland's Kray twins were hired to establish who'd set them up.

There was a further twist when, despite the news blackout, the *News of the World* ran a feature the following week about a drugs raid on a rock star's house party. It mentioned no names but was enough to jar already frayed nerves. Jagger began to consider a CIA plot to destroy the Stones. He also wondered at the timing of the bust, just when he had taken out a libel action against the *News of the World* to deny their assertion that he took drugs. He had no proof. But it was a theory he didn't drop.

Jagger and Richard consulted their lawyers and waited. But

nothing happened. They withstood the suspense long enough, then decided to leave the UK for a while. In early March Jagger flew with Faithfull to Morocco. As a relaxing break, it proved a disaster.

Trying not to involve himself in the fact that Keith Richard had started an affair with Brian Jones' lover Anita Pallenberg, Jagger found himself diverted by another hotel guest, Cecil Beaton. The bisexual photographer was an influential cultural force in British life with a colourful reputation for high-society escapades, stemming from when he was romantically linked with the actress Greta Garbo in the 1940s.

Despite concern for his recent, still phantom, brush with the law Jagger recommended LSD to Beaton. As an artist it would sharpen his appreciation of colour. Beaton didn't want to betray that his interest lay mainly in Jagger when he took the Stones out next day on a photo shoot. But he was clearly fascinated by him. At one point he photographed Jagger's nude bottom, which later sold for £2500. Beaton rated Jagger sexy yet sexless. 'He could nearly be a eunuch,' he said.

Back in the UK the press reports were that Jagger, Richard and possibly two others faced charges for drug offences relating to an incident at Redlands the previous month, maintaining that summonses were imminent. When they did it was for a hearing at Chichester magistrates' court on 10 May.

But before that a European tour was scheduled, which too had complications. Not able to handle his depression over Pallenberg's defection and Richard's betrayal, Jones had checked into the Priory Clinic, Roehampton. Any notion of taking this opportunity to oust him from the band was thwarted when Jones checked out to join them in Sweden. After two weeks in the private clinic, he was scarcely better.

The Redlands revelations had international repercussions. At the airport, customs were ready to give the Stones a hard time. They carried out a painstaking scrutiny of luggage and individual body searches.

On tour the police had started to get tough with riotous fans and were fighting back, using batons so freely that it led Jagger to snarl, 'Why do you have to hit girls on the head?' By the time the tour reached Italy it was Jagger who, according to Faithfull, was getting physical. Jagger has never had a reputation for using serious physical violence against women, so maybe it was the poisonous atmosphere on stage between Jones and Richard plus the violence that erupted each night at gigs that proved too much for him. Whatever the reason, after a particularly rough run at Rome's Palazzo dello Sport, he returned to his hotel suite and Faithfull, and allegedly went berserk.

Like the rock star babe she hated to be thought, she was waiting in bed for him wearing only a see-through negligée. To her horror his reaction to her surprise visit was, she has said, to slap her repeatedly across the face. According to Faithfull it was as if he had become momentarily a different person. After the initial shock she fled, but he came after her and allegedly continued to strike her. She later maintained he beat her badly. But that it was a one-off act of violence he never repeated.

His humour didn't improve as the tour progressed. In Paris he complained, 'I feel as if I am being treated as a witch,' after another heavy session with customs' officials. Unimpressed with the argument French officials delayed them so much at Le Bourget airport that the band missed their flight to Warsaw. Jagger lashed out in anger at one officer whose retaliation floored him. But he was lucky an assault charge wasn't added to his problems.

Fights broke out again, in Poland this time, when fans rioted outside Warsaw's Palace of Culture during the Stones' first visit to Eastern Europe. Steel-helmeted police clashed with fans who demolished crash barriers and tried to charge the iron gates. Coming under a hail of bottles and bricks, the authorities used water cannons to cope with the second performance.

The spiral of violence followed them to Zurich, where the precautions taken to protect the band at the Hallen Stadium were not adequate. One youth managed to scale the 20-foot stage and get close enough to Jagger to grab him from behind, pin his arms to his sides and throw him to the floor. He then tried to stamp on his chest. Chauffeur-cum-minder Tom Keylock went to his rescue and hit the boy so hard he broke his hand. Despite these experiences, when the tour ended at Athens' Panathinaikos football stadium, Jagger announced that the Stones would never tour America again because it had been one put down after another. They would instead concentrate on Europe. But he had no way of knowing that the Greek gig would signal the end of Stones' tours anywhere in the world for over two years.

Back in London that spring Jagger spoke out in support of teenage rebellion, and against politicians whom he dismissed as half-witted and authoritarian. This call for freedom of expression attracted the attention of Labour MP Tom Driberg, with whom he would go on to have a rather one-sided friendship. Claims that Jagger seriously considered standing for Parliament do not bear serious close scrutiny. The work involved hardly fitted with being a rock 'n' roll star, but he was a public figure, and people listened when he was reported by the press as saying, 'I see a lot of trouble coming in the dawn.'

His own problems came to a head on 10 May with his first appearance in Chichester Magistrates' court alongside Richard and Robert Fraser. The committal proceedings were brief. All were sent to trial at West Sussex Quarter Sessions in June and released on £100 bail each. A modest number of fans had gathered outside the courthouse. But hours later the scale of the Stones' plight was brought into sharp focus when news broke that Brian Jones had just been busted.

Jones' own problems had heightened when he'd tried and failed to woo Pallenberg back from Richard. He was drowning his sorrows in drink and drugs and had woken up that day amid the wreckage of a heavy night. One of his guests, Stash, otherwise known as the Swiss Prince Stanilaus Klossowski de Rola was still there too when Scotland Yard Drug Squad detectives had arrived. Jones could only watch as they confiscated various items for analysis.

What they'd found was enough cannabis to roll ten reefers. But when he was bundled outside to the waiting police car, he was mobbed by waiting reporters. It seemed inexplicable that practically the whole of London's press corps already knew about the bust. By 5 p.m. Jones was charged with possession of a quantity of cannabis and cannabis resin, and with permitting his premises to be used for the purposes of smoking illegal substances. He was to appear at Marlborough Street Magistrates' Court the next morning. That night as newspaper billboards announced THIRD ROLLING STONE ON DRUGS CHARGE, it was apparent that the police were out to break the Stones. Hearing about Jones' bust, Jagger feared that it would prejudice his own and Richard's trial.

Preparation for the trial took up much of the coming weeks as Jagger met with his lead defence counsel Michael Havers QC, later Britain's Attorney General. Publicly he adopted a carefree attitude, but privately he was aware that the outcome of no trial is a foregone conclusion. Havers wanted to have the two Stones' cases tried separately from Fraser's as he was up on more serious charges relating to possession of heroin. Because Jagger had admitted that the Italian travel-sickness pills were his, his defence was that they were of a type obtainable over the counter everywhere in Italy. Although they contained traces of speed and had not been prescribed by his doctor, he made the case that his GP could have prescribed him something similar. On this defence he went to trial on 27 June 1967.

Faithfull didn't attend even this first day. Instead with her son, Nicholas, and a friend she went into hiding at the home of Small Faces lead singer Steve Marriott. She had turned to drugs for comfort. While Jagger scanned the public gallery for her she was getting stoned somewhere in Richmond. What worried Jagger most is unclear, but when he had tracked her down she was found to be still tripping.

More sober, that evening Faithfull visited Jagger in Lewes jail remand cells with young photographer Michael Cooper. Jagger, still upset at a guilty verdict, was trying to put a brave face on things. Richard had been allowed home as his trial began the next day. Like Faithfull and Cooper, he'd initially romanticized the idea of lying low in their outlaw hideout, but with the stark reality of Jagger and Fraser both banged up, he spent an anxious night. Faithfull, lost and alone and under the influence of LSD, spent the night in the arms of Michael Cooper.

Next day Richard's trial opened. For its duration Jagger was held in the court's basement cell, brought there handcuffed to Robert Fraser. This extreme measure was captured on camera and shows him acting up, trying to get Fraser to smile along with him. But it was a different story once inside. Richard was found guilty.

In a last-ditch effort Havers protested on Jagger's behalf that over 100 varieties of pills similar to those involved in his case were obtainable on the NHS, but to no avail. The judge began his address with the comment that their offences potentially carried a maximum 10-year sentence. Richard came off worst – one year in prison with £500 costs. Fraser received six months with £200 costs, and Jagger was sentenced to three months with £100 costs. Reporters in court noted his distress at receiving a custodial sentence. Deeply shocked, he was led from the dock to Brixton Prison, while the others were taken to Wormwood Scrubs.

It was the biggest upset of Jagger's life. Years later he spoke offhandedly about it. Of how he had mentally prepared himself for the three-month sentence. But when Faithfull saw him that night, he was distraught, despairingly asking her, 'What am I going to do?' Perhaps upset for him too she hid it nevertheless by a display of toughness, calling him spineless. The experience proved salutary in that Jagger never let his guard down in front of Faithfull again.

In the event his ordeal in jail was a short one for on 30 June Havers managed to get both Stones released on £7000 bail each pending appeal. Fraser was refused bail. The next afternoon, spruced up and grinning again, Jagger emerged from Brixton to wave at press and fans. Immensely relieved, he was driven off in his limo for Shepherd's Bush, to pick up Richard from the Scrubs.

But Jagger was on bail and therefore not free. In the meantime though he would appreciate the groundswell of anger that had risen against the authorities, in this case largely dismissed as Draconian. The Who, not to miss a trick, on the day Jagger and Richard were sentenced had announced that they intended to release a series of Stones' compositions to keep them alive in the public's mind.

But it wasn't necessary. Stones' fans were already roused. Many had protested at the sentences outside the offices of the *News of the World*, broadly seen as involved. When police had moved them on they joined a bigger gathering at the Eros statue in Piccadilly Circus, chanting into the night 'FREE THE STONES!' But the most influential support came from an unexpected quarter.

Prior to the trial *The Times* had taken little interest in the Rolling Stones, reporting on the band as they had the Beatles, as an interesting development in popular culture. Now on 1 July 1967 its editor William Rees-Mogg weighed in with a leader famously titled WHO BREAKS A BUTTERFLY ON A WHEEL?

'It wasn't particularly related to supporting the Rolling Stones,' says Lord Rees-Mogg today. 'It was to address the injustice of the sentences. In Mick Jagger's case it seemed particularly clear that he was being singled out because he was famous and that nobody else in these circumstances would have been more than bound over. I personally thought it was wrong.'

Within days other papers followed his lead. Later Jagger went personally to see Lord Rees-Mogg to thank him.

Jagger now returned to Olympic Studios for recording commitments. Brian Jones, on the verge of a nervous breakdown, had just been re-hospitalized at the Roehampton clinic and did not join them. With pressure of every description closing in on him he was diagnosed as possibly suicidal. One of the hardest prospects he had to face remained working with the other Stones, particularly on their current project.

Weeks after John Lennon had made the shock announcement in May that they were done with touring, the Beatles released *Sgt Pepper's Lonely Hearts Club Band*. The product of 700 hours of studio time, the pioneering album unsettled and affected the creative output of every other band in pop, the Stones included.

The record labels for the Stones and the Beatles had deliberately ensured their releases rarely clashed. This neatly avoided the risk of chart defeat at the other's hands and could sustain the illusion of equality. Now this watershed album, which would spend six months at number 1, creatively put the Beatles in pole position. This, compounded by the failure of *Between the Buttons*, unsettled Jagger and Richard, and made them fearful of demotion in the songwriting league.

Unwisely the Stones decided to produce an album just like *Sgt Pepper*. *Their Satanic Majesties Request* was not the success they'd hoped for when it was released at the end of the year. And Brian Jones' opposition to it had marginalized him further. He was not the only one feeling isolated. Matters were coming to a head with Oldham, but the most compelling drama unfolded in an upcoming court appearance.

In the month since his conviction Jagger was concerned that he might lose his appeal and go to jail. Leaving the office for the High Court on 31 July, he wished the Stones' secretary well for her imminent wedding should he not be able to attend. But his anxieties were put to rest when the Lord Chief Justice, Lord Parker, although upholding the conviction, commuted the sentence to a conditional discharge. Richard's conviction was quashed, but Fraser's appeal failed. A great deal had been riding on the outcome of this appeal, and the media had anticipated it either way.

As soon as Jagger left court he attended a press conference at Granada TV studios. In releasing him Parker had advised that as a rock idol Jagger had social responsibilities. But high on freedom Jagger defiantly announced to journalists that 'My responsibility is only for myself.'

In previous weeks he had been invited by John Birt, then a young Granada researcher, to appear in TV's *World In Action*, to be filmed on the day of the appeal. Jagger had agreed, obviously without knowing if he'd be available. When the press conference ended Birt, now Director General of the BBC, Jagger and Faithfull were taken by helicopter to Spains Hall, Finchingfield, the home of Colonel Sir John Ruggles-Brise, the Lord Lieutenant of Essex, where the programme was to be filmed. Demob happy, Jagger's behaviour with his girlfriend in the aircraft and at Spains Hall was a source of some embarrassment. So much so that when the crew were ready to start filming, Birt had the unenviable task of trying to prise the lovers out of a bedroom they had commandeered at the mansion.

The idea was for a debate among Jagger and four leading figures in society, including William Rees-Mogg.

'I thought it was a very good idea,' recalls the *Times* former editor, 'as I was interested to find out basically what the ideas were behind the Rolling Stones, because of the great impact they were having on the young. The feeling was that the Stones had an emotional bridge to their audience. It was perfectly genuine, and in fact in the mid-sixties in British society a sort of struggle was going on against old paternalism and whatever the new society was going to be, and I feel that the Stones were more important in that respect than the Beatles.

'Besides myself there was old Frank Soskice, an ex-Labour Home Secretary, John Robinson, Bishop of Woolwich, who had written the book *Honest to God*. I thought him very superficial. Then there was a Jesuit priest, Father Thomas Curbishley, of the three the most intellectual and honest. I wouldn't mark Robinson very high on either and as for Soskice, high on honesty but not so high on intellect.'

Shrewdly Rees-Mogg assessed Jagger's response to the panel's questions.

'He was mildly contemptuous of Robinson,' he says, 'friendly but not overly respectful to Soskice and clearly identified Curbishley as the serious figure. I was impressed with the subtlety of his personal responses. He was much more intellectually gifted than I had expected him to be. He had a quick mind, and it struck me that he had an equally quick eye for the defects of the people interviewing him.'

That summer Jagger and Faithfull joined an ill-fated trip to Wales to attend a seminar by the religious guru Maharishi Mahesh Yogi. In August they moved, with Nicholas, into 48 Cheyne Walk, a house for which he paid £40,000 on the banks of the Thames at Chelsea. Faithfull had persuaded Jagger to buy the magnificent Queen Anne-style townhouse. Her strategy to get out of him whatever she wanted, one to which she openly admits, was to appeal to what she called 'his snobbery'. 'I had convinced him we had a duty to live up to his position,' she said. No doubt it suited her too.

Their life together continued its ups and downs. Jagger appears to have proved sexually tamer than Faithfull had imagined. Although he liked being in bed with two women, he usually took a back seat, rolling a joint and watching. His penchant for cross-dressing continued in the spirit of the times hallmark experimentation. He seems to have enjoyed sexually blurring the lines. Faithfull later spoke of her lesbian affairs, with which Jagger had no problem. He would be more concerned, she claimed, had she taken a boyfriend. But like Shrimpton, Faithfull would also come to remark on his diminishing interest in sex between them. There were occasions when he appeared to give off ambiguous signals. Such as the time Robert Fraser, who was gay, turned up at the house to find Faithfull alone and curiously made a pass at her just as Jagger walked in. From Faithfull's recollections her lover flew into a rage during which it was hard to work out of whom he was most jealous. Tremors in their relationship were thus faintly detectable.

They were more pronounced, however, in Jagger's professional life. Mid-month the single 'We Love You' had been released. It was hyped by the suggestion that Jagger had written it in jail. But that didn't help at all. Jagger's pride was dented. It was a competitive business with rival bands in adjacent studio space. Whilst *Satanic Majesties* was being recorded the Jimi Hendrix Experience were working on the follow-up to their début number-two album, *Are You Experienced*. Members of either band would drop in on one another during recordings, as Experience bass player Noel Redding recalls.

'While mixing was going on we'd wander through into the Stones' studio, where Jagger, Jones and Richard were usually pretty high. Michael [Mick] came through later into our studio, came up to me and asked if I'd like to smoke a joint with him. He had some wonderful stuff too! We sat down in a corner with the hash, just looked at each other and said, "Good luck."'

Such incidents may have contributed to a convivial atmosphere, but at its core the Stones were discordant. Press reports indicated Andrew Oldham was on his way out. In late September, having made the deal with Klein, it was made official.

But tensions among the band focused on Brian Jones, whose problems with himself and the others led to his collapse and admittance to St George's Hospital at London's Hyde Park Corner. When Jagger heard the news he was not best pleased. Faithfull later attested that the level of animosity towards Jones had now become ferocious, and it was barely concealed by Jagger when he called a press conference, at which he tersely declared, 'There's a tour coming up. There are obvious difficulties. One of them is with Brian who obviously can't leave the country.'

As it happened Jones had discharged himself from hospital within an hour of admission. His doctor reported that there was no cause for alarm. Jones was suffering from strain but was mainly just exhausted. But Jagger was right. There *were* difficulties, and they were a lot more fundamental than being able to go on the road.

7

RIFTS AND RIVALRY

I N 1968 AFTER an undistinguished year professionally, Jagger's subversive image was bolstered by his brief appearance at one of the anti-war demonstrations staged in the new year outside the American Embassy in London.

Equally, for months, it had pleased him to be friendly with Tom Driberg, the enthusiastic Labour MP who wanted to attract the youth vote. Jagger's influence among them was one way of doing this.

The previous summer the former war correspondent had championed the Stones in the House of Commons, criticizing the courts for their handling of the Redlands bust. And from their first encounter he had pandered to Jagger's vanity by repeatedly praising his physical attributes. Jagger listened to the man's impassioned monologues in public and in private. But he was no more than playing politics.

The idea of becoming an MP still attracted him, but the idea that any political affiliation might lie with left-wing doctrines was for some not credible. Lord Rees-Mogg's opinion of the Stones' beliefs was that 'Mick Jagger interestingly turned out to be basically liberal, against the nanny state, and really held to the classic John Stuart Mill view that people should have the freedom to do whatever they want unless it harms others when the State is then entitled to intervene. It was an argument he handled well and at a time when this kind of view was much less heard. It later became, of course, Margaret Thatcher's conservatism.

'Although the Rolling Stones were rebellious they actually represented a relatively right-wing position, and it was the Beatles who were truly left wing. Jagger appeared to me to be what he has since become – a successful businessman, building up his own fortune and believing in individualism.'

So Jagger liked the aura of anarchy but preferred to avoid lawlessness, as became evident when in mid-March he joined a particularly turbulent street demo heading for Grosvenor Square. It was chic to be radical. Several prominent film personalities were taking centre stage at these events, and Jagger wanted to be involved too. He was driven to its fringes towards the banners and slogans of its demonstrators. Instructing Keylock to come back for him in half an hour he surprised the crowd, quick to surround him, and thrilled to the buzz his presence provoked. In between mumbling responses to the man with the megaphone he signed his autograph and glared defiantly for the paparazzi who stumbled backwards before him, determined to capture him for the morning papers.

As soon as the first rock was hurled in anger he wisely left, and by the time the casualty and arrest tolls began to rise he was back in Chelsea. It was after this that he drafted the lyrics to what would become 'Street Fighting Man'.

The rest of spring was spent at Olympic Studios, laying down tracks for a new album, and holidaying in Ireland with Faithfull. It was on Jagger's return from there that the band filmed an exciting promo, which has come to be regarded as the forerunner to the video. It was to accompany a new song 'Jumpin' Jack Flash', which had originated weeks before from Bill Wyman and had been released with 'Child of the Moon' on the B-side. Wyman had been experimenting with an electronic keyboard and had stumbled upon what was perhaps the most interesting riff since 'Satisfaction'.

Recognizing its obvious strength Jagger worked on the lyrics, and by the end of April it had joined the Jagger/Richard canon. Its promo brought them back in touch with *RSG* director Michael Lindsay-Hogg.

'Mick called me up and said they wanted to film something different,' he recalls. 'I'd shot promos for Beatles' numbers including "Paperback Writer", but in those days not everybody could afford to do clips, because usually bands paid for them themselves. Also, only a few could afford the attitude, either you show our promo, or we don't appear at all. Like the Beatles, the Stones, especially Mick, were very much getting to be that they didn't like uncontrolled situations, and promos were a good way around that.'

Jagger and Richard, it seemed, were more in control of the band's affairs these days.

'I initially talked the idea over with Mick and Keith but not the others, and we decided to go for it. Back then there were no contracts involved. It was all a case of How much? £500? Done! A handshake, and that was it. There was no sense that these things would be seen in 5 months let alone 25 years.

'One thing I noticed at this time. Mick had previously always been cool, assessing a situation and using it to gain maximum leverage for himself. We had started at midnight and would work till dawn when, at one point, a policeman came in off the street. Just your average British bobby who had wandered in to watch a while. As soon as Mick saw the uniform he got extremely agitated and barked, "I'm not doing this in front of him. Get rid of him!" The whole Redlands experience and having come close to going to prison had been hard for Mick and still clearly haunted him.

'By half way through the night we had filmed it straight, just a performance with some flashing lights, and it was fine. But then Brian came up with the suggestion that they should alter their whole look by using dramatic make-up and, as it was a tough number, give it a harder edge. I liked it, so we shot a second version. When we'd finished *that's* the version everyone liked, and it was the very first pop promo that had that extra something in it, which set it apart from the normal performance clips.'

The next day Lindsay-Hogg, the Stones and Eileen Atkins, then a young actress, got together to finish filming footage for 'Child of the Moon'.

'We went into the country for the shoot,' says Lindsay-Hogg. 'In addition to Eileen, we also had a child, and Mick and Keith were to appear on horseback at one point.'

'It was filmed in Epping Forest,' Eileen Atkins recalls. 'I was paid fifty quid for an afternoon's work, and it was all rather glamorous to be working with the Rolling Stones. I was impressed with Mick that day, and I do recall that I did my first take very badly indeed. Michael gently said, "I don't think we want it quite like that. Let's do it again," and Mick never gave the slightest clue that he thought I'd just been terrible. He was very charming, and I came to the conclusion that he did have a brain after all.'

When filming ended it was minus one scene.

'Brian was to have been filmed in a tree,' says Lindsay-Hogg, 'but when the time came, we couldn't find him. He had wandered off and got lost.'

The atmosphere between Jagger and Jones was noticeable to the director who admits, 'I don't want to use the word ostracized, but Brian annoyed Mick, that's for sure.'

It had gone beyond annoyance. Lately a few guitarists, including Eric Clapton, had been brought in to the studio to contribute, which Jones took as an insult. He had cleaned up and was off drugs and had regained enough confidence to confront Jagger about it.

This unhealthy atmosphere made it hard for anyone close to the band to treat seriously the rumours that they planned to tour that year. Jagger began to develop his own ambitions. There had often been talk of a Stones' film, which had never been realized, but Jagger had a real desire to act and at this point almost got his first part.

'Michael Lindsay-Hogg was a friend of mine,' says Eileen Atkins, 'and at the time I took part in the "Child of the Moon" clip, he and I were about to do *Elektra* on TV. I'd said to Michael that it might be a fresh idea to work with people not normally associated with this kind of thing. I'd suggested we ask Mick Jagger to play Orestes, and Michael was all for it. But then over the next couple of weeks we had second thoughts. Mick was great as a Rolling Stone, but we just couldn't see him handling Greek tragedy.'

Nevertheless on 11 May Jagger's film début was announced, in the movie *Performance* that would star James Fox. Shooting was scheduled to commence mid-July. The next night the Stones appeared at an *NME* Poll Winners concert at the Empire Pool Wembley, where amid reassuring chaos they previewed their new single. It would be their only live performance of the year, just as 'Jumpin' Jack Flash' released at the end of the month would prove their solitary single. It soon reached the top on both sides of the Atlantic and was their first UK number 1 for two years. What spiked their pleasure, though, was the fact that just days before Brian Jones had been busted. And this time it was a set-up.

Jones had been buoyed up by his pride in their latest single. It had given him renewed professional optimism. His personal life had been less satisfactory, but he had not resorted to drugs to cope. He was alone at his Chelsea flat when a thundering on the door heralded the drug squad. The evidence – a lump of hash found stuffed in a ball of wool Jones hadn't even known was in the flat – was found instantly and in dubious circumstances.

No one close to Jones believed it was anything but a bad bust, a deliberate set-up. Jagger agreed with this, and still haunted by his narrow escape from a jail sentence, he was always aware that he could be next in line in the attempt to crack down on the Stones.

A distraction from such concerns came on 5 June when work began on Jean-Luc Godard's *One Plus One*. For a sizeable fee footage of the Stones at work in Olympic Studios was to be integrated into the rest of his feature film. The embryonic track was 'Sympathy for the Devil', the perfect vehicle for the band's demonic image. The satanic influence scenario was taken seriously by everyone but Jagger. Keith Richard believed that this number fixed them with the Lucifer tag for decades. But Jagger considered it nothing but play-acting. With his own acting début approaching he enjoyed his involvement with the filmmaker. In the end he confessed he never did find out what *One Plus One* was about. Jones, leaving a preview of it months later, put it more succinctly when he called it 'fucking shite'. Not many disagreed.

Jagger's determination to be at the forefront of dealings with the director reflected his desire to set himself apart from the band. Not so unusual in a flamboyant front man but undoubtedly irksome to the other band members. In a message in that month's *NME* Jagger called himself Jumpin' Jack Flash and spoke of how thrilled he was that 'he had made number one' adding, almost as an afterthought, that the Rolling Stones were also pleased. Some say that from as early as 1965 Jagger would have liked the band to become 'Mick Jagger and the Rolling Stones.'

NME also wrote of a new album, and throughout July this demanded most of Jagger's attention. Along with Faithfull, Richard and Pallenberg he shuttled between LA and London working on songs. Any free time was spent partying. After watching the Doors perform in Hollywood he attended a particularly riotous party with Jim Morrison. In London belatedly to celebrate his 25th birthday he went clubbing taking with him a copy of the as yet unreleased Stones album. Jagger treated its patrons to a preview of *Beggars Banquet*. He had a prime audience there, including rock's finest and society's greatest. But it was galling when Paul McCartney arrived and stole his thunder with the Beatles' new single 'Hey Jude'. When everyone took notice of it Jagger felt more than a bit upstaged. It is said he spent the rest of the night dabbling in drugs, applying, by his standards, less than his normal restraint.

He recuperated in Ireland with Faithfull, but trouble arose with the speculation that Jagger had invited Clapton to join the Stones later in the year. If true, unless there was the intention to increase the band to six, it is likely that Jagger had one of two possible scenarios in mind. Either that Jones would go or be asked to go, or that he'd be leaving anyway if he were to receive a custodial sentence for his supposed recent drug offences. Whatever, Jones felt destabilized by it all.

Problems, too, surrounded the Stones' new album. Its release had been delayed by a battle with Decca over the sleeve design. Jagger had wanted it to depict a graffiti-covered toilet wall, but the record company freaked. And then in America, their new release, 'Street Fighting Man', was banned by some Chicago radio stations in the wake of recent civil unrest there. Jagger hoped the ban would excite interest in the number, but by autumn it was obvious that wasn't going to happen.

In September the press discovered that Faithfull was pregnant, something Jagger himself had known for weeks. Initially ecstatic, and hoping for a girl, they had prematurely settled on the name Carrina. Jagger had already proved himself good with Nicholas, and when reporters sought a comment about the pregnancy he was positive about it. The idea that becoming a family man might blunt his Lothario image perhaps hadn't occurred to him. He even said they would have another three kids. But the fact was that the child would be illegitimate. Faithfull was still married to John Dunbar.

This fact didn't take long to spark controversy, and Jagger enjoyed refuting any hint of an idea that he might marry his lover. Something that tallied with his reputation as a non-conformist. But he was in fact pressurizing Faithfull to divorce Dunbar. This conventional side to him came as little surprise to Faithfull, who repeatedly turned him down. Her refusal seems to have been partly her fear that as Mrs Mick Jagger she would lose her own identity. But if so it was based on a strange logic. Her fame, after all, was closely linked to her life as Jagger's girlfriend, something that perhaps she was reluctant to acknowledge.

Some sections of society responded self-righteously. They made political and moral capital out of this domestic development in Jagger's life and roundly attacked Faithfull. She was depicted as a sexually promiscuous woman who'd abandoned her husband for a Rolling Stone and was now carrying his bastard child. The backlash was so pronounced that even the Archbishop of Canterbury expressed his abhorrence for this sinful display of a lack of moral fibre. As the row escalated, Faithfull, already vulnerable, leant more heavily on drink and drugs to cope with her emotions. While Jagger took the opportunity to argue for a more enlightened society.

When he was invited to debate his views on the *David Frost Show* with moral campaigner Mary Whitehouse, it was anticipated with some interest. But if Stones' fans were relying on their hero's hedonism to speak out against the outmoded institution of marriage, many were surprised when he talked of consecrating one's union to God and never breaking it. When asked why then he had decided against wedlock, he maintained that he didn't feel the need for it. After all, for years the Stones had been marketed as men behaving badly, sexually available and tantalizingly unattached.

As the TV debate heated up it turned ugly for Whitehouse, something Jagger appeared to enjoy. But later something happened that could be interpreted as gallant, as Mary Whitehouse recalls.

'I got a very rough time from the audience, but then as I was leaving the building Mick ran and caught up with me. He said how deeply sorry he was about how I was treated, that people had been extremely unkind, and he went out of his way to say how much he respected the work that I did. I was very touched.'

Jagger's acting career began that autumn with the Donald Cammell/Nicolas Roeg movie *Performance*. Part of his desire to act may well have evolved from an appetite whetted by Faithfull's two small film roles and West End stage appearances.

On 12 September shooting of *Performance* began, the very day the Anglo/French co-production of *Girl on a Motorcycle*, starring Faithfull, was premiered in London. Its American title, *Naked under Leather*, gives it away as a plotless piece of soft porn. During the three months it had taken to make Jagger had often dropped in on her on location in Switzerland and France. She was starring opposite French heartthrob Alain Delon, whom she claimed made advances to her. These she repelled. But not those of an attractive young photographer, to whom she confessed to being strongly attracted.

Jagger had organized fresh flowers to be sent to her daily at the film set. When filming ended he also took her on holiday to Brazil. But he was nevertheless as aware as she that their relationship had passed its peak.

It had been after Faithfull's return from shooting, and via her agent Robert Fox, that Jagger had met one of Fox's actor sons, James. Over subsequent months Fox and his girlfriend often met up with Jagger and Faithfull, but it was a strange friendship. They dined out often, though Jagger also enjoyed playing host at home. He liked courting Fox's friendship and would often entertain them over dinner with his talents as a mimic.

As time went on Jagger also enjoyed his habitual wind-ups. He and Faithfull were often out of it on acid, but Faithfull imagined that one of Jagger's aims at this time was to wife swap Fox's girlfriend. Maybe this was just designed to amuse but it tapped into Fox's vulnerabilities. As would the experience of working on the new Warner Brothers film. But even before that began Jagger had problems to surmount.

Scripts were sent regularly to Jagger. It was a gamble to take on someone like him with no experience, but, with a rock star of Jagger's status, one worth taking. Jagger had never had an acting lesson in his life, and when it came down to it he ran the risk of making a fool of himself, once the pre-release hype of Rolling Stone Mick Jagger met on-screen reality. Two unsuccessful acting attempts followed, but Jagger still believed he had it in him. He was never one to admit defeat. In this case it was wise that he did so.

Faithfull was supportive throughout and had moved to an old rambling house in Ireland's County Galway to nurse herself through her pregnancy. Jagger agreed to join her two weekends a month. His initial bravado about exploring his talents had evaporated as pre-production work brought the reality of filming into focus. And with some desperation he turned to his girlfriend to give him a crash-course in acting. Faithfull, prone to romanticizing, saw Jagger as a 'pre-Raphaelite Hamlet'.

It was a salacious mix of crime and decadence that formed the nub of *Performance*, but Jagger's agonizing about his role in it was mostly due to his overambition. He played Turner, a reclusive rock star with voyeuristic tendencies, who becomes entangled with Fox as a vicious gangster on the run. The film company had envisaged a Beatles-type production. What they got was a dense melodrama of alter egos sustained much of the time by shock value. The two women in Turner's life were to be played by French actress Michele Breton with Anita Pallenberg in the role of a drug-soaked seductress. The scene was set for some unpleasant game-playing, the more so when Jagger enacted the advice he had received from Faithfull on how to play Turner. He should see him as a hybrid of himself, Brian Jones and Keith Richard. Presumably she had not intended this to encourage him to take what appeared to be the short leap to discover an attraction to Pallenberg.

Roeg and Cammell had assembled a real-life motley cast, most of whom had nothing in common. Possibly as a consequence, filming was continually problematic. Tempers were often frayed, and Jagger was frequently bewildered by the whole process. Equally it must have been intensely frustrating for a professional actor like James Fox. For although Jagger threw himself into acting, he refused to rehearse much. Some of those on the set later alleged that he would sometimes only do so much then call a halt. Fox is said to have been heard often knocking on the Stone's dressing-room door, wanting to run through their lines just once more. But apparently the singer's response was a frequent 'Fuck off, Jimmy.' With no clear fix on his character Jagger appeared to accept the sexual bizarreness of Turner's persona that Roeg and Cammell wanted him to exploit. Destructive elements, powerplays and a general air of malaise infected the shoot, spreading as moodiness throughout the main players. But it was personal problems that proved the most damaging.

In view of their initial distrust and mutual dislike, Jagger possibly viewed Pallenberg as a challenge. At home Faithfull was pregnant, getting bigger and less attractive all the time. Perhaps telling himself that their relationship was heading for the rocks anyway, Jagger failed to resist a brief fling with Faithfull's best friend.

At first Faithfull never dreamt that Jagger would cheat on her with Pallenberg, but gossip worked its way back to her that he was proving as untrustworthy as she herself was. And she didn't like it. The news, though, could scarcely have come as a surprise given that Jagger, Jones and Richard often moved in on each other's women. In a sense the women had some control over the men's fragile egos, constrained as they were by fear that one band member might be thought of as sexually superior to another. For the women it seems as long as they had one Stone it was enough. For the men it was partly about which girl was the bigger prize, to be wrested from a rival suitor and held on to as some kind of personal trophy.

Fidelity had clearly never been a feature of Jagger and Faithfull's relationship. But the timing of the infidelity and the person he chose could hardly have been worse for Faithfull. Nevertheless he got off lightly. He escaped any fall-out over what did or did not go on with Pallenberg because Faithfull elected to disregard it. In time, though, the unspoken would help to poison their relationship. It didn't have to wait so long to affect the other player in the pack, though, but even the volatile Keith Richard shied away from confronting Jagger. It is said to have been hard on him. Some claim he avoided the film set not able to face his suspicions. Others maintain he tormented himself by sitting outside in his car while a runner acted as his personal spy. Either way, Richard bottled up his jealousy and anger. And Jagger also escaped a confrontation with his songwriting partner.

It seems possible that Richard was concerned with doing nothing that could further risk tearing the Stones apart. Jagger was preoccupied by his acting début. He had been restless for some time and felt there was more to life than leading the Stones. Perhaps he had seen broader horizons. Having betrayed Jones to get Pallenberg, Richard perhaps thought there was some kind of divine justice in what had happened. But Jagger wasn't looking for a serious relationship with Pallenberg. In any case there was an added dimension to it all. For if he had been at all turned on by seducing Richard's woman, he himself was receiving similar treatment. The film's director was engaged in a secret liaison with Pallenberg too. With so much intrigue and so many mind games many of those involved in *Performance* ended up suffering in some way. But it surprised no one who knew him that Jagger appeared to walk away unscathed.

With shooting over in November Jagger went into overdrive entertaining at Cheyne Walk. Until, that was, Faithfull returned from Ireland and thinned out the crowds. With the rot having set in over Pallenberg, combined with her troublesome pregnancy, feelings between the couple were tense. Jagger now shied away from all talk of marriage. Their sex life together was almost non-existent. And the joy at discovering they were expecting a baby was different from its imminent arrival.

Jagger liked his ladies svelte and began explaining his absences by claiming work commitments. When the couple did meet they rarely discussed anything in any depth. This, though, was not peculiar then. Jagger cultivated his image as cool and hip, and even in private there was no apparent desire to address anything of substance. Unfortunately, this was also true a couple of weeks later, when, in her seventh month of pregnancy, Faithfull miscarried. By bizarre coincidence, within hours of Jagger and Faithfull's loss, Yoko Ono also miscarried her baby by John Lennon, also in her seventh month.

Faithfull was devastated. Jagger was too, though later she accused him of a too swift recovery. She sought solace in the usual cocktail of drugs and alcohol to numb the pain. But this meant that she became an even greater burden to a man not known for cherishing a high-maintenance relationship. Jagger spent more time with Richard, and whenever the atmosphere became too gloomy at home he would buy Faithfull something to cheer her up. It seems clear they had turned another corner in their affair as he took his pleasures elsewhere. But, with typical male double standards, that didn't mean he would ever put up with being cheated on himself. After the miscarriage Faithfull maintained he didn't pay her proper attention, yet she was expected to live up to her name. She didn't. While Jagger was at the studio, she entertained a series of one-night stands at Cheyne Walk. Later she boasted that he had never guessed at the time how promiscuous she was. And that when he found out, it made him bitter.

Strong emotions of all kinds were a feature of the reception given to the Stones' only album of 1968. And of the appearance in court by Jagger and Richard to hear the verdict in Brian Jones' trial. The three Stones plus Jones' girlfriend Suki Potier posed in an obliging huddle for the cameras afterwards. Jones had been found guilty as charged, but got off with a fine.

Jagger had floated the idea on BBC Radio 1 that the Stones were discussing a major world tour, possibly for the following January. While it was not being aired publicly, privately much was made of the fact that Jones' two drug convictions could be enough to prevent the band from including the States in this tour.

Early in December, *Beggars Banquet* was released. The deadlock over the sleeve had delayed it to the point that it now met head on with the Beatles' new album, the double LP *The Beatles (White Album)*. Decca's design for the Stones' album, plain white and scripted like an invitation was similar to *White Album*. This was hard to countenance, just after accusations of copying *Sgt Pepper*. The Beatles went to number one, while *Banquet* peaked at 3, but it is still regarded as perhaps the Stones' finest achievement. What some believe irked Jagger most was that a great deal of this praise was once more reserved for Jones.

To launch the album the Stones held a beggar's banquet on 4 December in the Elizabethan Room of London's Gore Hotel, a lively affair, with serving wenches, a seven-course banquet and guests dressed in rags. It ended with a custard-pie fight, during which Jones pushed a pie into Jagger's face with what witnesses agree was near brute force. It all made the late evening TV news, and subsequently Jagger wrote an apology to the hotel management. But sorrier times were around the corner.

In a project dreamt up with Michael Lindsay-Hogg Jagger returned literally to centre stage as circus master. It was a two-day shoot beginning on 12 December at Intertel Studios, Wembley, and Lindsay-Hogg recalls its origins.

'By this time I'd filmed "Hey Jude" and "Revolution" for the

Beatles, and Mick asked me one day, "What about doing a TV show?" I was to direct, and it was all to be organized within the rock world, as opposed to nowadays when companies like Budweiser plonk down x amount of money and pull all the strings.

'The Rock 'n' Roll Circus was in effect produced by Mick. He was always shrewd with money. Some call him downright mean, but, over the years, in my dealings with him I paid for a meal one time, he paid the next. He drives a tight bargain all the same. He knows what everything is worth and tries to get it even cheaper.

'Anyway, after Mick's call I was doodling on a pad and drew a circle, and the idea evolved from that into creating a circus. I rang Mick back and suggested this as a theme, and it grew over the weeks. We'd meet roughly once a week over the next two months. All had their say, but the real pusher behind it was Mick. He had, even then, an entrepreneurial attitude. I thought him very smart and very driven.

'In the *RSG* days I didn't especially notice his ambition but Mick had long since grasped how powerful the Stones were, and *then* he had got more ambitious.'

Jagger discussed which bands would be invited to take part in the show and who'd form the supergroup. He also made up the numbers with a couple of less prominent bands. In the end the line-up included the Who, Clapton, Lennon and Ono, Mitch Mitchell, drummer with the Jimi Hendrix Experience, and Jethro Tull.

'Steve Winwood was originally going to be included in the supergroup,' says Lindsay-Hogg, 'but he dropped out.'

It had a doomed air about it even before filming finished and in fact would not be shown for decades.

'There were various reasons why it was decided not to put it out,' says the director, 'but mainly it was that the Stones thought the Who gave a better performance than them. The Who were recorded early evening, and the Stones didn't start until 2 a.m., then the shoot lasted for 5 hours. Everyone felt ragged by it.'

The tension wasn't just due to how late it was, however, as Lindsay-Hogg confirms.

'There had been a great deal of stress in the Stones, and all the drug-taking hadn't helped. Brian had hurt his wrist when he was in Morocco recording the Jajouka musicians. It still wasn't strong and was hurting him when he played. By now of course Jones always felt hard done by. He and I lived quite nearby in Hampstead then, and on the first night I had not long got home when he rang. He was upset and said that Mick and Keith had been mean to him all day, and he didn't think he was going to come to the studio the next day.

'I know we had all been pretty ratty and so I said, "You've got to come, Brian. We're shooting the Stones tomorrow and what are the Rolling Stones without you?" I think I managed to convince him that Mick and Keith hadn't been as cruel as he thought, that he was being over-sensitive and should put it down to everyone being frayed at the edges. I wanted to convince him that they weren't against him, but I think the more Brian believed Mick and Keith were ganging up on him, the more they were!

'Brian had been so beautiful in a masculine way with enormous sex appeal and really he had been ground down and was in a weak emotional state making him deeply unhappy when we recorded the Rock 'n' Roll Circus.'

For all Lindsay-Hogg's tact the hostile atmosphere wasn't unnoticed by guest musicians. Lennon is said to have advised Jones to leave the Stones, and Ian Anderson, lead singer of Jethro Tull, recalls how 'Brian appeared to me somewhat ostracized, both musically and socially from the rest. Doubtless the Stones view that particular period now with a mixture of sadness and perhaps guilt.'

As much as the rift with Jones was widening, so Jagger was working to repair the damage to his relationship with Richard. The guitarist had proved awkward over the single he was due to write with Jagger for *Performance*. Were he to become stubborn over Stones material, that could have been a problem that affected the band's viability. Jagger was too shrewd to allow a sexual conquest to come in the way of business. Richard was equally clear that their friendship was more important than hurt pride over a woman.

Days after filming for the Rock 'n' Roll Circus finished Jagger and Faithfull, Richard and Pallenberg went on holiday to Brazil. It was not happy families. Jagger enjoyed pretending to renew his seduction of Pallenberg. And she later claimed Jagger had wanted her to ditch Richard. But she was deluding herself. Faithfull stood it only so long, before returning to Britain.

The new year, 1969, brought little change in the behaviour of either Jagger or Faithfull. The drug-taking and the affairs continued. Faithfull's problems were compounded by the fact that she didn't have a steady income of her own. To feed her drug habits she began an unsavoury affair with a dealer. By the time she played Ophelia in a Roundhouse Theatre production of *Hamlet*, which opened in March and was directed by Tony Richardson, she was quite strung out. Jagger, now thoroughly despairing of her, had begun seriously to look elsewhere.

He also buried himself in work as the Stones returned to the studio to produce material for a new album. He and Richard had already written a few tracks, including 'Honky Tonk Women' and 'Let It Bleed'. With Richard now living in a house just down the street at 3 Cheyne Walk, they could collaborate more freely. Within weeks Jagger was convinced that the new album would outshine *Beggars Banquet*. Once again thoughts of touring began to dominate him.

For one thing, he wanted to raise some cash. Things were not working out with Allen Klein, and this had led to a great deal of dissatisfaction. By spring Jagger's concentration on the Stones' financial affairs bordered on the obsessive. To stem the flow of outgoings he insisted on a host of cutbacks. But financially things couldn't have been so bad. He had recently purchased Stargroves, a 16th-century manor house set in 40 acres near Newbury in Berkshire, as well as a country cottage for Faithfull's mother. Yet he complained of having no money. He had decided therefore that touring was the best way to raise revenue. But two developments then arose that might potentially stop them.

The first was a new film role. Tony Richardson offered Jagger the lead in a film about the 19th-century Australian outlaw Ned Kelly. Shooting would commence there in July. With *Performance* still under wraps – the development company had delayed its release over what they considered to be its pornographic content – Jagger was keen to advance his acting career. The second was his arrest on 28 May with Faithfull on drug charges, for which they were each released on £50 bail.

Just days before, Jagger and Richard had agreed that Brian Jones' two drug convictions did jeopardize the band's chances of obtaining the necessary visas to enter the States and was therefore sufficient reason finally to let him go. Ironically, with one existing conviction and a trial pending, Jagger himself posed as big a threat.

Nevertheless, with indecent haste, a list was drawn up, and within a week guitarist Mick Taylor, recommended by blues veteran John Mayall, was invited to audition at Olympic. Taylor had thought the invitation was to contribute to the Stones' new album. He hadn't dreamt it was an audition to join their regular line-up. All this had been decided before anyone had the courtesy to go and tell Jones he was fired.

Jones was then living in Cotchford Farm, Sussex. It was there that Jagger, Richard and Charlie Watts went to tell him. And the irony of Jagger trying to cite the two drug convictions as part of the reason why was not lost on Jones. The four spent a civilized day together while Jagger worked round to telling Jones he was out.

If they had expected Jones to disintegrate at the news they were wrong. Jones had expected it and had plans to audition for a new band. He calmly accepted a pay-off that gave him a settlement said to have been £100,000, on top of his royalty share. It was 5 June, and it had been agreed that the official announcement would follow in a few days.

The return journey from Sussex must have found them all in a strange mood. A long-held wish to get rid of Jones had been achieved at last, but not without some underlying anxiety. And the fact remained that Jones, as the founder member, had always been popular with the fans. There was some concern over how they would view his departure.

It was something no one had ever been quite sure of testing. Bill Wyman later confirmed that asking Jones to leave had been talked about for years but deferred because of fears that it could damage the Stones' image. But now it seemed that the band's fame was solid enough to be able to afford to let him go. There remained the risk, though, that if Jones formed a new band, he might exceed their own success, and take some Stones' fans with him.

If anyone imagined that Brian Jones could be sacked from the band he had started, and be truly so sanguine about it, they were mistaken. But a polite exterior would be put on the official parting, to be announced by the band's PR officer Les Perrin. In the meantime Jagger and the rest looked to the future. It was felt that they needed a boost in profile, and a Blind Faith open-air gig in Hyde Park had given Jagger an idea.

8

DEATH KNELL
OF THE SIXTIES

O N 8 JUNE 1969 the news officially broke
that Brian Jones had quit the Rolling
Stones. Musical differences were cited,
and both Jagger and Jones and the rest
concealed the underlying mutual resentment.
The façade was maintained that they remained friends. Two days
later, Jagger announced Mick Taylor as Jones' replacement. A photo
call in Hyde Park followed, which also announced their free gig there
on 5 July.

On the personal front, the cracks in Jagger's life with Faithfull
were now beginning to show. The strain between them had been
evident even on their brief appearance in court over their May
drug bust. Soberly dressed, pale and serious-looking, Jagger
strode in and out of court significantly separate from his girlfriend. His body language reflected the strain between them.

This was something for which he had lately begun
compensating in a relationship with another woman, albeit a
clandestine affair, known only to a few. She was singer/actress

Marsha Hunt, one of the stars in the controversial theatre production *Hair*. Hunt had also appeared nude in *Vogue* magazine and had posed naked for sessions with Jagger's friend David Bailey. An appearance on *Top of the Pops* had become a talking-point when her skimpy top had ridden up whenever she flailed her arms in the air, thereby partly flashing her bare breasts. The barrage of complaints about this had instantly given her a provocative and wayward reputation.

Attracted to this new bad girl on the block, Jagger had his office ring Hunt's record label to ask whether she would appear in the upcoming publicity photo to promote the Stones' new single, 'Honky Tonk Women'. Hunt had her own successful music career and an image to maintain. She decided against it, then Jagger personally rang her and invited himself over.

He arrived dramatically after midnight and talked of how lonely he was. She listened sympathetically as he complained of the burden Faithfull's drug abuse placed on him. And of worries he had with his band. If Jagger didn't seduce Hunt that first night, it was not long before they became lovers.

Their liaison was a clandestine affair. He would sneak out of Cheyne Walk or take a detour from the studio to meet with the woman with the startling afro hairstyle, whom he called Miss Fuzzy. Supportively, she encouraged him to talk to her about his troubles, later asserting that he invaded her life 'like a golden eagle with a broken wing'. Jagger much appreciated this outlet. There would be a later rude awakening, but by summertime their trysts had grown more frequent.

Apart from Brian Jones' refusal to accept a guest spot with the Stones in Hyde Park, there were other problems, this time of a financial nature. The price for Jagger of becoming more involved in the band's business affairs had been to face the shock that they were not as wealthy as he felt they should be. To put it simply, although the Stones were nearing the end of the Sixties as famous as the Beatles and had grossed several million pounds, they had very little of it remaining.

Help out of this tangle came at a party given by Christopher Gibbs. There Jagger met former merchant banker, now financial adviser, Prince Rupert Ludwig Ferdinand zu Loewenstein-Wertheim-Freudenberg. The son of Prince Leopold and educated at

Magdalen College, Oxford, he was in partnership with Jonathan Guinness, a family some of whose branches Jagger had long made every effort to know. On discovering the Stones' plight he agreed to look into their affairs. With hopes of a brighter future Jagger returned his attention to the goings-on in the studio.

For years it had been their practice to turn night into day, which included recording through the night when things were quiet. Jagger and the others were busy at Olympic Studios mixing tracks for their new album when in the early hours of 3 July he received a phone call to say that Brian Jones was dead.

The full extent of what happened may never truly be known. But, in keeping with the view that some still hold of his self-destructive image, the drink and drugs, it was easy to claim that his death by drowning in his pool was an accident waiting to happen. But Jones' death was no accident.

It was, whatever the verdict, a shocking development. As with any sudden death there was not enough initial accurate information to make much sense of it. It was hard enough for some just to cope with the fact that Jones was gone. But in Jagger's case, just as Chrissie Shrimpton and Marianne Faithfull both had occasion to believe, he often seemed incapable of being affected deeply by anyone else. The same appeared true of Jones' death.

Later in public Jagger expressed his grief, but his subsequent actions are hard to tally with any declarations of sorrow. Once, when caught off guard, he admitted to journalists that he had felt a little shock, but added of Jones, 'the guy was unbearable'.

For a time that night recording at Olympic stopped but not for long. A visitor there minutes later was told what had happened and was stunned when he realized the band would not stop recording that night. Jagger had snapped, 'No!', when asked about it, turning back to what he had been doing and making it clear that work went on.

Later that morning the news broke on billboards, radio and TV, numbing huge sections of the world's population. Jagger and the others met at the Stones' office. Some staff were upset. Various satellite employees, friends and others gravitated there. Tom Keylock is said to have described Jagger now as badly rattled and shaking, and others maintain that he paced the floor nervously.

Hard-headed business sense or a remarkable resilience are also

the kinder interpretations of what happened next. By mid-
afternoon there was a determination to go ahead with the
prearranged recording at a BBC sound stage of their new single,
for a spot that night on *Top of the Pops*. Publicizing 'Honky Tonk
Women' clearly remained a priority, but to many people it
indicated an insensitivity.

But the truth is there had been no love lost between Jagger and
Jones for years. The path of their relationship, dominated on both
sides by intense rivalry and frustration meant theirs was an
acrimonious alliance. Death doesn't rub that out overnight, and
therefore it can be argued that at least Jagger wasn't being
hypocritical.

Jagger and Faithfull attended a party in Kensington, not 24
hours after Jones' death. It was given by Prince Rupert
Loewenstein, and was the kind of glitzy celebrity affair that Jagger
adored. It was a wild night, with the police responding to scores of
neighbourhood complaints that had no effect on its noise levels. It
continued, in a marquee in the grounds of the Prince's Kensington
home, unabated. The dress code was white. In protest Faithfull
defiantly wore black. But Jagger turned up in a snowy outfit by
designer Michael Fish. It looked like a Greek army tunic crossed
with a dress.

On 4 July 'Honky Tonk Women', a number on which Jones had
originally played lead, rerecorded with Mick Taylor on guitar, was
released. It was a double-A side with 'You Can't Always Get What
You Want' and reached number 1 in both Britain and America.
That same day journalists pressed Jagger about the fate of the Hyde
Park concert; in the circumstances they would not be blamed for
cancelling. But Jagger was adamant that the gig would go ahead.
This, though, caused some consternation, even though Jagger said
that it would now be a memorial to Jones.

'I hope people will understand that it's because of our love for
him that we are still doing it,' he declared. This gratified public
perception, especially the fans, but did not impress some of those in
the know, Faithfull not least of all. She later said that from her
perspective nobody by then seemed to care about Jones. From what
she could see there was little grief over his death. She even went so
far as to say she felt it had been a relief.

'It solved a terrible predicament for them,' she said obscurely.

Faithfull herself was now edging toward the end of her time with Jagger and the Stones' circle.

The Stones were soon rehearsing at Apple Studios for their first live gig in over two years. On the Saturday Jagger woke complaining of laryngitis. In the preceding weeks he had involved himself with the mechanics of the Hyde Park concert to an intense degree, including the stage design. He insisted that a carpet should cover the 10-foot high wooden platform as he intended to dance barefoot. To his friends this was all a diversion from his feelings of anxiety.

Jones' death had increased interest in what would in any case have been a vital gig. It was moving into the realms of an historic rock event, which six TV companies were to cover live. Jagger was terrified of going on stage, something he admitted to Faithfull in the limo that took them to the Londonderry House Hotel, where the Stones were to gather. But she was in no condition to be supportive. Suffering from anorexia, and battling to kick her heroin habit, for years she had hated her public image of frail young thing. Now with her blonde hair hacked short, she looked pathetic clinging on to her bewildered son, Nicholas. That same day she had filed for divorce from John Dunbar. He had counter-sued, citing Jagger as co-respondent. Jagger, however, was too preoccupied to notice. Indeed if his mind strayed to a woman at all, it is likely to have been to Marsha Hunt. Would she, or would she not, turn up, as promised, to watch him perform?

On the hotel TV Jagger could see hundreds of thousands of people in the sun-drenched park. Beaded and bangled, carrying joss-sticks, they were preparing for the world's biggest wake. The concert kicked off at 1 p.m. with The Third Ear Band followed by King Crimson, Screw, Alexis Korner's New Church, Family and Battered Ornaments with a good-humoured crowd of dope-takers and day trippers. The one incongruous sight was the gang of Hell's Angels who had been hired as security. They were there to intimidate troublemakers, yet, according to Bill Wyman, the unorthodox bodyguards handled the fans gently and were, he declared, 'an asset'.

As the afternoon wore on, across London the Stones were joined at the hotel by manager Allen Klein. Two topics dominated the conversation: Jones' death and the upcoming gig. Jagger appeared to remain in a world of his own, detached from the others, presumably upset and nervous as hell and wondering if his voice would hold out.

His atrocious singing was only one of the factors that contributed to this concert going down in history as the Stones' worst ever live performance. Wyman wonders if the enormity of the event overwhelmed them, but Richard couldn't seem to cope in Jones' absence with live instrumental solos that lost direction so often that Jagger rasped, 'Tempo! Get the tempo together!' If anyone could be forgiven for being overawed it was Mick Taylor. Acutely conscious of comparisons to his predecessor he was visibly uneasy beneath a gigantic blow-up of Jones, high above the set.

The heat didn't help, affecting the electrical equipment and tuning of instruments. Jagger's arrival on stage in thick make-up, wearing the Michael Fish white mini-dress over trousers, had a good initial shock value. For the next hour he struggled to shine, prancing, squatting, twirling and strutting, hand on hip, through old hits and new numbers. Later, he stripped off the dress and tried to whip the crowd into a frenzy by lashing the stage with his studded belt. He dropped to his knees and appeared to suck suggestively on the globe-shaped microphone head gripped high between his thighs. It still had a dislocated feel to it.

Nothing seemed to gel. Not even that it was supposed to be a tribute gig. Jagger had opened the Stones' set by reading two verses from Shelley's 'Adonais', and thousands of white butterflies were released from cardboard boxes into the air as the band plunged into their first number. Michael Lindsay-Hogg speaks of the feeling in the audience that day.

'Things between myself and Mick had changed. Brian's death had knocked on the head my idea to reshoot the Stones' set in the Rock 'n' Roll Circus at the Coliseum in Rome, and Mick and I had had a falling out about that and a couple of other things, and we ended up not speaking for the next couple of years. I went to Hyde Park, although I was annoyed the whole time, because I'd wanted to shoot it myself. But people were very shaken by Brian dying, and there was a definite sense among the crowd of it being a special occasion for them.'

Phil May, Pretty Things front man and Jones' friend, agrees. 'There was an extraordinary feeling in the crowd, but I'm not sure about the taste of the tribute. Because I knew a lot of what had gone on, much of Mick's speech clanged in my head, and I just couldn't take it. In fact, a lot more people than Jagger and the others realized, knew about the animosity behind the scenes. If Jagger had confronted the reality and said about Brian, "Well, we fought like bastards, but we'll still miss him," more people in the know might have respected him, instead of expecting us to swallow all the bollocks he came out with. However, to some small extent it celebrated Brian.'

It was the absence of any obvious respect backstage that upset others. Special guests had been invited to the private enclosure before and after the gig, among them bass player Noel Redding.

'I'd been invited to the gathering backstage with the Stones,' he recalls. 'Personally speaking this whole idea of going ahead with the gig is not something I would have done, and I hadn't been sure till the last minute about turning up. But when I got there and saw what was going down, I was disgusted. I met Denny Laine [ex-Moody Blues singer] who felt exactly the same as me, and we both walked out and went to a nearby pub where we had a drink and talked about Brian.

'To me this business of it being a tribute to Jonesy was nothing but a big fat PR exercise. It was all wrong.'

One fan-club official felt similarly let down. Speaking specifically of Jagger she later revealed that she and many club members had been amazed in the first place at his determination to carry on with the concert. But what had dismayed them most was that it appeared to them that Jagger hadn't been at all affected by Brian's death.

'He seemed sort of heartless,' she recalled, 'as if nothing had happened. I thought differently of him after that, and I think a lot of Stones' fans did too.'

Someone whose devotion Jagger could count on was Marsha Hunt, who continued to enjoy the clandestine nature of their relationship. She clearly saw herself as a focus of positive energy in his life. She did not use drugs herself and gave him an escape to a drug-free normality.

One of Jagger's assistants privy to their affair had secured Hunt a vantage-point high on a platform of the scaffolding erected at the side of the stage. Jagger worked his way through the performance flanked by his two lovers; to the left, Hunt in a white fringe buck-skin outfit and Faithfull on his right, looking more ethereal than ever in an ankle-length white dress.

When the gig ended Faithfull returned with Nicholas to Cheyne Walk, and Jagger wound up that evening at Hunt's flat, where they spent the night together. The formal inquest into Jones' death was to be held the following Monday, 7 July, in East Grinstead, when the wholly inadequate verdict of 'death by misadventure' would be recorded. Jones' funeral was three days after that. Jagger's first day of filming for *Ned Kelly* was 13 July, but he left Hunt's apart-ment early on the Sunday morning, and collected Faithfull from Cheyne Walk for Heathrow and Australia.

'Mick likes to live in the present,' Lindsay-Hogg says of Jagger, 'not at all in the past. He is not nostalgic and doesn't go down memory lane if he can help it. It doesn't suit his nature or character.'

It had never suited his nature either to deal with any emotional upheavals.

Of the Stones, only Wyman and Watts attended Jones' traumatic funeral in Cheltenham, augmented by the thousands of sobbing fans who thronged the streets. Richard stayed away, spending time in the recording studio.

In the previous few weeks Jagger's visits to Hunt had provided relief from the disintegration that was going on around Marianne Faithfull, who seemed set on her own destruction. From the moment they boarded their flight to Sydney Jagger was thrown back into confronting the troubles in their relationship. On the plane she took over a dozen Tuinals, a strong barbiturate. By the time they checked in at the Chevron Hotel, Jagger had difficulty hiding from the staff his girlfriend's zombie-like condition. Once in the suite, he fell asleep. Faithfull, left to her own crazy devices, went over the edge.

She took the rest of the Tuinals, all 150 of them. In her already weakened state they did not take long to wreak their havoc. But first in that peculiar semi-limbo before unconsciousness, she experienced a maelstrom of emotions. Unhinged, she believed she had some weird, other world connection with dead Stone Brian Jones.

'After his death I felt we were all in terrible trouble,' she would later say. She also maintained that she attempted suicide to take revenge on those around her, whom she believed were not showing sufficient concern over Jones' death. The view from their top-floor suite overlooked Sydney Harbour. While Jagger slept on the bed behind her, she tried to open a window with the intention of jumping out. Fortunately it was not the type to open, and she soon sank into a coma that would last six days.

Jagger found her when he woke up. He held her and shook her, but when that didn't work he called an ambulance. Faithfull was rushed to St Vincents Hospital, where despite having her stomach pumped her condition was diagnosed as critical. A local newspaper broke the news worldwide, and in the first couple of days the reports were bleak. On the morning Brian Jones was buried a hospital spokesman grimly revealed that she might die. Newspapers had a field day, one tabloid not shy of pointing out that Faithfull was Jagger's second serious girlfriend and apparently the second to try to kill herself. Hurt by the bad press, Jagger phoned Hunt, whose concern for him acted as a balm, much needed when the Sydney drug squad pulled him in for questioning. But the pills Faithfull had taken had been legitimately prescribed, so no action was appropriate.

Jagger visited Faithfull in hospital, but he didn't, as has been suggested, keep a vigil at her bedside. He had a film to make, and there was the added complication that Faithfull's role had to be taken by Diane Craig, who had trouble learning her lines at such short notice. The reality of acting once again proved daunting for Jagger, who quickly found that he wasn't having as much fun as he had imagined.

His monosyllabic lines were delivered in a bad Irish accent, and Jagger is said to have found the script and the rest of the cast wanting. It was not a recipe for contentment. Then a prop gun accidentally backfired on Jagger, and the wound required 16 stitches. It could have resulted in him losing a hand. The one plus was that due to the unhappy circumstances, Jagger didn't have the worry about perhaps being shown up by his girlfriend when it came to acting. Friends of the couple have been vocal in their opinion that Jagger had been somewhat jealous of Faithfull in this respect. While John Dunbar openly expressed his view that the one thing with which Jagger would have been not able to cope was to be upstaged by his woman.

Faithfull's occupation of this post had been already under threat. Her suicide bid drew another line in the sand. At first Jagger wrote her loving letters, which she cherished. But she was not aware that he was also writing lovingly to Marsha Hunt and calling her long distance. When Faithfull was fit enough to leave St Vincents she moved to an infirmary, then a ranch close to the film's location. Jagger paid for all her medical costs, which later included trips to a Swiss psychiatrist. But with recovery came the realization that the gulf was widening between them.

Jagger was also disillusioned with acting, bored and wishing it would all come to an end. With little going right for him, an important development in rock culture had also eluded him. On 15 August there was Woodstock with its 400,000 people, and at the end of the month Dylan headlined at the Isle of Wight. Jagger was sick to have missed it, and it was only some consolation that, in his absence, *Through the Past Darkly (Big Hits Vol. 2)* was released in Britain in mid-September. The album was dedicated to Brian Jones. And it made number 2 in the UK and the States.

It was shortly after this that *Ned Kelly* was wrapped up, and Jagger flew with Faithfull to Indonesia for a holiday to try and pick up the pieces. He arrived home in October, still dissatisfied, to face a pile of problems. Faithfull was still using heroin, as were neighbours Richard and Pallenberg. Financial affairs were not healthy either, and with the medical fees from Australia to pay Jagger kept to a tight budget. The cash he gave to Faithfull was carefully monitored as he dreamt of a way out of the band's commitment to Allen Klein. Possibly via Prince Loewenstein, whom Jagger saw as Klein's replacement as their business manager. It was around this time that the idea of tax exiles was first mooted.

In mid-October the band flew to Los Angeles to prepare for their first American tour in three years. Jagger and Richard stayed with Stephen Stills at his palatial Laurel Canyon home. Wyman and Taylor opted for hotels, and Watts rented a mansion near Sunset Strip for him and his family, which doubled as the Stones' HQ. Not able, for peace of mind's sake, to leave Faithfull behind, Jagger had her fly over. A roadie met her at the airport to take her to a rented house. His brief was not to allow her to be seen in public until she was fit. Faithfull felt like a prisoner in a plush jail, but Jagger, trying to concentrate on the band's imminent tour, didn't want her around him until she had recovered. When her health had improved later she became a rock widow while recording and rehearsing took precedence.

Despite their poor showing at Hyde Park, the pre-tour weeks were not all spent in rehearsal. There were the usual diversions, including the habitual surfeit of groupies. One in particular caught Jagger's eye. Pamela Miller, later Des Barres, was a selfstyled Queen of Groupies. She maintains she headed to Hollywood armed with old-fashioned values and in search of her rock prince. This was a goal she achieved. But in between she slept with rock stars galore and kept detailed diaries.

Perhaps in this calculating streak lay part of her attraction for Jagger, or maybe the appeal was more basic. Seducing someone else's woman made him feel powerful. Miller, when Jagger met her, had just got her prize – Jimmy Page, and had hopes for a ring. She called Led Zeppelin's lead guitarist 'the most beautiful Englishman alive', and from the moment Jagger spotted her on a club dance floor he made up his mind to have her.

The country-rock band playing was the Flying Burrito Brothers, whose vocalist Gram Parsons had become friends with the Stones. Over the mike Parsons, also close to Miller, warned Jagger to watch out for the tender beauty 'Miss Pamela'. Jagger approached her soon after, kissing her fingers and bowing gallantly. An invitation to her and friend to come back to Laurel Canyon was accepted, and by dawn they were dancing close. No one could say he didn't try hard. But when he invited her to join him in bed she declined.

In the next couple of weeks he went into a charm offensive but while she responded to his overtures, she found him easy to resist. It wasn't that she didn't fancy him. Miller called Jagger 'number one on my far-fetched fuck list.' And let him go as far as kissing her inner thighs, leaving as she put it 'a sticky trail like a snail had been crawling into my panties'. But at the last moment she backed off. The truth was that sex with Jagger wasn't worth risking her relationship with Page. And that drove him mad. Miller confessed she feared Jagger dubbing her a 'prick tease' after that night but, nevertheless, two days after the Stones opened their sixth tour of

America on 7 November at State University, Fort Collins in Colorado, he sent a limo to take her to the gig as his guest.

It was already a record-breaking tour, with ticket prices to match. Unfair jibes at the Stones and their management for 'fleecing' the US public was only one source of discontent. Another came when radical groups looked to the Stones to live up to their outlaw image. At Oakland Coliseum they found themselves in a difficult political position when the Black Panthers reportedly demanded backing from them. Refusal supposedly brought death threats serious enough to make support artistes Ike and Tina Turner insist on armed protection.

Politics aside, this trip, Jagger focused on his performance. His style had become androgynous. Dressed in slinky black with a stack pipe hat, waist sash and floaty scarves, he twirled and twitched, ducked and dived his way barefoot through each night. Audiences hardly knew what to make of him at first, an unnerving experience when Jagger himself was already uneasy. His fear of being upstaged almost became a reality with Tina Turner on the bill. But the trick was to delay their appearance by nearly an hour, by which time the fans were baying for them. Five months on since Hyde Park it must have worried Jagger that they were still incohesive. 'Ragged' was the word he later used to describe their performance. It was all disappointing after such a long absence and the subsequent build-up. American audiences had anticipated better.

It didn't help that personal problems flared up then too. On the way to the Moddy Coliseum, Dallas, a reporter at the airport asked why Marianne Faithfull had left him for Italian painter/filmmaker Mario Schifano, someone who had once dated Anita Pallenberg. Despite the fact that he had been having an affair with Marsha Hunt for months and was currently pursuing Miss Pamela, Jagger was angry, mostly because of how it made him look.

He was barely a week into a vital tour. Every night on stage he was whipping the audience into a sexual frenzy. Now Don Juan had been discarded in public for another man. Not even someone famous. It got worse. Jagger discovered that Faithfull was no longer in the LA hideout but already installed in her new lover's Rome apartment. From there she had given a press interview, in which she had professed undying love for Schifano. Jagger's fury rapidly produced the Italian's home phone number, and he made tearful pleas to Faithfull to return. They went unheard. So he promptly rang Hunt.

He wanted some immediate solace and with his ego bruised he went in search of Pamela Miller, determined to seduce her that night, which he did. Fortunately for him the Queen of Groupies was angry with Page, perhaps sensing he was altar shy. She had begun instead to focus more on Jagger. At the Whiskey A Go Go, to background music by the Kinks, Jagger finally got it on with Miller in one of its red plastic booths. 'He gave new meaning to giving head,' she later crowed, her most vivid recollection the sight of Jagger down on her between her legs.

The tour was drawing capacity crowds. Throughout Jagger built up his androgynous image, which began to attract a gay following. So far as it is known he rejected any and all homosexual overtures, but the ambiguity of his act caught press attention and created a stir.

None of this deflected from complaints about the exorbitant ticket prices. On 28 November, after the Stones had played four shows at Madison Square Garden, it was announced at a press conference that they were to play a free open-air gig on 6 December, as a thankyou to the fans. The venue was mooted as Golden Gate Park, San Francisco, but that turned out to be impossible. That same day the Stones' new album *Let It Bleed* went on sale in America. The title proved gorily apt.

The free gig was never well conceived, and the subsequent lack of adequate preparation made disaster on some scale inevitable. It was not until the last minute that an announcement was made about where they'd play. American teenagers sat by their radios awaiting hourly bulletins. One ex-hippy, Robert Woods, vividly recalls the chaos.

'One report would say the Stones' gig would take place in such-and-such a place to be confirmed in an hour's time, but when the time came, that was cancelled, and it was a case of stand by your wireless for news of the next location. I remember when it was finally announced that it was to be at the Altamont Speedway in Livermore we all gasped, "What? Jeez, man, where's that?!" So there we all were, trying to find maps to track down this place, and I couldn't guess how many got lost. Whole pockets of fans never got there, after heading off in the wrong direction, most of them already stoned into the bargain.'

Altamont Speedway occupied a natural bowl reached only by dirt tracks. It was virtually hidden from sight. Of the near half million fans who did find it, hundreds of them abandoned their vehicles in 20-mile long traffic jams. They arrived on foot over the rise of the bowl in shadowy waves throughout the night. In the early hours of the morning of 6 December the Stones flew in by helicopter to view the site. In a long velvet cloak Jagger walked among the fans huddled round camp fires, stopping and speaking to some, stepping over sleeping figures wrapped up against the night chill. In the background the noise of the stage still being erected could be heard. San Francisco-based filmmakers Albert and David Maysles were to film the gig, and it was Jagger's hope that it would upstage Woodstock the movie.

Indeed, it was billed as Woodstock on the West Coast. The support line-up included Santana, Jefferson Airplane, the Flying Burrito Brothers and Crosby, Stills, Nash & Young. The Grateful Dead were also expected. It was the Dead's manager Rock Scully who suggested the Stones should give the job of security to the Californian counterparts of the Hell's Angels who had policed the Hyde Park security. The Stones agreed, and so in payment for all the beer they could drink they were hired.

The omens were bad from the start. Moments after the Stones officially arrived at the site, a teenage boy had rushed towards Jagger, screaming hatred at him and punching him in the face. The spontaneity of the gig had not prevented the dealers from making it there, and a lot of bad dope had been circulating for hours. It only added to the event's latent instability.

In a black and orange Ossie Clark creation Jagger had intended to look like Lucifer, but by the time the Stones began to play the horrors going on around them were hellish enough.

In the middle of 'Sympathy for the Devil', Meredith Hunter, an 18-year-old black youth, was savagely beaten to death by a handful of Hell's Angels.

The band played on, unaware of the fatality, and Jagger ended by telling the crowd how beautiful and groovy they'd been. 'We're gonna kiss you goodbye,' he yelled and with that rushed off stage to the helicopter that would take him and the others to safety.

American press coverage next day compared the gig favourably to Woodstock, and in Britain too the tragedy initially remained untold. It was *The Times*, on 8 December, that reported the four fatalities and countless injuries, some serious, as well as the treatment of thousands of drug overdoses. Jagger later admitted, 'We were partly to blame for not checking it out,' and the ripples from it would continue to spread out for years.

In 1964 Andrew Oldham had described the Rolling Stones not just as a band but more a way of life. Now as the decade entered its final days neither the Stones, nor the times, had a chance of ever being the same.

9

HEART OF STONE

I N THE AFTERMATH of the disastrous finale to their US tour Jagger flew to Switzerland on private business. Perhaps he was suffering a crisis of confidence or possibly the events had sobered him. Whatever, it was a time in which he was uncommonly frank about himself. He admitted that he wasn't a good enough vocalist to derive much pleasure from singing. He said he liked playing the guitar more, adding, 'And I can't play the guitar. But I know that if I keep on playing guitar I can get better, whereas I can't improve much as a singer.'

The last three weeks of 1969 was a time Jagger would probably rather forget. *Rolling Stone* magazine described Altamont as the result of diabolic egoism. There were accusations that it had been a determination to film footage to rival the Woodstock documentary that had prevented the gig from being stopped before the bloodshed began. The hunt for who to blame got under way.

Let It Bleed was released in Britain on 5 December and topped the album charts and is now considered the peak of the Stones' achievements in the sixties. But it was widely criticized when it emerged that one track was about Albert de Salvo, aka the notorious Boston Strangler. Nevertheless its success was not enough to raise spirits.

One situation at least was resolved when on 19 December the seven-month-old drug charge was heard at Marlborough Street Magistrates' Court. Jagger was fined £200 with £52 costs, and Faithfull was acquitted. Still not able to accept that Faithfull had dared to leave him, the previous week he had gone to Heathrow to meet her on her return from Rome. She did not dash into his arms as he'd expected, instead she told him calmly that it was all over between them and he'd left with his tail between his legs.

He was far from friendless, though, and it was around now that Jagger asked Marsha Hunt to move in to Cheyne Walk, which she did not do, moving instead into a St John's Wood flat.

Jagger had known for some time that he and Faithfull were drifting apart. But he just couldn't accept that she had left him. As Christmas approached Faithfull, Nicholas and Schifano were staying at her mother's country cottage. One evening he turned up there unannounced, and a big scene followed between the men. For a liberated woman, Faithfull took surprising pleasure in seeing herself fought over. Although she says she no longer loved Jagger, she was impressed by his determination. And slept with him that night.

The newly reunited couple returned the following day to Cheyne Walk. But behind closed doors there were new pressures. Having sampled the delights of Pamela Miller and other practised groupies, Jagger had acquired a wider sexual palate. Faithfull was no prude, but his suggestions shocked her. She gave him a straight no. But it left her demoralized. Jagger simply reverted to his regular visits with Hunt.

'I would have died for him,' she declared, but what he asked of her was less final. Hunt is adamant it was Jagger's idea that they try for a baby.

Jagger had no intention at this stage of becoming a family man. Just as ego had triggered his desire to retrieve Faithfull, so the same reason probably lay behind his desire to father a child. It no doubt stoked pride in his prowess when just weeks later Hunt had news for him. It was in Hyde Park, en route to the Dorchester Hotel to attend a meeting with head of Atlantic Records Ahmet Ertegun,

'I don't believe in monogamy,' Jerry Hall once said. It was a view that she would need to believe in absolutely in order to survive the two decades of her relationship with Jagger. Just 20 when they first met, the blonde Texan's recipe for a successful marriage is to 'Be a maid in the living room, a cook in the kitchen and a whore in the bedroom.' She would require all these skills and more to stand by her man.

Above: Jagger stands top right, school Basketball Team, 1960–61. Jagger's father was a keen sportsman who encouraged his son's natural athleticism for which he is now famous.

Right: Olympic pentathlon gold medallist Mary Peters met the Stones during their tour of Ireland in 1965. 'I had just won Sports Personality of the Year Award after the Tokyo Olympics,' she said, 'and had been invited to have my photo taken with the Rolling Stones.' She'll never forget the crowds of girls who mobbed the band's dressing room and the hordes of fans in the streets that day.

Phil May of the Pretty Things, left, and Dick Taylor, on stage. Taylor, once in the original Rollin' Stones line-up, is a childhood friend of Jagger's, and it was his band that Jagger first joined when he was at school.

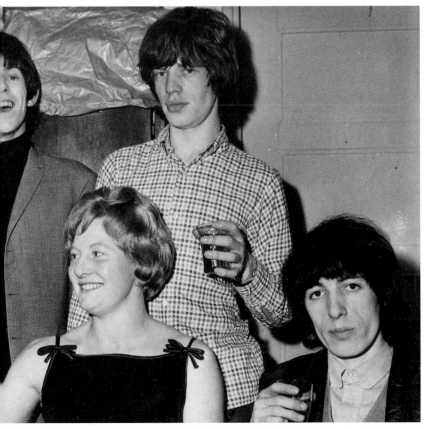

Above: Jagger *(centre)* with Mary Whitehouse and David Frost on his show in 1968, when he was invited to debate with her his views on marriage and morality. Whitehouse recalls the experience as tough but ultimately found Jagger charming.

Right: The Stones in Paris with support band Gun, June 1990, just before the show at the Parc des Princes. Joolz Gizzi *(fourth from left)* holds a guitar given to him by Ron Wood.

Left: In conference at Regent Sound Studios, 1964. *From left to right*: Allen Klein, Brian Jones, Jagger and Andrew Oldham.

Jagger in 1966 with Chrissie Shrimpton. She was his first serious girlfriend. But it was a relationship that started with passion and ended in tears.

Above: With his first wife, Bianca. Some say Jagger's feelings ran deeper for her than for any of the others, that she touched him in a way that no woman had ever done before or has done since. But ultimately it was not a marriage made in heaven.

Left: Jagger's lover Marsha Hunt, seen here with their daughter and Jagger's first child, Karis, born in 1970. Hunt adored Jagger but, although a strong and independent woman, her feelings for him were to cost her dearly in the years to come.

Marianne Faithfull became almost as famous as Jagger in the sixties. Her life and their relationship was marred by her drug addiction and his at times emotional indifference. But, as can be seen here, there were lighter, more pleasurable moments.

that she told him she was pregnant. In a display of self-sacrifice she assured him that if he had changed his mind about wanting a baby she was prepared to have an abortion. Jagger said he was happy, if she was. In fact for a brief, initial spell he warmed to the role. He toyed with naming the infant Midnight Dream, but overall he talked of it being a boy, a son he dreamt of sending to Eton. It was an ambition that didn't surprise Marsha Hunt. She knew of his upper-class aspirations.

While Jagger insisted that the handful of people privy to the pregnancy be sworn to secrecy, he continued to indulge that interest by attending every debutante ball and garden party he could, with Faithfull of course. But she was a reluctant, on occasions embarrassing, partner. Jagger had been ecstatic at Lord David Brooke's invitation to a formal dinner at Warwick Castle. While Jagger enjoyed the splendid surroundings, Faithfull found them overwhelming. To cope she had taken Mandrax. As a result she passed out during the meal, her face in her food. Jagger carried her from the formality of the state dining room with its liveried footmen to an upstairs room to recover. After that, he attended blue-blood gatherings unaccompanied.

Marooned at Cheyne Walk, Faithfull sank deeper into depression. Once she was in such a chronic state of confusion she found that her mother had placed her in what Faithfull called a 'loony bin'. In a panic she rang Jagger who came and had her released. By any measure it was a difficult domestic situation for Jagger to endure. But he had no intention of allowing her destructive behaviour to drag him down, a fear voiced by Ahmet Ertegun with whom the Stones were in deep negotiation over a multi-million dollar deal with Atlantic Records.

By late spring his love life was a disaster zone. Faithfull, alternating between heroin and cocaine, was a physical and mental wreck. Jagger often came home to find her collapsed or in tears and distraught, yelling at him. She'd lately found out about Hunt's pregnancy. But her jealousy was misplaced. Hunt's condition was showing, and just as he had done when Faithfull was pregnant, Jagger began to look elsewhere. He used his country home Stargroves to entertain a succession of one-night stands, mostly Americans, for whom he had a penchant. Often after these meaningless encounters, a woman would approach him in a restaurant, only to be rebuffed when he claimed no recollection of her.

Someone who knew the score was Pamela Miller. Still carrying a torch for Jimmy Page, she was living in London with the co-owner of Granny Takes A Trip, one of King's Road's most fashionable boutiques, which Jagger frequented. There, at the end of May, she contrived to bump into him. Dismissing his minder Jagger took Miller for a walk and ended up round the corner in Edith Grove, where inside the derelict flat he had once shared with Jones and Richard, according to her, they 'checked out each other's buns'. Soon after that he dropped by her flat when the boyfriend was working, turning her, as she put it, 'into a cheating trollop'. With Jagger, Miller maintains, she had some great laughs.

At home Faithfull was beyond laughter. She would later swear she had no regrets about her involvement with Jagger, but she had by then reached the conclusion that she had to leave him. This, she has maintained, was an act of self-preservation. She feared becoming another Rolling Stone casualty, although, she conceded, her drug abuse shouldered much of the blame for driving a wedge between them. Her addiction to heroin, she admits, turned life into a nightmare for Jagger. Yet she also claims he made no real effort to stop her. He would comment on the amount she was using but never seriously hooked into her troubles. As it happened, had Jagger felt the need to make her choose between him and drugs he would have lost. She valued being a junkie more than being his girlfriend, she once confessed. It was a sad comment on her state of health, and their rotting relationship.

When Faithfull left Jagger again it was for another man, Lord Rossmore.

'I first met Mick and Marianne in May 1969 when they were among various guests at Glin Castle in Ireland,' he says. 'Later when I ran into her again she was already attending a Harley Street psychiatrist whom Jagger was paying to try to get her off drugs. When she left Mick and came to me, I then took over the medical bills.'

He dismisses claims that Faithfull and he became engaged.

'We talked about marriage but there was no formal engagement. In the circumstances that would've been impossible. Marianne was really quite ill and had great difficulties. I tried to support her, but it was tough and so sad because she did try very hard.

'She is a wonderful character and has an extraordinary ability to survive. Most people would've crumbled under a quarter of what she has gone through. She has terrific weaknesses and enormous vulnerability, yet incredible strength. I saw that when we were together, and she fought hard against addiction.'

True to form Jagger did not like the fact that she had left him, and this time for a lord. He didn't actually want her back, yet he bombarded her with calls and letters asking to see her. Faithfull saw through it all. She had a lot of resentment towards him. Later she revealed she considered him deeply conceited about himself and the way his women looked. She charged him with feeling contempt for women, maintaining that to him they existed only as a reflection of himself. In so doing she was echoing the sentiments of her predecessor, Chrissie Shrimpton.

Faithfull gained several stones in weight, cropped her hair and developed all the signs of a heavy drinker. To hit home best she reckoned she had but to target his vanity by presenting herself as fat and unsightly. She knew he would rather die than be seen with her. When she appeared unannounced on his doorstep one day, looking a sight, Jagger apparently froze her out and never bothered her again. Faithfull continued to use a variety of drugs long after their split. For his part Jagger claimed it was she who had nearly killed him.

On 24 June 1970 *Ned Kelly* was premiered at the London Pavilion. Jagger had known in advance just how awful it was. At a private screening he had burst into tears. With *Performance* still unreleased, this would be the public's first chance to assess his acting skills. Little wonder he was a worried man. Under the circumstances Jagger had little choice but to concur in its universal condemnation. In an attempt perhaps to save face he said that making the film had been something to pass the time.

Despite the aftermath of the première he still seemed to be far from a flop with women. First he drove leggy Californian blonde Janice Kenner from the studio to Stargroves, where she was ostensibly installed as housekeeper. Her true position revealed itself at the jealous outburst that erupted when Jagger briefly added another American blonde, Catherine James, to his household. There was a brief affair too with a former girlfriend of Brian Jones,

Suki Potier. Then came the ever imaginative Miss Pamela.

Miller fancied filling Faithfull's shoes, but there was no chance of Jagger choosing such a celebrated groupie as his girlfriend. For a few hours instead, the painful humiliation of *Ned Kelly* was erased as they walked, talked and returned to Cheyne Walk where they got high on especially fine marijuana, then, says Miller, 'We fucked on a pile of pillows.'

Miller may have begun attaching special significance to their sexual encounters, but four days later Jagger was reported to be dating Patti D'Arbanville, a 19-year-old New York actress/model, who had posed for top photographers and completed her first feature film. On the day this liaison hit the papers, Marsha Hunt became the centre of attention too.

For a charity fashion event Hunt had been modelling a Thea Porter maternity dress. Her pregnancy was advanced enough to show, so she told the press she was expecting a child, but tantalizingly refused to name the father. Lately there had been gossip that Jagger had once secretly dated the ex-*Hair* star. Inevitably one journalist guessed correctly and threatened to run the story. As soon as the newspaper looked set to print their suspicions, the Stones' publicity machine swung into action. Photos of Jagger with another woman were released, someone with whom it was claimed he had a strong attachment.

Marsha Hunt attended the *Ned Kelly* première seated next to Jagger's parents, aware that he hadn't told Joe and Eva they were to become grandparents. He must have been sure that Hunt would not tell them herself. During a mid-August press conference, Jagger commented that while it wasn't impossible he'd get married, he'd never settle down. Then he added, 'I might have kids.' As if it were a distant prospect.

Ten days later another press conference in Copenhagen heralded the start of their first European tour for three years. While Jagger's personal life had been convoluted, the summer had been busy professionally. Throughout July the Stones had cut tracks for a new album at Olympic, as well as in the recording studio they had had built for them in an articulated lorry known as 'the Mighty Mobile'. The band's contract with Decca expired on 31 July, subject only to the delivery of one final single. Relations between the two sides were far from good, and nothing said this better than

'Cocksucker Blues', the number with which the Stones fulfilled their contractual obligations with the company who had launched them. It was clearly unreleasable.

The end of July also saw the start of legal proceedings against Allen Klein. Colossal amounts of money were involved, and it looked set to be a tough and protracted battle. Prince Rupert Loewenstein's advice to the band was to cut their losses and settle out of court for $2 million. A $1 million split between Jagger and Richard in recognition of their majority stake due to songwriting royalties and $1 million divided between Bill Wyman, Charlie Watts and Brian Jones' estate. Mick Taylor, as a salaried employee, was not entitled to a share.

But Jagger had identified an opportunity. Released from Decca, record companies were now queueing up for their business. Jagger took care to be involved in any negotiations. He would later complain that he had little choice but to keep a close eye on the band's affairs. But as Richard, Wyman and Watts saw from the way he behaved at the subsequent business meetings, the truth was Jagger thrived on it. Eventually Atlantic Records survived his scrutiny – offering the most money. Not an unreasonable choice. Jagger had already spent time with its chairman Ahmet Ertegun. The son of a diplomat, Ertegun moved in high-society circles. Jagger was altogether content with the Stones' fresh start.

Their sell-out tour began on 2 September at the Olympic Stadium, Helsinki. Innovative, among rock shows its elaborate design involved a stage set that would be dismantled and erected for every venue. What remained the same were familiar problems with hotel accommodation, rioting fans and authorities resorting to tear gas to control the crowds.

Four days into the tour Decca released the album *Get Yer Ya Yas Out!* in both Britain and America. It was material recorded live at New York's Madison Square Garden the previous November and became a UK number 1. The tour ended in Munich on 11 October, but not before scores of fans had been arrested, and Jagger himself involved in a punch-up with a reporter in Rome.

Jagger continued vigorously with his pursuit of pleasure. 'If you don't have fun on the road, it's your own fault.' And for the duration of the trip he had been as good as his word. Marsha Hunt and their unborn baby were largely forgotten. He did phone, but less often and when he rang it was to entertain her with tour anecdotes, sometimes including stories of sexual conquests, often with someone else's woman. But he had been steadily changing over the months in his relationship with Hunt. The novelty had to some extent worn off, and he scarcely mentioned the pregnancy any more. His talk was almost all of performing, and plans for the band to go into exile.

The golden eagle was, after all, a bird of a different feather. Perhaps Jagger feared it heralded the end of his footloose behaviour with Hunt, but if so, he was wrong. Their relationship had been uniquely open, each independent of the other and Hunt had no desire to tie him down. Or possibly he thought she might become demanding when she had not been before. But, whatever the reason, according to Hunt, Jagger became almost like Jekyll and Hyde.

Erratic behaviour was a device Jagger often used when he wanted to get out of a relationship of which he had tired. Another was increasing an awareness of a new woman on the horizon. That way suspicion and jealousy would work its way into his current lover's emotions, and thereby relieve him of the distress of breaking the news himself. But it was perhaps not quite so calculating and conscious as that. The fact was Jagger was not ready for commitment. There were too many distractions. Although he sometimes felt the need for it, settling down was not a dream he found easy to make real. So there was nothing innocent about it when he blithely told Hunt of a woman called Bianca, whom he'd met in Paris. She would, he said, be travelling with him to the tour's end.

Bianca Pérez Morena de Macias was born in Managua, Nicaragua. She was 26 when she persuaded her former boyfriend Donald Cammell to introduce her to Jagger at a post-gig party at the Hotel George V. She described herself, however, as 21. This disparity was just one of many obscurities about her past. A lot of misinformation originated from various sources, presumably in an attempt to create an alluring mystique to match the sleek raven-haired beauty she had become. Her father, although credited with a range of exotic occupations, was at any rate not poor. But her parents split up when she was young, and Bianca had been raised by her mother.

Like Faithfull and Shrimpton, hers was a Catholic upbringing, complete with the teaching that inclined towards sexual repression. She later claimed to have been brainwashed into believing that virginity was a woman's biggest asset.

Her mother ran a small snack bar and struggled to make ends meet. Yet it is said that at 17 Bianca, who had never been expected to dirty her hands with chores, secured a scholarship to attend the Institute of Political Science at the Sorbonne in Paris. There, soon after her arrival, she was drawn into the world of fashion. But reality couldn't match her dreams and short of money she ended up back home, where she refused a desk job in the civil service, soon to return to the Parisian fast track. How she financed her life in this whirl is unknown. Her new job on the Nicaraguan Ambassador's staff gained her entry to the diplomatic party circuit certainly. But her salary scarcely seemed up to supporting the *haut monde* lifestyle she adopted.

Then in 1966 while living in London, through a friend she met and quickly became involved with Michael Caine. It was a volatile relationship and though she moved into his Dorchester Hotel suite they existed on a spate of spectacular fallings-out. In the sixties film and music often meshed. Caine and Jagger socialized at the same places, and as Caine starred in *Alfie*, one of the decade's biggest box-office draws, it is odd that Jagger never noticed the actor's fiery girlfriend.

By the time of their introduction Bianca had moved on to become involved with music executive Eddie Barclay, an older man. She claims she had been searching for a father figure until she met Jagger. This was fortunate, for eyeing the poised and disdainful woman who epitomized Parisian chic, Jagger's feelings were strictly unpaternal. Many say that when he looked at Bianca, he saw himself. As for Bianca, she maintained it wasn't his physical attributes she appreciated as much as his vulnerability, to her an unexpected bonus. Friends considered them mirror images in that they could both be moody, sullen and secretive.

When Jagger returned to Britain with Bianca on his arm it was to a barrage of questions from journalists and a blitz of flashbulbs. Everyone wanted to know who Faithfull's mystery successor was. In the final weeks of the tour foreign photographers had gone to such lengths to capture her that Jagger had again hit out. This time it had cost him a £500 fine for assault. Now they remained hidden behind a phalanx of bodyguards. At Heathrow the drama heightened when Jagger declared, 'I can't tell you who she is,' and Bianca would only say, 'I have no name.'

They did have a hideaway, however – Stargroves. On their return from Europe the Stones had begun to work on an album for their new label. The time was right. In America in recent weeks music magazines had hailed the Stones as the epitome of sex and drugs and rock 'n' roll. They were described as unique among their peers, and it was predicted they would never fade away.

A new album was desirable to exploit this, but Jagger, in the throes of his budding romance was possessive and didn't want to spend time away in London. He had persuaded the band to use a makeshift studio at his country home. This proved difficult when it came to work. Whenever Bianca appeared Jagger and she couldn't keep their hands off each other. They would disappear for hours. All of this caused delays and resentments.

Bianca's arrival is said especially to have annoyed Anita Pallenberg. She viewed her status as Keith Richard's common-law wife as somehow placing her above all other Stones' partners. But her attempts to stifle the newcomer were wasted. Bianca had spirit, and it is perhaps more accurate to say that it was she who intimidated Pallenberg with her impenetrable air of self-assurance. Richard, too, is said privately to have intensely disliked his friend's new lover, though publicly proclaiming otherwise. But nothing much cracked the Nicaraguan's cool aloofness.

Bianca was nothing if not adept at eliminating competition. And she saw off even the most assiduous attempts by her lover's past flames to rekindle old embers. When Pamela Miller, believing she had a real hold over Jagger, rang Stargroves, she was simply frozen out. In all of this Jagger left Bianca to it. He felt she had no need of advice from him. Especially on how to handle or defuse the hostility from Pallenberg and Richard. Bianca made the best of it. But when the phone rang one day in early November she was in for a shock.

Marsha Hunt was a name Jagger had omitted to mention, and he certainly hadn't warned her that she was about to make him a father. In the latter stages of her pregnancy Jagger had visited Hunt infrequently. Their understanding had been that they, whilst living separate lives, would yet share the responsibility of having a child. But it was hard not to see Jagger's moodiness whenever they met.

It had also been difficult for Hunt to cope financially. Pregnancy had put a hold on her singing, modelling and acting career. Yet according to Hunt, she was receiving no money from Jagger. The most she said he had done was send his housekeeper to stay with her as the birth approached. As October ended Jagger received a reluctant request for a contribution to help with the forthcoming child. He sent her £200 with a note acknowledging that he hadn't done his best for her. He also loaned her a ring to wear during the birth.

Hunt's decision to have a home delivery had been to keep it out of the papers for Jagger's sake. It was abandoned, however, when a potential complication sent her to St Mary's Hospital in London's Paddington. There on 4 November 1970 she gave birth to a baby girl. The days when they had good-naturedly argued over what to call their child were distant now. Hunt named the baby Karis. With no expectant father in the delivery room Marsha was trundled alone back to bed, but despite everything she couldn't wait to use the portable pay phone to tell him. Jagger was at Stargroves with Bianca when the call came through. When he replaced the receiver he calmly announced that Marsha Hunt had just given birth to his daughter. Bianca's astonishment was overtaken by a distinct sense of being disadvantaged by this woman, now the mother of his child.

Jagger sent a limo to meet Hunt and the baby at a hospital side entrance a couple of days later. He had arranged for red roses to await her at the flat. But it was a week before he turned up to see Karis. He arrived bearing gifts, from champagne to trinkets. But he was not her sole visitor. The midwife was there, and she recognized him and looked astonished to see him. He kept a low profile in another room until she left. But after she had, Jagger appeared to want to be anywhere but where he was. He was edgy and distracted, taking little interest in the infant and finding it hard to meet Hunt's eye. He made his excuses and left soon after. When he paid a second visit a fortnight later his detachment was even more pronounced. In the intervening time he had also recalled his housekeeper. Hunt began to feel increasing sense of isolation.

The veneer of civility between them peeled away when Hunt, having put up with enough chitchat, flew at him. She berated him for not phoning and for his generally uncaring attitude. It was a vulnerable time and she was amazed when Jagger lashed back. He told her she was a fool if she had imagined that he had ever loved her. But, as she burst into tears, he had saved the worst for last. According to Hunt, Jagger then threatened that he could take Karis away from her if he chose. Why he should say such a thing is perplexing, especially as he had no intention of taking on the responsibility of a child. But he was angry and defensive. However, if he thought he had had the last word, it was his turn to be shocked. Sobered instantly, Marsha warned him that if he dared try, she would 'blow his brains out'.

Putting distance between himself and Hunt suddenly seemed like a good idea. Soon after, Jagger left with Bianca for a holiday in the Bahamas. In fact he spent most of the winter showing off his exotic companion to his smart friends. One in particular, Prince Loewenstein, was preoccupied by arrangements with the French authorities for the Stones to emigrate there in the spring. Jagger was becoming increasingly involved in the Stones' business affairs and would chair meetings at Cheyne Walk, often to Bianca's annoyance. She was well ensconced there now, and her influence was showing. Her desire to change things included getting rid of the hangers-on and freeloaders the drug parties attracted, and she became adept at freezing out the most undesirable ones.

Those suffering from drug addiction were to be beneficiaries of the charity premiére on 4 January 1971 of *Performance* at the Warner West End cinema. It received mixed reviews, which after Jagger's universal panning for *Ned Kelly* had to be an improvement. Its run, however, lasted only weeks after which the film was withdrawn due to its excess of sex, drugs and violence. It was never put out on general release.

But news from America lifted Jagger's spirits when, amid rumours that the Stones were quitting the UK, *Billboard* voted them third bestselling artistes in the USA for 1960–70. Those rumours became reality when it was announced in early February they were leaving to live and work in France and that a British farewell tour would begin the following month. As the stampede for tickets began, Jagger denied accusations of abandoning home territory for tax reasons, though later admitted that the Stones had owed the Inland Revenue more money than they could earn. With the level of taxation for high earners at above 90 per cent, it was difficult to blame the band for becoming the first British rock 'n' roll tax exiles.

But still Jagger didn't like the talk and tried to put a respectable face on it. Both he and PR man Les Perrin were fighting a losing battle, though. Just over a week after the tour began on 4 March with a gig at Newcastle City Hall, inflated figures of the band's earnings were freely published. Jagger was moved to sign an advert that the Stones placed in all the major music magazines, which cut the speculation. Decca cashed in on the publicity by releasing an album, *Stone Age*, just as Atlantic Records revealed their plans to distribute the Rolling Stones' own label.

The ten-day tour ended with two gigs at the London Roundhouse before capacity audiences of 4000. Among them were many celebrities, including Eric Clapton, the Faces and DJ John Peel, but the friends and family farewell party was not held until the end of the month, at Maidenhead's Skindles Hotel. Emotions ran high that night, and the music was loud and the dance floor crammed with people. It marked the end of the Stones' permanent residency in Britain.

Before leaving the country, Jagger asked that a nanny should bring Karis to see him. His request was made easier by knowing it would not be refused, as Hunt had for months let it be known indirectly that Jagger was welcome to see his daughter. She was therefore delighted when the call came. Jagger's paternal urges perhaps also stemmed from the fact that he was about to have a second child. Although not widely known, Bianca was pregnant.

By April the band and their families had relocated to the South of France. All five Stones settled there, within travelling distance of Nellcote, Keith Richard's mock Roman villa in the harbour town of Villefranche-sur-Mer. This was to double as the band's base. Jagger and Bianca opted initially for a suite at the Byblos Hotel, St Tropez, although they would later move into a house in Mougins, once the home of Picasso.

Even before arriving in France, encouraged by Bianca, Jagger had adopted Parisian chic and had recently been voted one of the world's best dressed men. The French Riviera and Bianca suited Jagger. He enjoyed the glamorous social whirl of the pampered and pretentious St Tropez set. And his apparent joy in Bianca's company sparked speculation that they might marry. He denied this, despite the fact that plans were already under way.

He had already asked Bianca, at four months pregnant, to marry him, and she had said yes. But she had her misgivings. She was frightened by the idea of marrying him, aware that it was his nod at convention that wanted to make an honest woman of her. When it went wrong later Jagger ungallantly recanted, citing the excuse he often used – it had just been something to do. At least he owned up: 'I've never been madly deeply in love. I'm not an emotional person.'

On 16 April their new single 'Brown Sugar'/'Bitch', with a Chuck Berry oldie 'Let It Rock' also on the UK version, was to be released. It was the first on the Rolling Stone label and peaked at number 2. To promote it the band appeared on *Top of the Pops*. Marsha Hunt was proudly convinced that the song had been inspired by her. She didn't know that its working title had been 'Black Pussy', the subject of much studio ribaldry. But it wasn't Hunt Jagger picked up on during his brief British trip, but Faithfull.

It was to be their last intimate encounter. They met by chance in Chelsea's Kings Road outside Granny Takes A Trip. Faithfull had smartened up since he had last seen her, and he publicly embraced her. When he had left Shrimpton, Faithfull had arrived home one night to Harley House to find Jagger and his ex in the lounge, looking interrupted and guilty. Now about to marry Bianca, Jagger suggested he and Faithfull should retire to a room above the boutique for old times' sake. She agreed. There they had sex, dressed and parted with a kiss. While Faithfull invests an air of romance to this, it can be seen as an aspect of his territorial nature.

Days later, on 23 April, the album *Sticky Fingers* was released and went to number 1 in the UK and the USA. The highly original album sleeve, designed by Andy Warhol, showed a jean-clad crotch with a real zip that when pulled down revealed a pair of Y-fronts. Combined with their new logo, of big lips and a slavering tongue, also by Warhol, it reinforced the message that sex was still what sold the Stones.

Just over a year now since the Beatles had disbanded, something John Lennon said came to mind, identifying basic differences in the bands: 'We were never dependent on fans being in love with us so much as others are. Not like Jagger. Now *he* can't afford to get married. The Stones would be all over.'

But the taboo about Mick marrying and so diluting their pulling power was about to be broken. Still denying rumours of marriage, on 2 May he flew across France to present Bianca on her birthday with a stunning diamond bracelet. A week later he collected two specially designed wedding rings. That, and the discovery that he had applied for special dispensation to marry without the usual posting of banns, finally reached the press. But with such a secretive start their wedding was bound to produce a few hiccups.

Because they were to be married in a Roman Catholic church, Jagger, officially Anglican, had taken private catechism lessons, not only from Rev Lucien Baud, the pastor who would marry them, but also from the Bishop of Fréjus. The intention to have a small wedding, with only Keith Richard from the Stones invited to the marriage ceremony, upset the rest of the band. Witnesses were to be Nathalie Delon and Roger Vadim, and in addition to Jagger's family, friends who flew over by chartered jet at short notice included Paul McCartney and Ringo Starr with their wives, Eric Clapton, Keith Moon, some members of the Faces, Ossie Clark, Donald Cammell and Ahmet Ertegun.

The wedding on 12 May 1971 in Nice would be a two-part affair, a civil ceremony before Mayor Marius Estezan at the town hall, followed by a church service in the 17th-century St Anne Chapel. But before either could take place a prenuptial agreement had to be signed.

Jagger informed Bianca of this with just hours to go before the marriage. Under French law one of two types of agreement had to be signed, stipulating either that all property is held separately, or that it is all joint. Needless to say Jagger expected his bride-to-be to sign the former. This caused a row, during which Bianca later claimed she was put under incredible pressure to sign. Each was as stubborn as the other, and at one point she threatened to cancel the wedding.

Jagger had known long in advance what he was going to do and had gauged that his best hope of her acquiescing would be to tell her when she was in her wedding outfit with guests waiting. Only then perhaps would she have been likely to forgo her rights.

No sooner had Jagger got what he wanted than Les Perrin had

to break it to the irate groom that as the council chamber was a public place it was full of photographers, journalists and sightseers. Jagger, furious sent Perrin back with a warning that he was not coming unless the place was cleared. Meeting total resistance, now *he* threatened to call it off. The Mayor issued his own ultimatum. If bride and groom did not present themselves in ten minutes, there would definitely be no wedding.

It ended up a chaotic hippy event. Bianca wore a wide-brimmed stylish hat, and a white Yves St Laurent suit with a neckline so low that in her braless state it revealed her nipples, Jagger a cream three-piece suit with floral shirt and sneakers. Flashbulbs popped as guests tried to glimpse what was going on, distracted by Richard and Pallenberg having a private row in the background.

The chaos deepened when the wedding party proceeded on to the St Anne Chapel. Its old door had been barred because of the crowds, and Jagger found himself battering on it to be let in to his own wedding. By the time he reached the altar he was still angry and stressed. The Earl of Lichfield gave away Bianca to Bach's wedding march and the theme from *Love Story*.

The reception was held in a disused theatre at the Café des Arts. Drinking and dancing Jagger was at last able to relax, jamming along with Steven Stills and other musicians. Richard, having changed his combat-style clothes for Nazi uniform, crashed out and ruined any hope of an impromptu Stones performance. The hired reggae band kept things going. Not able to resist, Jagger later clambered up drunk on stage, and for almost half an hour cavorted with P. P. Arnold with whom he's said to have once had an affair. Sick of the thick dope haze and semi-conscious bodies scattered indiscriminately about the floor the bride, still smarting from the prenuptial stunt, danced just once, with Jagger's father, then left alone. Her husband appeared not to notice her departure.

Back in London Marsha Hunt heard the news of Jagger's wedding but had her own preoccupations. Among Jagger's presents to Karis on his first visit had been a silver spoon, but there were no signs that the girl was headed for a privileged life as the daughter of a wealthy rock star. Hunt was living frugally, hoping to get work to ease her escalating money troubles.

Across town Marianne Faithfull had problems of a different kind. She later called Jagger's marriage to Bianca an act of ultimate narcissism. She hadn't seriously expected an invitation but celebrated anyway, ending up spending Jagger's wedding night drying out in Paddington Police Station. Her descent into living rough as a heroin addict was perilously close.

The next day the newlyweds left Cannes by yacht on their honeymoon, their destination a chateau near Micinaggio, accessible only by sea. From there they sailed round the world, returning to the Riviera at the end of the month, where recording commitments at Nellcote anchored Jagger until late July.

But these sessions soon became fraught. The further Bianca got into her pregnancy, the more fractious she became. Jagger often had little choice but to call it a day with the band and fly to Paris, where Bianca preferred to stay. This caused some resentment. His close friendship with Richard came under a lot of pressure as a result of the demands of an increasingly discontented wife, and Jagger felt pulled in opposite directions. He would look back on his first year of marriage as being the only happy one. It was downhill after that.

10

DUCKING 'N' DIVING

I T WAS EN route to Ireland to stay with the Guinness family that on 30 July Jagger announced to reporters at Heathrow that he and Bianca were expecting a baby. Personally he was looking forward to relaxing at Leixlip Castle, viewing it as a welcome break from Nellcote, which had degenerated into a den of dope dealers and other unsavoury characters. Working in the fetid atmosphere of the poorly ventilated basement there had become more than he could bear, as had Keith Richard's erratic behaviour. The primitive recording conditions appealed to the guitarist. But Jagger was less impressed, and the friction between the two was tangible, affecting the band and making those around them edgy. The tension cranked up a notch every time Jagger seemed to put his wife before the Stones. Richard was jealous of what he thought were Jagger's new priorities.

But there was another annoyance. In June Decca had released 'Street Fighting Man', followed by an album of old numbers called *Gimme Shelter*. Under the new Rolling Stones label so far only one single and one album had come out. The Stones had left Britain to make more money, and the potential of this new company was not being realized. Blame for this seems largely to fall on Jagger as the other Stones appeared frustrated at what they believed was his reluctance to sign up other bands.

Possibly this stemmed from his old fear of risk-taking, but supposedly several bands destined for superstardom – later said to have included Queen – slipped through their fingers. Then again maybe there was method in his madness. The music business is a constantly changing world and, for most of those in it, perennially insecure. Why, therefore, encourage the nurturing of future competition?

Jagger purposely left Bianca out of all business matters. This didn't worry her. What did upset her was her pregnancy. She hated it, and at this time there seemed to be very little Jagger could do right in his wife's eyes. He also couldn't help but be aware of the band's rancour towards her worsening. Bianca apparently added to this herself, though. Just as Richard was put out by her, equally she felt threatened by the hold he and those in the Stones' circle had over her husband. Bianca didn't endear herself to them either by behaving some said, in an arrogant, high-handed manner towards them. The root of it all could have been insecurity.

She was already vulnerable when she began to harbour a suspicion that Jagger had resumed his former brief interlude with Anita Pallenberg. He had not, but to disabuse Bianca of this meant paying her extra attention. This, in turn, displeased the band. By the autumn for the first time in his life Jagger must have felt like a break from the constant hostility. To try to ease the situation and cut down travelling time, he persuaded Bianca to return to their rented St Tropez villa for a while.

It was in September, against this backdrop of unrest and with Bianca eight months pregnant, that Jagger invited Marsha Hunt and Karis on a weekend visit. He sent his driver Alan Dunn to meet them at Nice airport. His orders were to take them, not to any one of the spare rooms in his own palatial home but to Mick Taylor's house in nearby Grasse. Later that evening Dunn drove them to dinner with the Jaggers.

Throughout the visit Jagger had eyes only for Bianca. At dinner they nestled against each other, whispering in French and ignoring their guests as if they were invisible. It was fortunate that Karis was too young to realize how completely irrelevant she appeared to be to her father. The next day was no better, and before long it was time for Dunn to take them to the airport. Hunt's reasons for enduring this display of shocking manners were simple. She was in rent arrears, which potentially threatened her daughter's security and welfare. She had hoped an offer of help might have been forthcoming, but when it wasn't she steeled herself to ask, again for the child, for a modest loan. Jagger gave her £200 but could not look her in the eye as he handed over the money. Whether or not he had staged the whole charade to show off his pregnant wife to his erstwhile lover, or to prove to the jealous Bianca that he was indifferent to Hunt, it was not well done.

Hunt and Karis returned to London, Jagger and Bianca to Paris, where on 21 October 1971 Jade Sheena Jezebel Jagger was born at the Rue de Belvédère Nursing Home. Mick was thrilled. He phoned his parents, then Richard. He told the latter not to expect him for a month. Richard was not thrilled. In early November the trio flew to Britain for Joe and Eva to meet their granddaughter. The press got in on the act.

'I've always been a good father,' Jagger boasted, presumably feeling he had discharged his paternal obligation to his eldest child by having recently had delivered to her a rocking horse for her first birthday.

Jagger returned to Villefranche just before the recording sessions ended. Surprisingly, in the less than propitious circumstances, they had produced enough material for a double album, with the working title *Tropical Disease*. Then Jagger publicly outlined plans for spring 1972 with a 40-venue US tour. Altamont still cast its shadow over them. Mindful of this, they planned to play in smaller, more controllable venues. Work was still required to finish off the new album, and it was decided this was best done in the secure environment of an LA studio.

Profanity and violence preoccupied the lyrics of much of the double album now entitled *Exile on Main Street*. It was then under production at Sunset Sound Studios, where worked carried on beyond December. The new year, 1972, had begun with an old irritation. The Stones were due to release the new single 'Tumbling Dice'/'Sweet Black Angel', under their own label, and Decca had recently issued an anthology album, *Milestones*. But in America

London Records had put out *Hot Rocks 1964–1971*, and the Stones sued ex-manager Allen Klein for releasing material without their agreement.

This action came on top of a clutch of law suits issued months before when Jagger, Richard, Wyman, Watts and Brian Jones's father filed a High Court writ against Andrew Oldham and Eric Easton. They claimed that they had made a deal with Decca that had deprived the Stones of certain record royalties. Simultaneously they filed an action against Klein for failing to represent their best financial interests, resolved later in the year when both sides announced they had settled all outstanding differences.

Jagger and Bianca were back in London. Since their marriage the media had fêted them as society darlings. Bianca's unique sense of style had further influenced Jagger, refining his off-stage image. Outdoing each other in sartorial elegance, both were included in the year's respective best-dressed categories. In private it was another matter. A flying visit to LA overlapped 12 May, their first wedding anniversary. Some wondered how significant it was that Jagger spent the day lunching with Rudolph Nureyev, before joining John Lennon and Yoko Ono for their recording session at Record Plant Studio.

A week later Jagger was back in London, attending the US Embassy to collect personally the Stones' work permits for their upcoming tour. As last-minute preparations got under way for this, with estimations of gross earnings of around $4 million, Jagger received another request for help from Hunt who had continued working, going from a West End musical to setting up the group 22. She had calculated that £600 would provide the necessary costs for taking Karis on the road in Europe with a nanny. It was the third time she had asked Jagger for help. This time he wasn't easy to track down, but she proved persistent. After a series of difficult phone calls, he sanctioned the handout. His women trouble didn't end there, though.

He had taken Bianca on a quick holiday to Asia, partly as a sweetener for the fact that he preferred she should not accompany him to America. It was more appropriate that she should stay at home to care for Jade. The road was not the best place for a mother and child, but Bianca was furious, and they were still battling it out as Jagger stood in his hallway among his suitcases awaiting transport to the airport.

When he proved impervious to all argument, Bianca shrieked that if she wasn't allowed to come, he could hand back a scarf of hers he had packed. Jagger complained that he had wanted to wear it on stage. But she was immovable, and he ended up rifling through each suitcase to find it. According to Jade's nanny, Jane Villiers, who witnessed this, Jagger was so distraught that he burst into tears. Eventually, though, he produced the scarf and handed it over. He may have lost the battle, but he had won the war when he left alone to join the others at Heathrow.

Exile on Main Street had been released on 30 May. Attracting polarized reviews, it topped the UK charts, as it would Stateside, and made a good launch pad for their North American tour. They opened on 3 June at Vancouver's Pacific Coliseum to the usual accompaniment of riots, injuries and arrests; a pattern repeated elsewhere in the coming hectic weeks. Joining them for a handful of shows was legendary bluesman B. B. King, an early hero of the band's, who in turn respects the Stones.

'I'm a big fan,' King says. 'I met them for the first time in the early seventies just when I had a big record out. My agent was able to get theirs to let me open their show.'

'They were extremely energetic,' he says of the band's performance that tour. 'I call it a lotta electricity movin' around on stage. Mick Jagger, for me, was the centre of that energy, but having said that really from the beginning it seemed that they handpicked each other and gave folks exactly what they wanted – great entertainment.'

With the Beatles disbanded, the Stones had the chance to consolidate their position and reign supreme. Nevertheless new challengers appeared all the time. It was the dawn of glam rock and bands like T-Rex and Sweet, with sexually ambiguous stage acts and flamboyant visual imagery, were increasingly popular. David Bowie, too, whose new album, *The Rise and Fall of Ziggy Stardust and the Spiders From Mars*, achieved incredible chart success.

Jagger monitored all developments in music. He felt he had been first with an androgynous stage style but vulnerable in the face of these new invaders. He was conscious too, that at almost 29 he had to work at keeping his image potent and determined to prove he had more than ever to give on stage. His slinky jumpsuits (later favoured by Queen front man Freddie Mercury, Jagger's one serious rival) in flimsy material were slashed to the navel and strewn with gaudy spangles. His make-up he applied more heavily. To size up to his promiscuous reputation he put a rolled-up sock down the front of his near diaphanous outfits. These, he said, 'make me look like I have a permanent hard-on', useful when he went out each night to stir up the audience into a sexual frenzy. Was it fear of losing his crown that made him perform with such zest that critics called him possessed? Or was he just high on performance and drugs taken during backstage breaks? Whatever the reason, before each show was through the stage was pitted with holes where he had thrashed it with his studded belt as he snarled his way, demented, through the songs.

It was a winning formula, and success bred success. Delirious fans stormed the record shops, which ensured extensive radio airplay and fed back into a string of sell-out gigs. Trouble came with the territory, but venue management tried to curtail it with body searches for arms on entry. But none of this prevented a celebrity turn-out at concerts, among them Jack Nicholson, Orson Welles and Britt Ekland, Ike and Tina Turner, Truman Capote and Princess Lee Radziwill. By half way through the tour the press were salivating.

'They were famous, now they are a legend,' cried one critic, while some appointed the Rolling Stones the top music attraction in the world. But it was rock promoter Bill Graham's view that caused most comment when he overreached himself by proclaiming, 'They are the biggest draw in the history of mankind. Only one other guy ever came close. Gandhi!'

But this was not how everyone saw them. Owners of land surrounding Altamont had been waiting since 1969 to make a claim against the Stones for damage done to their property. The US tour was just days old when they made their move. Having played the Winterland in San Francisco, the band had just boarded the plane for LA when a curvaceous young woman in hotpants and a tight tour T-shirt pushed her way through the fans and charmed Ian Stewart into letting her on to the plane for Jagger's autograph. The sight of her sashaying down the aisle caught everyone's eye. As she knelt on the seat in front of Jagger she leant sensuously forward and purred, 'Mick Jagger?'

Jagger nodded, only for his leery grin to freeze on his face as in a very different voice she said, 'I am hereby serving you Michael Philip Jagger –' And then began to list the charges. Then everything happened at once. One witness claimed she was thrown down the aircraft steps, while Richard tossed out her sheaf of papers after her on to the tarmac. The woman herself, Vivienne Manuel, later testified in court in Alameda, California, that Jagger had struck her several times; a charge he admitted. His explanation was that it had been a kneejerk reaction when she had thrown the papers at him, but one he claimed, he had quickly regretted. Eventually an award of damages to the landowners was overturned on the grounds of improper service, and an out-of-court settlement was finally reached.

But trouble followed for those in charge of the band's security, given that they had considered it now to be run along the lines of military precision. This tightening-up had been done to ensure no repetition of 1969. But another, more sinister legacy of Altamont had already appeared with talk of death threats against Jagger from Hell's Angels aggrieved that they had been left to take the rap for Meredith Hunter's murder. When asked by reporters if he was frightened by this, Jagger displayed a false bravado, but later admitted to being 'scared shitless'. He was also said to have packed a loaded .38 revolver for use as a last resort. In time his fears for his own safety would become all-consuming, but for now he had to be content with a small army of bodyguards hired to protect them wherever they went.

No security system is perfect, however, as was proved when the Stones were due to perform in Canada. On 17 July at the Forum in Montreal, a bomb exploded under an equipment truck. It had nothing to do with the Hell's Angels; French-Canadian separatists later claiming responsibility for destroying the band's gear and shattering Jagger's brittle nerves. With replacement equipment the show went on late, which, though unavoidable, heightened tempers among fans cheated by the black-market sale of hundreds of fake tickets. The atmosphere was more than usually volatile. Jagger did well to be hit by only one bottle hurled on stage, although he had a moment's panic when a firecracker went off.

The triumphalism of earlier weeks looked to be turning sour as the aggressive behaviour continued next day. They had to fly south for a Boston gig, but fog caused a diversion to Green Airport, Warwick, Rhode Island. One local press photographer began snapping happily at the unexpected celebrity visitors, until Stones' minders tried to stop him. When the scuffle escalated, airport security rushed in, arresting Keith Richard for assault.

Their gig in jeopardy, Jagger argued so vehemently with the officers that he ended up in the back of the police van too. He was joined by Marshall Chess who ran the Rolling Stones label and a third man, Robert Frank. All three were charged with obstructing police. They were only in custody for a short while before Boston's mayor secured their release, but were set to appear in court on 23 August. Meantime, for a second night, the show started hours late.

The tour ended on Jagger's birthday with a gig at New York's Madison Square Garden, followed by a glittering reception at the St Regis Hotel on Fifth Avenue. Guests included Bob Dylan, Carly Simon, Andy Warhol and other celebrities, among them Truman Capote who had been assigned to cover the trip for *Rolling Stone* magazine. Jagger disliked Capote, doubtless not unconnected to the American writer's contempt for him. Capote had witnessed the band's excesses in hotels and on planes, especially the drug use (one tour film, commercially unshowable, is said to show Jagger ready to go on stage snorting a line of coke through a rolled-up bank note).

But Capote restricted his notes to Jagger's professional life, and they were none too complimentary. He damned Jagger for not being able to sing or dance and having no talent, adding, 'That unisex thing is a no-sex thing. Believe me, he's about as sexy as a pissing toad.' He also predicted, 'He will never be a star,' about which, long before his death in 1984, Capote will have conceded he was wrong. But he also identified that 'Jagger could, I suppose, be a businessman.'

It had been shrewd to punctuate the US trip with doubts about whether or not, after 10 years, this was to be the Stones' last tour. It would have done no harm to ticket sales. When the interest had waned, Jagger had injected new life into it by predicting that before he was 33 he would be out of music. He should by then be doing something else. He shuddered at the prospect of ending up like Elvis Presley, singing in Las Vegas to housewives with handbags. Still eschewing the idea that he enjoyed the business side of music, not acceptable for an artist in those pre-Thatcher days, he made it his point to stress in interviews that he had no interest in being rich. Yet at the same time he insisted on knowing exactly how much he was personally grossing each day on the road.

By refusing to allow Bianca to join the tour Jagger had ensured nothing cramped his style. The fact that he was married put no brake on the one-night stands. They had their uses, and he knew their place. But almost on arrival in America, at a post-gig party, he had had his whip hand snatched away when he ran into Pamela Miller for the first time since Bianca had warned her off.

Miller had been involved with actor Don Johnson, but was fast losing him to Melanie Griffith. Upset over this she was drunk when she turned up at the party. Seeing her, Jagger called out but was hardly prepared for her response. She ran through the crowd, pushing film stars, politicians and other American glitterati out of the way, to knock her ex-lover to the floor in her exuberance where she promptly, in her own words, 'plunged my hand down his pants and into the crack of his sweet famous ass.' It was as well for both Miller and Jagger that that night was not one of the few occasions Bianca made a flying visit to join her husband or her now trademark ebony and ivory walking cane might have proved more than an elegant fashion accessory.

Bianca was present at the final New York party and accompanied Jagger when afterwards the band scattered. News had just come through that the Rhode Island court case hearing had been postponed to 13 December, so the couple headed to Ireland before resuming their jetsetting and meeting up with friends, one of whom was fashion model Amanda Lear.

Lear had worked for the same model agency as Pallenberg and it was through her in the mid-sixties that she had met Brian Jones. 'At the time my boyfriend had been Tara Browne,' Lear says. 'Tara and Brian were very close friends, and after Tara was killed I was desperately unhappy. Brian was wonderful and strong for me during that time, and for a long while we remained just friends, then later I became his girlfriend. Through Brian I met Mick Jagger at various times, but this was late 1968 and a very shaky period. Brian was planning leaving the Stones. He spoke to me about it only a little but told me, 'They don't want me any more.' Because I was on Brian's side I didn't want to see Jagger or any of them then.

'In 1972 I was living in Spain with the artist Salvador Dali, whom Brian had previously introduced me to. I modelled for Ossie Clark and had appeared on an album cover for Roxy Music, the first girl in black leather. David Bowie saw this photo. He liked the look and wanted to meet the girl. One night I got a call from my friend Marianne Faithfull. I was in London, and it was late but she said a friend of hers was dying to meet me. She sent a car to fetch me, and she introduced me to Bowie.'

Lear and Bowie began an affair (he was married by now to Angie Barnet) and often made a foursome with Bianca and Jagger.

'After dinner one evening we all went to Tramps, then to a cinema in Leicester Square to see a big boxing match live from Las Vegas, I think it was Cassius Clay, but I can't recall who he was fighting. Anyway Bianca wouldn't talk to me. She sulked the whole night. Mick ignored her and was very pleasant to me, but Bianca could be like that, on and off. You would wonder what you had done wrong, then the next time you could be at a party and she'd be all over you. I think she lacked confidence, and of course it was hard living with Mick Jagger's ego.'

Bowie and Lear were together a year and during that time Jagger dropped by their flat often.

'David particularly copied Mick a lot. He was jealous of Jagger's success and badly wanted to be as big. To him Mick represented the top entertainer in the world, and David was very ambitious.' Bowie according to Lear, hugely admired Jagger.

'It's been alleged that Bowie and Jagger had something going homosexually. I believe David was madly in love with Jagger during the time I knew him. Mick might've crashed at Bowie's flat on the odd night when he'd had too much drugs or drink, but as far as I saw Mick always had an eye for a pretty girl. Personally I never witnessed anything gay between them. David was a different matter. He liked boys and girls. I suppose to Bowie, the ultimate trip would have been to get Mick Jagger into bed, but I don't believe he ever did. I do know there was a lot of rivalry underneath their friendship as far as David was concerned.'

The only rivals Bianca deigned to acknowledge were female. Mindful of his tax situation Jagger kept on the move, often travelling without his wife. In November while in America he guested on a Carly Simon single 'You're So Vain'. His participation wasn't publicized, but word got around. Inevitably there was rumour of an affair. When Jagger had met Simon she seemed happily involved with James Taylor. That alone would have been a challenge to Jagger, and certainly Simon found Jagger exciting and worldly. She was also said to have been impressed by his fabled promiscuity – something that had also been an attraction of one of her former lovers, Warren Beatty. But although talk of an affair between them was only conjecture, it was enough to inflame Bianca.

Faithfull had seen herself as restoring calm to Jagger's world after his combative union with Chrissie Shrimpton. Whether or not Jagger had anticipated it, with Bianca that balance had tipped again. It took only a suspicion of adultery for Bianca to prove she was more than a match for him. Her Latin rages were becoming legendary. When Jagger went back home to the South of France it was to find himself locked out. He talked his way in eventually. But the fragile truce soon collapsed, and he was out again.

Anyone really close to Jagger would have seen the writing on the wall. Emotionally troublesome women were undesirable and as such expendable. Even a wife. By autumn it was obvious that Jagger had grown tired of Bianca. He had briefly thrived on a return to volatility, but the relationship had turned a corner. In the coming months if they were seen in public together at all, it was rare to glimpse a trace of affection. In private they fought bitterly, and staff dreaded their appearance in the office.

Just when it seemed the marriage could hardly get any worse, the relationship sank to an all-time low when Bianca opined on a US chat show, 'Mick doesn't think much of women.' Jagger's clash with her over the remark was incendiary, but she was never under his thumb. She was stronger than his previous women and determined not to be subservient to him or his public image. She refused to stoke his ego.

'Mick's accomplishments are his. Nothing to do with me,' she stated. 'I must achieve my own.' Like Faithfull, she did tend to overlook the fact that it was her association with Jagger that had gained her visibility. But no one could say she did not make something original of her enhanced public profile. As much as she enjoyed her life as an international jetsetter, all the concurrent attention did not blind her to the fact that she felt neglected.

By this time Jagger had two discontented women on his hands, the other being Marsha Hunt. In Hunt's case it was at last clear to him that things had changed. Struggling single-handedly to bring up their child, that summer she had decided to find out about how to get financial support from Jagger. As they had not been married, and their daughter was therefore illegitimate, her one legal appeal was to bring a paternity suit against him. This was a big step, that would undoubtedly attract media attention. Whilst Hunt considered her options, Jagger, perhaps acting on a tip-off, had called her, hoping to talk her out of doing anything he might consider rash.

He invited his ex-lover to a lunchtime *tête à tête* only to find Hunt in a militant mood. Cutting through his attempts to soften her resolve, she demanded directly why he had not helped her meet the £150 hospital bill with which she'd been faced when Karis had suffered burns from an accident involving scalding tea. Jagger made the mistake of replying offhandedly that she would most likely have spent the money on herself. That remark was enough for Hunt to have a writ raised against him.

Jagger had unsuspectingly agreed to meet Hunt one afternoon on the steps of the Albert Memorial in Hyde Park, unaware that her lawyer was in the vicinity, waiting to make service. Moments after Jagger arrived, the man, clearly unhappy at the set-up, moved in to take Jagger so by surprise that he had accepted service of a writ before he could gather his thoughts.

It probably scared Jagger most, once his initial anger had receded, to see how coolly determined Hunt was about the establishment of a trust fund for Karis. She suggested a sum of £25,000, which would release him from any future financial responsibility. It would also avoid her ever having to ask him personally for assistance. He did not acquiesce which led to Hunt's affiliation order the following year.

By the end of November, feeling besieged on all sides, Jagger must have been happy to have a legitimate excuse to get away, to join the Stones in Jamaica for a four-week recording session at Kingston's Dynamic Sound Studios. There was also talk of a Far East tour. In the meantime, on 2 December French drug agencies were closing in on Keith Richard and Anita Pallenberg, and in their absence warrants for their arrest were issued in Nice. The press went mad and the whole situation threatened to blow out of all proportion.

Jagger was furious. Days later he took the step of publicly distancing himself, Watts, Wyman and Taylor from Richard's troubles, denying that any charges had been laid against the four of them. His fury was personal and professional. Just the hint of drug trouble was enough to jeopardize the Japanese tour, which had shown signs of being record-breaking. Stones' tour manager Peter Rudge was despatched to reassure the government and nervous promoters trying to finalize details.

With all this hanging in the balance, Jagger returned to Cheyne Walk for Christmas. On 23 December a massive earthquake hit Bianca's birthplace of Managua. Communications were cut, and it was difficult to get news. Initial bulletins spoke of over 6000 deaths. Devastated, Bianca looked to Jagger who, despite pulling strings, was not able to find out what she wanted to know about her parents. As no commercial flights were scheduled to the area he chartered a private jet, loaded with 2000 anti-typhoid vaccine syringes, and flew to Nicaragua to search for her parents. Her mother's diner was now lost in the rubble, but by New Year's Eve, after several agonizing days, her parents turned up having been out of town when the quake hit. The new year then began with reports that Mick and Bianca Jagger, having made a mercy dash to Managua, were themselves now missing. Thankfully, four days later it was announced they were safe.

Jagger returned to Jamaica to continue work on the album while Bianca remained with her mother, renting temporary accommodation. The distance between them made communication difficult.

In the aftermath of the disaster, a relief fund was set up. Jagger decided to help. On 10 January he announced that the Rolling Stones planned to play a benefit gig in aid of the earthquake victims, to be held in eight days hence at the Forum in LA. He had been obviously moved by the devastation he had witnessed.

The LA charity gig raised over $500,000, after which the Stones flew to Honolulu. Their Australasian tour started there with two gigs at the International Sports Centre on 21 January. Through Hong Kong, Auckland, Brisbane, Melbourne and Adelaide they played, ending in Sydney on 27 February.

The performance, so well received in America, did not take off in Australia. Jagger wore the rhinestone jumpsuits, now with a matching mask, and performed with the same sexually magnetic energy, though sometimes he seemed to tire more quickly. The only real change, picked up on by fans and press alike, was that he had cut his long hair. Asked why, he replied brusquely, 'Because I had begun to feel like an old tart.'

This kind of sharp rejoinder, which once fed his bad-boy image, now seemed to turn against him. Critics accused him of a dated performance in a dated style. Clearly there were dissatisfactions he had to address as the band nevertheless went from strength to strength.

11

BAWDY LANGUAGE

ESPITE THE CANCELLATION of the Stones' Far East tour because of previous drug convictions, advance ticket sales had been phenomenal. Japan's influential *Music Life* magazine voted them Best Group of the Year and Jagger Best Male Vocalist. He was fêted too in Washington when in May he and Bianca went in person to present the Senate with a cheque for £350,000, the money raised by the band's charity gig in aid of Nicaraguan Aid. Bianca was a big draw in her own right, as, with mixed emotions, Jagger found out when he saw her described in the papers next day as 'the newest superstar in the family'. In return they were presented with a Golden Key, an honour that upset Bill Wyman. None of the other Stones, he later pointed out, had received so much as a thankyou.

Jagger's very public appearance at the seat of American government was, on the face of it, something of a gamble. The previous month Judge Orton of Warwick, Rhode Island, had rejected a motion to dismiss charges following the July 1972 airport incident and insisted that Mick Jagger and Keith Richard stand trial the next time they were in the States. But a fire at Stargroves gave Jagger the excuse to return promptly to London.

By the end of May he was committed anyway to sessions at London's Island Studios in Notting Hill Gate, mixing their new album; sessions that were often minus Richard: this absence initiated rumours that he was leaving the Stones, which quickly gained credence. By the following month Jagger denied, via *NME*, that Richard was to be replaced by Ron Wood of the Faces. Richard declared that the story had come as a complete shock to him, but thereafter he made sure to turn up at the studio. When tour manager Peter Rudge had revealed that the Stones would not be touring the US that year, it was Richard who announced that they were to embark on a major European tour instead.

Jagger, still trying to play happy families, planned to take Bianca and Jade to Italy. But on 18 June, the day they were to fly out, he learnt that Marsha Hunt had filed an affiliation order at Marylebone Magistrates' Court.

Through spring into summer 1973 Jagger had been slow legally to recognize Karis as his child. The previous November he had allowed Jade to attend her half sister's second birthday party, but for months he avoided answering all requests to sign the straightforward trust-fund document to which he had originally agreed. If he thought by ignoring the issue it would go away, he now found out he was wrong. But he was not about to make it easy for Hunt.

Ever conscious of his bad-lad reputation, Jagger knew that to be known to have fathered an illegitimate child could only boost it. But Hunt was not able to depend on that to help her. When news of the paternity suit hit the papers, the clandestine nature of their affair became a problem for her. No one believed her claims and tended to see her as a money-grabbing single parent trying to pin paternity on a rich rock star. She had a rough ride of it, mainly from the press who laid siege to her home. It says much for her strength of character that she weathered the storm and stuck to her guns. Whereas it does Jagger little credit that when asked to comment he remarked that it was possibly a publicity stunt by Hunt to revitalize her ailing career, so strengthening the perception of her as a gold-digger. Most of the few people who could have supported Hunt's claim worked for Jagger and were therefore no help. The next day the court upheld Jagger's lawyer's request for blood tests, and the hearing was adjourned. In further evasive action, a spokesman issued a statement on Jagger's behalf to say that the allegation was not admitted. Discussions were taking place between the parties about the merits of the claim. In fact Jagger left for Italy.

But sunnier climes did not breed warmer relations. By early July, though both parties denied it, talk that the Jaggers' marriage was on the rocks made newspaper headlines. For Jagger there was no escape into work this time. Details of the European autumn tour had just been released, and he was conscious that France was a no-go area with Richard's legal problems there. Richard had been arrested again in June when a drug squad raided his Cheyne Walk house. He, Pallenberg and Prince Stanilaus Klossowski had been charged with possession of drugs, and Richard also faced charges of possessing a handgun and ammunition without a firearms certificate. He had been remanded the next day on £1000 bail. He was allowed to keep his passport to honour recording commitments, but the hearing was set for the end of July, and the tour began 1 September.

Where Brian Jones had once been seen a liability to the band, now it was Richard's turn. Jagger, who felt that he was often left to bear the burden of the band's worries, tried to get away from it all by watching the Test Match at the Oval in July. But he only found himself the focus of new rumours, this time of a merger between the Rolling Stones and the Faces. This idea had grown from Jagger and Richard's recent recording session with Ian McLagan and Ron Wood at the latter's Richmond home studio. But before it could be verified, the next day's events diverted everyone's attention.

The paternity suit came back to court only to be adjourned again until 6 November to await results of the blood tests. The case, now on hold, was pushed aside when Jagger heard that Richard's troubles had been added to by a devastating fire at Redlands. All occupants had escaped unhurt, and some possessions had been rescued, but the 500-year-old house was razed to the ground. While Richard and Pallenberg wandered around dazed, trying not to get in the way of the firemen battling the blaze, at Marylebone Magistrates' Court they were further remanded on bail in their absence until 22 September.

Before that the Stones' new album was due for release. Jagger had been engaged in heated discussions about it with Atlantic Records supremo Ahmet Ertegun. The problems centred on a particular track, the title of which Ertegun wanted changed. Ertegun had also identified a possible libel problem with its lyrics over a reference to actor Steve McQueen. Jagger is said to have solved this by sending McQueen a tape of the song and receiving back a written guarantee that he would not sue. Ertegun, however, insisted on the name change, adamant that 'Starfucker' was unacceptable. Though not best pleased, Jagger relented and changed it to 'Star, Star'. Even so, on the album's release the track still drew a lifetime ban from the BBC. Irritated, Jagger argued, 'I'm not saying all women are star fuckers, but I see an awful lot of them.'

Goats Head Soup, recorded the previous autumn in Jamaica, was released on 31 August. 'I really felt close to the album, and I put all I had into it,' Jagger said of it. 'But whatever you do it's always wrong.'

He was referring to criticism levelled at the album over what was perceived by some as its sloppy execution and Jagger's sometimes arrogant yawning of the lyrics. As never before there were doubts voiced about his ability to structure a song, and the album was dismissed by some as a waste of vinyl. Yet other reviewers liked it, believing it a return to the band's roots. It became a dual UK/US number 1, trailered by 'Angie', the only single released from it. While it stayed at number 5 in Britain, it mirrored the album's achievement in America and went top. The promotional video was filmed by Michael Lindsay-Hogg, who had recently healed his rift with Jagger, and it later became one of the Stones' most recognizable film promos. The acoustic love song was said to have been inspired by David Bowie's wife.

Jagger had continued to develop his friendship with David Bowie, monitoring how his fortunes had changed, with a sell-out world tour and *Aladdin Sane* topping the charts in April 1973. Though Jagger disliked sharing the spotlight, he found himself drawn to the attractions Bowie represented, particularly his promotion as a solo performer. Lindsay-Hogg corroborates Amanda Lear's assessment of the Stone's feelings.

'Mick's friendship revolved around a rivalry he felt with David,' he says. 'Jagger clearly envied Bowie's freedom. David didn't have a band to handle or share royalties with. He also had a chameleon character and career and over the years it made Mick really frustrated at his own lack of acting success.'

This rivalry was not one-sided. During Bowie's UK tour Jagger visited him backstage, and onlookers to the exchange maintain each spent their time weighing up the other. It was the same story after the Stones kicked off their tour on 1 September at the Stadthalle in Vienna and wound their way around Europe to Newcastle in the middle of the month. David Bowie dropped by there to say hi. For Jagger the company of the star on the rise was not always desirable, especially the moment Bowie became visible that night at the edge of the stage. All eyes left Jagger and turned instead to the wings, where Bowie stood with his crown of orange hair. Needless to say, one backward glare from Jagger, and Bowie was moved out of sight.

Their apparent mutual fascination did cause comment. Jagger knew that while his androgynous image was just that, Bowie was open about his preferences. That was a risk Jagger would not have taken at any price. Not renowned for his generosity with money, still it is said that Jagger treated Bowie and his male companion to accommodation after that north of England gig, in a classy hotel with flowers and wine. It was always possible that Jagger courted Bowie and became seemingly inseparable from him, because he was not prepared to let him steal the limelight. Over the years he would often ally himself, even temporarily, to someone at the top.

Approaching Bowie's hotel suite later that night in Newcastle, Jagger, in company, is said to have overheard Bowie decry the Stones' act as stale. But before Jagger could take offence it all turned into a joke. Or was it? There was no way of knowing that Jagger would be a superstar two decades on, and with the ruthless nature of the music business there were always new contenders. Some around Bowie worried that Jagger had peaked, that Bowie ought not to be so freely associating with him.

Clearly Bowie didn't listen. In fact he and his wife moved to a house near Cheyne Walk in Oakley Street, which is where Angie Bowie later claimed she returned one morning unexpectedly to discover Bowie and Jagger naked, lying side by side in bed. Her sudden entrance, she said, woke the two up. Lost for words she adjourned to the kitchen before returning with a breakfast tray. She did not witness them engaged in any sexual act, yet later stated, 'I never even considered the possibility that they hadn't been screwing.'

Whatever the truth about what Angie Bowie witnessed, it would come back to embarrass Jagger years later when she told US chat-show queen Joan Rivers and millions of American viewers about it.

This claim of a bisexual attachment was not the only one. Andy Warhol is said to have maintained that he and Jagger had had something going. For a certain period it was hard for people around Jagger to know for sure, but the majority view was that it was all an act. Jagger perpetuated the uncertainty because he wanted it that way. Perhaps he came to wish he had not been quite so thorough. 'Is he, isn't he?' preoccupied those around him, each determined to make what they wanted of it to suit themselves. While there will always be those who choose to believe there is no smoke without fire, there has never been any proof that Jagger has ever been anything other than heterosexual. Indeed while debate simmered, Jagger was said nightly to be out and about with numerous women. Some turned, out, not unexpectedly, to be former, or current, lovers of rock star friends. As was the case with Bebe Buell.

By the time the Stones' tour ended in Berlin in mid-October, Jagger already knew the 18-year-old *Playboy* centrefold model. Buell was involved with Todd Rundgren and had a lengthy affair going with David Bowie. He, like Jagger, had not been able to resist the challenge of getting her to cheat on her rock-star boyfriend. Jagger had first met Buell earlier that year, backstage at an Eric Clapton concert, and had made an immediate play for her. At the post-gig party that night he flirted outrageously, making her the centre of his attention and urging her to ditch Rundgren. Disappointingly, although Jagger could see that his tactics thrilled the young woman, he failed to succeed.

'I thought he was kind of cute,' Buell confessed, 'but not enough to leave Todd for.' Apparently resigned to his fate Jagger abandoned his quest to talk to Clapton in the corner, amid a haze of dope smoke and people chattering louder the more drunk they became. The moment Buell left the room to wander into a deserted kitchen Jagger went after her. Rundgren, however, was not far behind. During the ride home Buell maintains that he lectured her on how

Jagger was as bad as Warren Beatty, to be avoided at all costs.

With his reputation to uphold Jagger naturally set out to get Buell, wearing her down until she accepted a dinner date. He applied his not inconsiderable skills at seduction, and Buell was impressed, especially with his chameleon-like adaptation to different social circles. His masterstroke seems to have been to say how desperately he had wanted her after that first date, but how he would control himself, not wishing to scare her. She fell for it.

After that their affair was a foregone conclusion. Perhaps he would not have felt so confident had he known what went through the model's mind as they stripped off in Jagger's suite at New York's Plaza Hotel. Her first glimpse at the superstar naked made her 'very shocked by his smallness.' He seemed to size up between the sheets, however, proving himself a demanding lover. As their affair developed, there was no exclusivity with Buell. She carried on her affair with Bowie at the same time. She freely confessed that it was accepted in those days, in these circles. If a lover introduced you to a friend, the likelihood was that you would end up sleeping with him too. 'Fidelity,' she said, 'was not the call.'

Jagger's affair with Bebe was long-standing enough for him to be concerned that she always looked right to be seen out with him. He demanded a certain chic of his mistresses and would inspect what they intended to wear before leaving the apartment. If not up to his exacting standards, they would be sent back to change. Buell found him a generous lover who regularly lavished expensive gifts on her. But he could be mean too. After spending hundreds of dollars on wine at dinner he might only tip a cab driver a quarter for the drive back to his Manhattan apartment. What surprised her about him was his knowledge of cosmetics, an expertise equal to that of a beautician. If her face had the slightest blemish, he would produce the exact cream to cope, and he tutored her in the art of facials and the use of herbal lotions.

Just as Buell was not Jagger's exclusive property, so the reverse was true. Leaving aside his wife, Jagger conducted liaisons with several women during this time. Buell claimed to love Jagger without being in love with him and could therefore see him objectively. Though Jagger referred to Bianca dismissively as 'his old lady', Buell believed that she was the one woman capable of hurting him emotionally. Buell thus joined a growing number of people who believed that the Stone's feelings for his wife went deeper than he was prepared to admit. Perhaps it was because he could never fully be sure of her. She had hidden depths that he either never took the time to explore or was prevented from so doing.

Michael Lindsay-Hogg recalls Bianca's unusual qualities.

'She was, of course, incredibly elegant,' he says, 'carried a cane and so on, but she had a boldness about her that was attractive and more than a little unnerving. She was also very secretive and never revealed too much about herself. Now she's a dedicated person politically, but then she was always smart. A lot of people used to think her an extremely frivolous woman but really she only grew up in a frivolous world. Mick wouldn't have married someone who wasn't smart.'

Two years into that marriage Bianca had emotionally moved on. Her growing indifference to her husband's extra-marital affairs allowed her to tolerate Buell. The younger woman was surprised that Bianca could treat her with equanimity whenever they met socially, even going so far as to allude to Buell as Jagger's 'little friend'. It also kept Jagger on his toes, but the fact was that Bianca was beyond caring. This probably punctured his pride, but what upset him more was the realisation that he was far from indifferent.

In the past Bianca's 'tricks', as Jagger called them, to ensure she kept him at her side, usually centred on a peculiar practice she adopted of losing a valuable piece of jewellery he had bought her and insisting he help her search for it. If in the mood, which was often, Jagger played along. The thought of losing something for which he'd paid good money forced him to. However, when Bianca tired of her own games she decided to beat her husband at his own. That provoked a reaction.

Outwardly Jagger appeared nonchalant when Bianca's name began to be linked romantically to various leading actors. Responding to comments about his wife being photographed dancing close to eligible men, he dismissed them by saying, 'I think women should do what they want. After all, men go around doing what they want.'

But his laissez-faire attitude was largely a front, and he was particularly angry about the reported attachment between Bianca and Ryan O'Neal. The actor had a fiery reputation to match his looks, with a list of glamorous conquests longer than Jagger's, and it was probably the fact that Jagger conceded him a worthy rival that infuriated him most. Bianca and Jagger were on a collision course, but for now they made a point of rarely being seen together. During their later divorce proceedings Jagger would contend that to all intents and purposes they separated in 1973.

The more immediate court case concerning Jagger took place on 6 November, when Marsha Hunt's paternity suit came up for a second time. She was hosting a successful talk show on Capital Radio at this point, and sensational headlines followed. It was tougher on her than she had anticipated, and counsel's advice to her was to consider settling out of court. It wasn't easy getting blood from a Stone and the best offer that could be got from Jagger was maintenance of just over £9 a week with a £10,000 trust fund which Karis would receive on finishing school.

But there was a catch, Hunt alleges. The offer was made on the condition that she authorized her lawyer to sign a document that stated Jagger was not her child's father. It was a difficult decision, and one about which Hunt had to think hard. Hard times lay ahead for her, and it would be January 1975 before she saw any money.

Jagger turned his mind to problems within the band. Days before their tour had ended Keith Richard and Anita Pallenberg had each been fined £500 with a 12-month suspended sentence for the Nice bust. A week later Richard admitted possession of the drugs cannabis, Chinese heroin and Mandrax, as well as a revolver, shotgun and ammunition and was fined £205 at Marylebone Magistrates' Court. For possession of 25 Mandrax tablets, Pallenberg drew a one-year conditional discharge. But while Jagger had been considering the potential repercussions of this for the band, rumours had grown that Mick Taylor was about to leave. These seemed to be corroborated when Taylor did not join the band in mid-November to begin cutting a new album at Munich's Musicland Studios.

Jagger returned to Cheyne Walk for the charade of a family Christmas, but though he avoided confrontation as much as possible, the freezing atmosphere in the house aroused no festive cheer. The façade finally cracked one week into 1974 when Bianca seized the high moral ground by telling *Viva* magazine about the poor state of their marriage. Her misplaced suspicions about

Carly Simon, despite the fact that the singer had recently married James Taylor, seem to have been largely behind her decision to go public.

Jagger thought that he was adept at press manipulation, but while he hadn't been looking his wife had been learning. In a soulful outpouring she revealed Jagger as not the man she had thought she was marrying. Throughout the piece her admissions were subtly loaded to show him up in the sweetest, sorriest possible way. One of her most damning comments was that she could no longer trust him not to lie to her. She laboured the point that she knew when she was being deceived, but suggested that what hurt most was her husband's presumption that she was ignorant of his behaviour. She dramatically predicted, 'Maybe tomorrow I'll be out on the streets.'

Wrong-footed, Jagger hit back by saying he had only married Bianca for something to do, adding that deep love was not a natural emotion to him. In an attack on his wife he condemned those who acted out their private lives in public, perhaps not aware of the irony of this remark. After all Marianne Faithfull had reckoned he liked to lead his life as if on the pages of a Sunday supplement. His last word on the matter was that for his marriage to stand a chance they would have to compromise. It became clear that by that he meant it had to be played his way.

Needless to say such a response inflamed gossip that the marriage was over, though Jagger simply turned his attention elsewhere. He had still not given up ideas of becoming an actor and was delighted to learn that Ken Russell was considering him for the role of Franz Liszt in his next movie. Jagger's excitement was shortlived when the part went instead to Roger Daltrey, but later relief set in when *Lisztomania* was dismissed as an unmitigated disaster. As other potential film roles hovered, only to vanish, he concentrated instead on what he knew best.

He had lately spent time with friends, attending David Bowie's recording sessions and seen often in John Lennon's company. Accounts vary over whether Lennon genuinely liked or merely tolerated Jagger, but at the end of March Jagger joined him at Record Plant Studios to cut material with Harry Nilsson. Lennon was producing an album for him, released later that year as *Pussycats*.

Jagger's New York visit was brief, as Stones' commitments tied him to attend Island Record Studios. The earlier uncertainty surrounding Keith Richard's tenure in the band was brought again into sharp focus. Richard had moved in with Faces guitarist Ron Wood and in his home studio had contributed to a Wood solo album and joined him on stage a couple of times. Jagger, George Harrison and Eric Clapton would also visit the home studio, but that didn't stop the rumour.

Renewed speculation about the Stones' future line-up continued alongside gossip about Jagger's marriage. Bianca appeared regularly in society columns, photographed out on the town on the arm of a variety of men. Communication between Bianca and Jagger had become bitchy. She said he was not able to grow up, and he responded by coming up with a number that said it all, 'It's Only Rock 'n' Roll (But I Like It)'. Released 9 July 1974 the single had moderate success in the UK Top 10 and America's Top 20. It was considered another step forward in the abandonment of the old satanic image, especially in light of the video that accompanied it.

'We wanted to inject a slight rough-trade element into the video,' director Michael Lindsay-Hogg recalls, 'which suited the band's image and also the song, so we had them all dress in sailor suits. I filmed them performing inside a giant balloon, which was originally to have contained mud, but that turned out a bad idea because it would've made the capsule too heavy. There was a risk it could burst and go all over the cables and perhaps electrocute everyone. So we changed it to foam, which, of course, altered the whole thing again as all the bubbles created a sense of having a lighthearted time, which was no bad thing. It got right away from the demonic attachment to the Stones.'

Distancing themselves from that look could only help in their battle with US Immigration as come autumn lawyers tried to find a solution. As early as February 1973 the Stones were said to have been banned from entering the country although they had travelled back and forth several times. To stand a chance of performing there, though, they needed work permits and appropriate visas, and, while hard won, eventually they were secured. During this period Jagger had tried to relax at a rented beachfront house at Montauk, Long Island, where ostensibly reunited with Bianca and accompanied by Jade, he stayed until early October.

In private the pair bickered relentlessly, but together attended Eric Clapton's comeback with *461 Ocean Boulevard* at the Nassau Coliseum New York gig to show support for their friend after his electro-acupuncture treatment to overcome drug abuse. They put on an artificial display of togetherness there for the press. It didn't last long. Within a week Bianca was openly musing that Jagger's sole reason for marrying her had been because he thought they looked alike. Jagger retaliated by spending a week in Paris, where he was said to be dating Nathalie Delon, one of the witnesses at his St Tropez wedding.

On 18 October *It's Only Rock 'n' Roll* was released, stalling at second place in Britain, but topping the America album charts. Greeted as fresher than *Goats Head Soup*, it didn't go unnoticed that Ron Wood had guested on the title track. Any renewed speculation as to his association with the Stones was overshadowed, however, when according to US radio news, the band's career was over. While Jagger was celebrating at a film première party in the Four Seasons restaurant, a Californian radio station, KTIM, announced that he had been shot dead on stage in London. Without verification, a string of stations interrupted their programmes with the shock newsflash.

At this point in 1974, despite everything, Jagger had rarely felt more alive. In November he called a meeting for the band in Switzerland, where they discussed the following year. They could now include the States in plans for a world tour. But before that there would be recording sessions at Musicland. But on 12 December, just as work got under way on what would become the *Black and Blue* album, there was Mick Taylor's announcement that he was leaving the Stones to join the Jack Bruce Band.

Taylor had always had a low profile with the Stones, but he had now been with them more than five years. Like Brian Jones he had engaged in run-ins with Jagger and Richard over their songwriting monopoly and had experienced as much luck in breaking that grip. He had not been happy in the band for a long time. The drug culture that surrounded them, mirrored in the lifestyles of many of their friends, was not to his taste, and concern for his physical well-being had made him realize it was time to bale out. Not naturally garrulous, he approached Jagger at a party and curtly informed him, 'I'm out.'

The formal announcement was the usual anodyne statement of Taylor leaving to explore new ventures and how sorry the band were to lose him, but wishing him well. The guitarist concurred that no personal animosity guided his decision. It was only later that the discontent leaked out. Taylor is said to have considered himself badly paid, and in any case he'd wanted to leave the band alive. Jagger is quoted as criticizing him for his lack of stage flair, plus citing objections about too much rhythm guitar, partly a result of Richard's withdrawal into a lower profile.

Talk of his replacement began with Ron Wood, Jeff Beck, Jimmy Page and Peter Frampton as favourites. Speculation continued into spring 1975 as music magazines came up with other potential replacements. By March, Jagger in New York with Peter Rudge, working through details of the upcoming tour, denied that they'd already reached their decision. But in LA he jammed together with Wood, among others, at Record Plant Studios. Wood also joined the Stones in Munich at the end of the month, by which time Richard appeared to have clarified the confusion by saying that after playing a single number with the band, it was obvious Wood was right for them. Jagger appears to have been unsure, typically resisting the move, almost considering a foursome. Nothing was officially resolved when rehearsals got under way at Montauk, Long Island, in April, until on the 14th it was announced that Ron Wood would play guitar for the Rolling Stones during their forthcoming American tour. He would not, however, be joining them on a permanent basis.

Jagger then turned his mind to the last-minute rehearsals and was taking a long hard look at himself. Analysing his sexually charged performance style he likened himself to a stripper up there doing the bumps and grinds to music. Ageing, or loss of his sex appeal, had always preoccupied him. Even at 32 he had his fears. He denied that he tried to project himself as an eternal 20 year old, yet he regretted having said a couple of years earlier that he would retire from music at 33. He now declared that he would go on for ever.

Jagger has a strong face with prominent features that could be considered ugly, but he had turned it round and made an attraction of unusual looks. His body, always toned, was subjected to a rigorous fitness regime.

'Mick has a body like a circus tumbler, sinewy and deceptively strong,' says Michael Lindsay-Hogg. 'He's also surprisingly fast on his feet. I remember in New York City at a street corner as the lights were against us we were standing talking. I took my eye off him for seconds, and when I looked back he was at the other side. Jeez, had he manoeuvred the traffic at speed!'

But no matter how good he looked to himself in the mirror there was something threatening to rain on his parade. Bianca.

He could not help but be aware of the splash she was making among the international film community at the annual Cannes Film Festival. Aware of Jagger's frustrated movie star ambitions she drew as much attention to herself there as possible. Her aim without doubt was to woo the right people, encourage them to believe she had screen potential, probably knowing that nothing would wound her husband more than if she succeeded where he had so far failed. She was also out to reinvent herself and told reporters that she wanted to bring some quality into her life.

'The press turned me into something I was not,' she maintained. 'They wouldn't accept the fact that Mick had married a foreigner. So from that moment on I was a bitch.'

Jagger's thoughts might have hovered ungallantly around the word as he helplessly watched Bianca's involvement with the Austrian actor Helmut Berger, whom the European press hailed the world's most beautiful man. She had often complained in company at home that Jagger did not pay her enough attention. Although Jagger tried to hide it, this had embarrassed him. Now he was about to set out on the Stones' most ambitious tour yet, and much of his sex appeal still lay in his raunchy reputation. It would undermine his credibility considerably if it looked as if he were not able to satisfy his own wife.

When it came to upstaging tactics, though, the Stones did just that on 1 May when they brought New York traffic to a standstill by slowly driving down Fifth Avenue playing on the back of a flatbed truck. People hung out of high storey office windows, pedestrians stopped to stare, and motorists' bewilderment turned to fury at being caught in a massive traffic jam because of a publicity stunt. Journalists and camera crews had been called at short notice to the Fifth Avenue Hotel and had just begun to feel cheated of a story when the unmistakable strains of 'Brown Sugar' had everyone out into the street. They had borrowed the idea from old-style travelling jazz bands, and it proved an outstanding piece of PR strategy.

Not long afterwards the new stage design was also unveiled. Shaped like a lotus flower with five giant petals that stretched out into the audience, it operated hydraulically. All was ready, the only hiccup being twenty stitches to a gash on Jagger's right hand that he got following an accident with a glass door when leaving a Montauk restaurant one night.

Wood had slid into the line-up naturally. Jagger called both him and Richard brilliant and complementary rhythm guitarists. Wyman's verdict was that, though not a fantastic musician, Wood was great fun.

The tour started on Wood's 28th birthday at the Louisiana State University, Baton Rouge. A fortnight later the compilation album *Made in the Shade* was released. The response on tour this time was different. Audiences still reacted with adulation to the extent that Jagger described the feeling he got each night on stage as orgasmic. Perhaps it was precisely for that reason that some sections of the press decided to revile him. Whatever they flung at him he appeared to let it bounce off.

'As long as my picture is on the front page, I don't care what they say about me,' he remarked. Which was just as well when an article in the *National Star* described Jagger as an example of how decent parents might fail. It called him 'a simple-faced disciple of dirt' and asked how he could have become such a hero to the hitherto wholesome all-American youth!

During a six-gig run at New York's Madison Square Garden *Metamorphosis* was released by Decca, which peaked in the American album charts at number 8, while *Made in the Shade* reassuringly edged two places higher and went gold. During this tour Jagger's stage style kept changing as if he were not willing or able to decide on his stage persona. His gut reaction was a retreat from his earlier campness, although glam rock was still in vogue.

Jagger wavered between styles, sometimes falling back on heavy make-up and shock value. In contrast to the stylish lotus petal set, a stage prop wheeled out at the first gig was a 40-foot inflatable penis that Jagger would straddle during certain songs. The shocks were not always for the crowd. Still playing with a bisexual image, Jagger would brush up against guest musicians, and once took Ron Wood by surprise by sticking his tongue in the guitarist's ear.

Off stage on-tour behaviour hadn't changed much, though the drug taking had escalated. By now lines of coke were laid out on amp tops hidden behind the curtains to accommodate an off-stage snort by Jagger and Richard. It was this kind of behaviour that had disgusted Bianca, and she now refused not just to go on the road, which wasn't unusual, but also to make her customary stopovers along the way.

Jagger didn't care about that, but he did mind that while the Stones were appearing at the Capital Center, Washington DC, his wife, with Andy Warhol were guests of President Gerald Ford's son Jack at the White House. His annoyance didn't so much stem from the distinguished visit as much as from Bianca's connection to her host. She was now linked, even if briefly, to 23-year-old Jack Ford, spotted dancing flamboyantly with him at a New York club. Lately she had been commissioned to write for Warhol's *Interview* and much to First Lady Betty Ford's distress had persuaded Jack Ford to be interviewed in the White House.

There was little time to dwell on his wife's latest activities, however. Between gigs at Memphis and the Cotton Bowl in Dallas, Keith Richard was arrested on 6 July by traffic cops in Arkansas. He was charged with possessing an offensive weapon. Wood, travelling with him, was also held but released without charge. All this detracted somewhat from the news that the Stones had surpassed a Beatles' record of twenty of their albums having made the Top 30 in America. *Made in the Shade* had made their total 21.

After the tour ended on 8 August at the Rich Stadium in Buffalo, New York, where hundreds were arrested and even more fans injured, Jagger remained in the States. He stayed on despite coming under fire from a pressure group known as the Coalition Against Macho-Sexist Music. They accused him of perpetuating sexist rock, against which he neither had nor desired any defence, especially considering his recent statement to journalists. A woman had no place on a rock tour he had said, in response to their questioning, unless it was to run errands for a man, make his meals, tidy his clothes and 'the only other reason is to screw'. It was enough to inflame the feminist lobby, just as, with impeccable timing, Decca rereleased the old sexist number 'Out of Time'.

When it all became too much he left America and travelled via

Ireland to Montreux, where a six-week session had been booked at Mountain Recording Studios. Two days after work ended in Switzerland Rod Stewart announced on 18 December that he was leaving as lead singer of the Faces. He was unsettled, he said, by his band's guitarist seemingly being on permanent loan to the Rolling Stones. Jagger had been in Paris and about to fly on to New York when he heard about this. He refused to confirm that Ron Wood would automatically become a full-time member of the Rolling Stones.

As the year drew to a close the Stones topped various popularity polls. *Creem* magazine voted them Best Group, Best R&B Group and Best Live Band. *Made in the Shade* also picked up Best Re-Issue LP. But in Britain the 1975 Christmas number 1 single was the unique 'Bohemian Rhapsody', written by Freddie Mercury. To accompany it Queen had produced what became the very first pop video. A landmark in itself, its innovative content had caused a stir in the music industry. It was the most momentous development in rock since *Sgt. Pepper* nine years before. Like then, the change was a warning shot across every performer's bows. No one could afford to rest on their laurels. Not even the Rolling Stones. Not if they wanted to remain on top.

12

TROUBLE AND STRIFE

JAGGER REMAINED UNPERTURBED by attacks from an increasing number of pressure groups angry about the misogynistic lyrics of his songs and even about his lifestyle. It was only rock 'n' roll, and in common with millions of fans, he liked it.

He also claimed not to be affected by the now almost daily press coverage of his stormy marriage. But photographs of Bianca dancing intimately with yet another young man at yet another nightclub did test his resolve to keep his cool. It is possible that all this plus travel fatigue contributed to a high level of stress.

There was also the strain Jagger had been under over Richard's continual battles with the law, as well as the overall pressure and uncertainty surrounding the Rolling Stones' future. Their last two albums had come under fire, and the face of popular music was changing. It was essential to move with the times, yet his and his band's image was such that there wasn't much room for manoeuvre. It was perhaps these factors which led to press speculation when, in the early hours of 27 February 1976 Jagger was admitted to Lennox Hill Hospital in New York.

Jagger was registered under an alias, but the press still found out. First reports suggested that he was suffering from a drug overdose, and that by noon he was out of danger, but this was denied. He was said therefore to be suffering from severe flu. Whatever had ailed him, when he learnt that a press contingent was about to besiege the hospital, he discharged himself. Less than 24 hours after admission, he was thus able to leave.

The next day, to signal that the Stones were very much in business, it was officially announced that Ron Wood, or Woody, as he became known, had joined the Rolling Stones. Soon after that they also announced their new tour. Leaving Bianca to her domination of the Manhattan social scene, Jagger headed with the others back to the French Riviera to rehearse, during which time the album *Black and Blue* was released on 20 April. It made number 2 in Britain and topped the US charts, but, although, in step with the times, it was more dance oriented, to hard core fans it was their weakest album yet.

By contrast it provoked a strong reaction from the Stones' old protagonists, the feminist lobby. Almost as if designed to bait them, the album poster depicted a scantily clad girl, her body crisscrossed with rope, her bound wrists stretched above her head.

It caused an outcry. The single from the album released the same day 'Fool To Cry'/'Crazy Mama' peaked at number 6 and slipped even further back in America, just scraping into the Top 10. Joining in with the feminists' jeers the music press began attacking the Stones, dismissing them as redundant.

'They really don't matter anymore,' cried *Creem*, adding, 'It's all over.' Weathering the flak Jagger kept watch on ticket sales, assured that fans around Europe didn't agree when he saw the phenomenal demand for each gig; they received over a million postal applications for the British gigs alone.

The tour commenced on 28 April at Frankfurt's Festhalle and proved as eventful as ever. Concert venues were altered at the last minute causing confusion. Unsettlingly, news filtered through while in Germany that UK police had raided Wood's house and somewhere Keith Richard had briefly stayed. This stoked fears that the Stones were again public enemy number one to the authorities. This led to increased tension within the band, and by the time they hit Britain in May internal hostility began spilling out into backstage aggression. After a gig at Glasgow's Apollo Theatre Billy Preston, their current guest keyboard player, and Wood got into a fist fight. The venue manager had to grab Preston, while Jagger restrained the guitarist. It was solved only when Jagger arranged for Preston to be flown back to London.

Jagger was also busy fighting off the critics. *Black and Blue* was accused of being unstructured and coming on top of the accusation tagged to *It's Only Rock 'n' Roll* he went on the defensive. As reporters provoked him during one press conference he retorted, possibly partly tongue in cheek, certainly irritated: 'People overestimate us. We are not as good as people think.'

He would normally have shrugged off such attacks more cutely, and though this almost humbling admission of defeat at the impossibility of pleasing everyone all the time was not entirely new to Jagger, it was rare. But he had been distracted by news that the terrorist faction the Baader Meinhof Group had issued a threat that they intended to blow up Munich's Olympiahalle when the Stones played there the following month. Jagger's nerves were further stretched with the news of Richard's car crash near Stafford, where he wrote off his Bentley and fell foul of the law when cocaine was found in his car. By Jagger's accounts the running expenses of this tour were so high that they were working just to break even. Richard's arrest brought with it fears that the rest of the tour dates could be in jeopardy.

Jagger's patience with Richard was wearing thin, and the fractures that had started to appear during recording at Nellcote five years earlier were increasingly apparent. But if old friendships were beginning to fall apart, a diversion came in the shape of someone new. At one of a series of shows at London's Earls Court, a 20-year old Texan model, Jerry Hall, sat watching him perform. She was with her boyfriend Bryan Ferry, who had lately fronted Roxy Music. Ferry had spotted Hall on the cover of *Vogue* the previous autumn and had invited her to pose for the sleeve of Roxy Music's album *Siren*. One thing had led rapidly to another, and, within weeks, they had become engaged.

Jagger had always had a weakness for long-legged Americans, and he first met the young woman from Mesquite, Texas, when she appeared back stage after the show. In contrast to dark petite

Bianca, Hall was big boned and towered over him. She had once performed a risqué double-act cabaret with Grace Jones in a sleazy Paris club, and she had no difficulty in interpreting the gleam in Jagger's eye. The daughter of a truck driver and one of five sisters, her party piece was to regale people with the story of how she had lost her virginity at 15 in a hayloft. It was during a storm, to a rodeo rider, who kept his boots on. Like Jagger, Hall was ambitious, and the ease with which she had achieved catwalk success had generated so much envy among fellow models that an unkind rumour had circulated that she was actually a man in drag! Jagger was instantly attracted to her mane of blonde hair and blend of down-to-earth manner and loud sense of humour.

She was also no ice queen, as he found out when he changed into seduction gear. Inviting Ferry and Hall to join the Stones for dinner, he fixed it that Hall sat next to him in his limo. During the ride to the restaurant, he pressed the length of his thigh against hers. From the accommodating way she shifted against him in the darkness of the car, Jagger was confident that she welcomed the advance. Hall later said that her first close-up of Jagger was in the dressing room, where he sat drowned in a robe. He looked to her much smaller than he appeared on stage. Yet she sensed an electricity between them at that first touch.

With Hall in his sights Jagger accompanied her and Ferry back to their home that night. There, undeterred by Ferry's presence, he continued the overtures he had made earlier. He made her laugh, and they fooled around. Ferry was apparently not amused.

'Bryan freaked out about the whole thing,' Hall said. But even for as bold a seducer as Jagger, there were limits to what he could achieve as a guest in the man's flat, with his fiancée. Nevertheless he took it as far as he could, following Hall when she went out into the kitchen, where she later claimed she tried to behave. Finding them together moments later it is surprising that Ferry didn't throw Jagger out. Instead he stormed off to bed. Sobered at last by her boyfriend's anger Hall asked Jagger to go. As he was leaving he tried to seal what he considered to be his triumph with a kiss, but, she says, she didn't let him.

For all his ardent attention it is probable Jagger never gave Hall a second thought after that night. As soon as the Stones headed back into Europe on tour his focus would have totally changed.

'When I go on the road I just go crazy. I become a total monster,' he has confessed. 'I don't recognize anybody. I don't even see them.' Again drugs played a part in this, both in the variety and quantity on offer. Nick Kent, a journalist who joined the Stones' entourage, saw it all first hand and claims that Jagger not only matched Richard's drug intake but appeared not to care about the risks they were taking.

The casualty of this indulgence was often the performances. Jagger began to bear out *Creem's* recent accusation that he seemed to have run out of ideas. His stage act had a more acrobatic aspect but still boiled down to a repetition of old poses, exaggerated strutting and preening, close to self-parody. He was jolted out of his self-absorption just before going on stage at Les Abattoirs in Paris when he was rushed at by a young man with a loaded pistol. The gunman was overpowered by several of the bodyguards that Jagger had kept since the death threats over Altamont, and it was all over in a minute.

Jagger was naturally shaken. He had been in danger for no more than seconds, but then seconds is all it would take four years later to murder John Lennon. Still, the vulnerable aspect of performing live could not have sunk in too deeply for as the tour ended late June in Vienna he would take the stage again in two months' time in a huge open-air gig in Hertfordshire.

The impressively crenellated Knebworth House in Stevenage, an hour's drive from London, had played host for two years to rock festivals. Past headliners had been the Allman Brothers and Pink Floyd, but 21 August 1976 would see their biggest act yet with the Rolling Stones. Unlike previous bands they visited the Cobbolds' ancestral home prior to the gig, and so the family got to know the band a little; Jagger in particular made his mark, as Lady Chryssie Cobbold recalls.

'They came a couple of times to acclimatize themselves with the grounds,' she says. 'Mick was very interested in the history of the house, and my husband and I were most impressed with him. He's very bright, and it seemed to us that he held the whole group together.'

Still haunted by Altamont, Jagger was keen for this gig to be its polar opposite.

'He was determined to have a carnival atmosphere,' Lady

Cobbold confirms, 'with clowns mingling in the crowd etc. We were surprised at how involved with the whole thing he became.' That carnival touch began early when the Stones sprang a few extra promotional ideas.

'They had arranged for two people dressed as harlequins to rush on to Centre Court at Wimbledon carrying painted placards 'STONES AT KNEBWORTH 21 AUGUST,' says Lady Cobbold. 'The only thing was, my father-in-law who was Lord Chamberlain to the Queen was sitting in the Royal Box, and he nearly died. He stormed home roaring that he had never been so embarrassed in his life. It took us some time to convince him that we'd had nothing to do with it.'

The tennis-court PR stunt was not the only one. A cricket match in Sussex brightened up when live TV cameras picked up two topless girls hoisting a similar banner. And a flag with the relevant information was briefly draped over wrought-iron gates at Hyde Park Corner before a policeman ripped it down.

At Knebworth preparation began with the construction of the stage. Its design incorporated a huge inflated-rubber upper lip. With orange back lighting it looked like a giant mouth, while the extended catwalk jutted out to resemble a protruding tongue.

'There were very long sidewalks too,' Lady Cobbold adds, 'so long in fact that Mick borrowed my pushbike because he thought he might have to bike down one of them to get to the stage.'

Other acts on the bill included 10cc, Hot Tuna, Lynyrd Skynyrd, Todd Rundgren's Utopia and the Don Harrison Band. With tickets at £4.25 a big crowd was anticipated. Staging these gigs requires the cooperation of several agencies, and it was while Lord and Lady Cobbold were in conference with the police and the concert promoter that the meeting was rudely interrupted.

'The Stones were having a sound check a couple of nights before the gig,' Lady Cobbold explains, 'and at the same time there had been a Girl Guides camp on the grounds all week. This night they were to have their campfire singsong, but they couldn't hear themselves for the Stones playing. We were just discussing the safety and security arrangements when the Guides Leader, a formidable woman, burst into the room.

'She raged, "How can we hold our singsong with that dreadful racket going on?" 'David said, "Well, you know, the girls might like to listen to the Stones."

'Nonsense!' she thundered. 'I want it stopped!'

'As we were in the middle of a meeting I suggested that she ought to go and have a word with Mick herself. So she did. She stormed out of the house to the stage, climbed up, elbowed her way past burly security men and jabbed Jagger, mid way through a song, in the ribs demanding, "Look here, my man, this noise has got to stop!" Jagger replied, "Fuck off, lady! I'm singing!"'

Actually he did stop and later that night adjourned to the house. He hadn't had the stomach for a battle with the Guide commandant, but he did eventually realize he was famished and tentatively asked about food.

'He was worried that our cook had gone to bed as it was 3 a.m. He was astounded to discover that we didn't have one,' said Lady Cobbold. Cooking bacon and eggs themselves, the band and their hosts gathered around the kitchen table eating and chatting until dawn when Jagger went off with the others to the studio.

On Saturday around 200,000 fans turned up. The Don Harrison Band kicked off at 11 a.m., after which there was a long delay before the second act came on. This set the pattern for the day. While celebrity guests including Paul McCartney, Jack Nicholson and Jonathan King milled about back stage, the audience grew increasingly restless. After waiting two hours for 10cc, when they did appear the crowd vented their frustration by lobbing missiles on stage. The day progressed with one band after another drawing varied receptions. Despite a dread of the mass mood turning ugly there was a third delay before finally the Stones appeared at 11.30 p.m., half an hour after the event was supposed to end. They were greeted by slow handclaps, jeers and whistles, all of which reassuringly dried up at the first strains of 'Satisfaction'.

Wisely they played a set of old favourites, closing in the early hours of Sunday morning amid rumours that this was their last ever gig. The Cobbolds meanwhile feared that this would be their last ever festival.

'I suspected some of these delays were down to bands waiting for darkness so that it would be more effective,' says Lady Cobbold, 'but the Stones coming on so late meant it hugely overran, and that caused us a heap of problems. We were taken to court for overrunning our licence for starters.'

The Stones had a rule that any women on stage were restricted to the far reaches. As Jagger strutted his stuff, Bianca, who had flown in specially from America, watched sullen-faced from the wings. Her mood had partly been set by Jagger's flirting that afternoon with Bebe Buell, there with Todd Rundgren. Waiting until Rundgren was on stage with Utopia, Jagger began to torment the singer, first with loud camp compliments, then by monopolizing his girlfriend.

In Buell's words her lover, as he was meant to, could see from the stage what Jagger was up to. Though angry, he was impotent to do anything while he was performing. That Jagger enjoyed teasing Rundgren like this was apparent. Bianca was less amused, however, and while Jagger retreated to the house while the fans dispersed in the early hours of the morning, she, it was claimed, was seen hitching a ride back to London.

When Jagger returned to the capital he booked into a hotel, aware that there was no welcome awaiting him from his wife at Cheyne Walk. It was already old news, but the papers hadn't yet tired of describing Jagger's marriage as a disaster zone. The rancour between them had descended to such a level that each was glad that the other continued to fail in their aspirations to break into acting.

Jagger had been anxious that his photogenic wife might have succeeded but two projects with which she had become involved since her charm offensive at Cannes had fallen through. He was in no better position, though. There were two possibilities with Franco Zeffirelli and Roman Polanski respectively, but each had come to nought. He also turned down another two projects, one of which was to star opposite Barbra Streisand in the third remake of *A Star is Born*. Jagger claims he had no regrets rejecting $1 million for the part when he discovered the character, ultimately portrayed by Kris Kristofferson, was a has-been rock star!

Fear of ageing still plagued Jagger. 'I don't want to play when I'm old,' he declared, adding that growing old was too awful to contemplate. This was an anxiety Michael Lindsay-Hogg had a chance personally to observe in his friend.

'He was at the height of his powers,' says Lindsay-Hogg, 'the height of rock 'n' roll excess, and I'd had an idea for a rock movie called *Golden Oldies*, which would feature Mick Jagger and John Lennon. At first they'd be seen sitting on a park bench, and as the camera comes round front you'd see that they were old men with grey hair. Then it would throw back to the sixties and seventies.

'Basically it was intended as a vehicle to get all these great songs into a movie and build a story around it. Mick was keen at first. He had put up the seed money for me to write a script, but then he became hugely depressed by it and wouldn't go ahead. He has enormous willpower and is tough minded, but he doesn't like to look forward, and I think it really alarmed him to envisage himself old.'

None of this, however, dulled his overall appetite for acting. But he had revised his agenda. He would indulge this desire only so long as the roles offered in no way threatened his rock-star status. In LA he rejoined the smart set, rubbing shoulders with the likes of Peter Lawford.

But Jagger wasn't always socializing. He attended a series of meetings with the head of MCA Records, with whom the Stones were discussing a possible contract. Several other discussions would take place over the coming months, until eventually EMI sold them a deal to distribute their records worldwide except USA and Canada, where the future of the Rolling Stones label remained undetermined.

With no Stones' activity Jagger fell back on entertaining at his newly purchased East 73rd Street New York town house. John Lennon was a neighbour, reunited by then with Yoko Ono. Jagger was still not prepared to acknowledge publicly that his own marriage was empty. He would go further and proclaim that all rumours of a split were false. He appeared distressed at the upset all the gossip was causing Bianca, who played along with the charade. In answer to the allegations of her romantic interludes with other men she now maintained that everyone had read more than there was into it. Her behaviour sprang from an innocent desire to offset the loneliness caused by Jagger's absence due to work commitments by dining with male friends.

Perhaps appeased that this explanation made him look less cheated, Jagger was content. Until, that is, he learnt that Chrissie Shrimpton was considering publication of his love letters to her in a UK tabloid. To put it mildly, he went berserk. His lawyers instantly started a lawsuit against the newspaper on the grounds that publication would be a breach of confidentiality and copyright.

Unfortunately for Shrimpton, who might have made some money from this exclusive, the UK courts agreed with Jagger.

With this victory under his belt Jagger began the new year. It was a time to reinvent himself a little. With this in mind he had a hole in which to insert a gem stone drilled in his front tooth. He first tried an emerald, but when people thought he had a rotten tooth he replaced it with a ruby. Bleeding gums wasn't the image he sought either and eventually he settled for a diamond. This, he felt, gave his smile an extra glint.

It was the familiar twinkle in his eye that upset Bianca soon after when she chose to believe that her husband had started an affair with Linda Ronstadt, the singer with whom Jagger had recently duetted on stage. Bianca in turn started to see Ryan O'Neal again, which in turn ignited Jagger's temper and set them at loggerheads again. With the new flare-up Jagger was glad of the excuse to leave New York for Britain, though it could have been on a happier mission.

On 10 January 1977 Keith Richard appeared before Aylesbury Crown Court for possession of cocaine and LSD, and Jagger attended the hearing. After two days Richard was found guilty of possessing cocaine, though cleared in respect of the LSD charge. With a £750 fine plus £250 costs he was free to join Jagger for a celebratory drink in a nearby pub. Despite the outward camaraderie a chasm was widening between them.

Jagger knew Richard had had his problems. The previous year a son born to him and Pallenberg had died at three months, and since then his drink and drug consumption had worsened. Jagger's increasing absorption with his new friends had left Richard rudderless and maybe feeling threatened. As Jagger refined his social skills, Richard went the other way, coarsening every aspect of his worst behaviour. Much to Jagger's horror he was soon to surpass himself.

The Stones were due to play at a Toronto club in early March, and on 24 February Richard flew in with Pallenberg. On arrival they were stopped at customs and searched. A quantity of hashish was found in their luggage as well as traces of heroin. On this occasion it was Pallenberg who was arrested and promptly released on the proviso that she appear in court. Jagger had just heaved a sigh of relief when three days later the Canadian Mounties raided Richard's suite at the Harbour Castle Hotel. Placing Pallenberg instantly under arrest they had to sit it out first with Richard, as he later revealed.

'They had to wake me up to formally arrest me, and that took about two hours to do.' Turning to Pallenberg he quipped, 'See you in about seven years.' But it was no joking matter. The quantity of heroin discovered, one ounce, elevated the plight from mere possession to the serious charge of possession with intent to traffic. He was also charged with possessing one-fifth of an ounce of cocaine. Released on $1000 bail, Pallenberg was released without bail, due to appear in court in March.

The media created an atmosphere akin to hysteria, and Jagger despaired. Apart from putting future deals at risk, under Canadian law a charge of trafficking heroin carried the threat of a life sentence. It was impossible to put a brave face on it. As word leaked out the Stones must have contemplated the end of their career. Jagger in particular was depressed, to the point of desperation.

Press headlines announced that surely this time the Rolling Stones were finished, and on 2 March the record label RSO announced that they were withdrawing a $7 million offer for the Stones' US recording rights. Jagger was stalked by journalists who tried every conceivable trick to get to him for a comment. Not surprisingly then he was despondent when two days later the band regrouped for the first time since Knebworth to play the El Mocambo Club. There more trouble arose.

Among the 300-strong audience was Margaret Trudeau, wife of Canadian Prime Minister Pierre Trudeau. Her presence at a Stones gig in the glare of the worst possible publicity would have provoked comment anyway. But it became more personal than that.

'I've always been a Rolling Stone fan,' Margaret Trudeau claimed. But this seemed insufficient reason for some not only to throw a party for the band at the same hotel in which Richard had been so publicly busted but also to book into the suite adjacent to Jagger's. She registered under her maiden name, coincidentally on her sixth wedding anniversary.

Margaret Trudeau was several years younger than her husband and judged by some to be extremely headstrong. Undoubtedly she did not intend to spark an international scandal that many believed rocked her husband's already precarious government and affected the Canadian stock exchange. But that is what happened.

At the next night's gig at the club Jagger fanned the controversy during his performance of 'Star Star', the song originally entitled 'Starfucker'. He made a point of singling Trudeau out, drawling contemptuously from the stage, 'Awright, Margaret?'

The morning headlines made grim reading for Pierre Trudeau. Jagger just joked about how he had had great fun performing in the intimacy of a club that had allowed the women, he said, to grab his balls.

'Once they started they didn't stop,' he said. 'It was great up to a point, then it got very difficult to sing.' But what everybody was interested to learn was whether the PM's wife had been at all inclined to do the same back at the hotel.

The storm did not die down. Apparently Mrs Trudeau had been troubled since an earlier hospitalization for emotional problems and so far the country had made allowances for any odd behaviour. It soon became clear, however, that this was different, and Pierre Trudeau felt obliged to make a statement. Speaking from Ottawa, he declared though that he had no intention of suggesting to his wife that she should come home. Seeing how out of control it was all getting Jagger, by this time in Manhattan, issued a statement that, though an attractive woman, Margaret Trudeau and he were not having an affair. Since she had also travelled to New York it hardly helped, and one newspaper led with 'MAGGIE, MICK IN NY DENY HANKY-PANKY'.

It was later contended that Jagger had never been the object of Trudeau's affection and that it was been Ron Wood who had caught her attention. Still, it was another drama Jagger could have done without. Although Bianca assisted by ridiculing any suggestion of a liaison, in private it had given her cause to berate him. Jagger reacted to the rumour somewhat ungallantly. 'I wouldn't touch her [Trudeau] with a barge-pole.'

This latest episode left the atmosphere at home unpleasant. Bianca later revealed that Jagger denied that he had affairs, period. To which she commented, 'Mick is not famous for being the most honest person.'

But there seems to be an odd logic to her version of the truth as regards her own behaviour. She felt different from him because she openly told Jagger about her extramarital exploits. It is unclear whether this was honesty Bianca-style or a desire to remind him unkindly of his failings and draw attention to her response to them. Either way she went on to be linked with a string of names. It marked the beginning of the end for them now.

All this women trouble hadn't blinded Jagger to his real difficulties. At a brief court appearance on 7 March, Richard had been sent to trial a week hence. When asked directly whether the band would tour if the guitarist were jailed at that time, Jagger replied, 'Obviously we wouldn't if Keith were only in jail for a short period of time. But we can't wait five years.'

In fact, he had already decided that come what may the Stones would not fold without Richard and had begun making contingency plans. When the 14th arrived Anita Pallenberg appeared at Brampton Courtroom in Toronto to be fined $400, while Keith was remanded on bail until 27 June.

As Richard's fate hung in the balance, Jagger was still smarting at the loss of RSO. So his spirits were considerably lifted when on 1 April Atlantic Records re-signed them for North American distribution of their Rolling Stones label. The deal was purported to be in the region of $21 million for six albums. As such it made the band, the focus of so much controversy, the highest-paid recording artists in the world.

Despite all the strife his buoyant mood was maybe a factor in the startling gift of a white horse that Jagger gave Bianca for her birthday on 2 May. The magnificent stallion made an unusual entrance into a new nightspot in New York called Studio 54, led in by a black man covered only in gold leaf. Studio 54 was to become very popular and decadent, soon gaining a reputation as the place for celebrities to have fun. It particularly became a personal battleground between Jagger and his wife.

Each caught up in a struggle for supremacy, Studio 54 gave them a public arena in which to flex their respective social muscle. Both had their own sycophantic hangers-on, and on the occasion of an especially high-profile party, each would try hard to upstage the other's entrance.

It irked Jagger that he invariably lost out to Bianca who, it was quickly acknowledged, had become Queen of Studio 54. For a brief stretch in the mid-sixties Jagger had tolerated the idea that

Marianne Faithfull had been considered almost as important as him. But 10 years on, current drug bust notwithstanding, the Stones were nowhere in the shock value stakes. There was more emphasis on social status. What Jagger failed to appreciate then was that Bianca Jagger, by attracting such attention, helped keep his name in the limelight. It was not something with which he felt comfortable. Often on arrival at the club he would glare across at his wife surrounded by her court and head straight for the exclusivity of the VIP-only basement.

Jagger lived at the heart of the Manhattan social whirl, where one night in May at a dinner party he ran into Jerry Hall again. They were seated next to each other at table. On her other side sat Jagger's friend and rival for roué of the year, Warren Beatty. Between them they did wonders for Hall's morale as they not so subtly locked horns over who would win her. Hall coyly flashed her engagement ring, a detail neither man acknowledged.

Using fair means and foul eventually Jagger wrested her away and took her to Studio 54. He was intrigued to hear that she was now earning enough money as a model to have bought herself a Texas ranch. Her mother had impressed upon her from an early age that a woman's sexuality could be a valuable tool, and the adolescent Jerry, as she later admitted, became more than healthily curious about sex. With this she combined a belief that a woman's financial independence meant that no man could buy her. This would all have been a lethal-enough attraction for Jagger, but he then discovered that she was on the verge of marrying Bryan Ferry, currently on a solo tour of Japan. It became almost his duty to steal her away.

On leaving the club Jagger invited Hall to his apartment, where he made a pass at her. At first she resisted his attempts to kiss her, but despite her obvious nerves she still gave out the right signals. It was then easy for him successfully to manoeuvre her in time into the bedroom. Hall later recalled that her first thought the following morning was, 'Oh, no! What have I done?' She had hurriedly dressed and fled the building, hailing a cab and leaving before Jagger was awake.

Jagger continued to romance her with flowers and dinner invitations, even serenading her once in a Thai restaurant. In the first intense days Hall, heady from it all, avoided Ferry's phone calls from Japan. She did not know what to do. Her friends revealed that although she felt it was lust not love, she was increasingly talking of Jagger as the man of her dreams. Jagger favoured a discreet affair at first. By the end of June, though, they showed up as a couple at a society birthday party.

It was little consolation to Bianca to know that though Jagger had chosen openly to flaunt his mistress, he was at the same time unfaithful to Hall. In his mid-thirties he liked girls half his age. On occasions he had brazened it out when the mother of the target of his attentions turned out to be a woman he had once known as a girl. He also carried on affairs with more mature women, preferring the company of socialites to whom he would talk emotionally about the deterioration of his marriage. What he omitted to tell them was that he considered he had just become a father for a third time.

On 1 July 1977 Bebe Buell had given birth to the girl who would become the beautiful actress, Liv Tyler. Jagger, she claimed, rang her declaring, 'I'm coming over to see my child.' She says he was her first visitor in the maternity hospital. The previous year, while continuing her relationship with Todd Rundgren, Buell claims she embarked on an affair with Aerosmith lead singer Steve Tyler and that she had become pregnant by him in October 1976. At Knebworth, according to her, Jagger had taunted Rundgren by saying, 'You better hold on to your girlfriend. I'm a bigger star than you. I'll nab her.'

Whatever induced Jagger to imagine himself broody evaporated when on arrival at the nursing home he had to share Buell's attention with the baby.

'He said, "All right, put her away now. I can see you're a mother,"' says Buell. Jagger's willingness to claim paternity not surprisingly had limits. He liked the general speculation that Buell's baby was his and was even known to introduce her as 'the mother of one of my illegitimate children'. But he was hugely relieved that Buell had no intention of seeking financial assistance from him to support the child.

Before his sex life could become any more complicated, Jagger's attention was diverted by something else. 'Since the age of 14 I haven't taken anything really seriously,' Jagger once boasted. With the exception, that was, of his personal safety. In early July all his energies went into preventing publication of *The Man Who Killed Mick Jagger*, a novel by one David Littlejohn, Associate Dean of the

University of California. His very reasonable grounds for objection were that some madman could be inspired to try to accomplish the deed. Friends already knew that Jagger's recurrent nightmare was of being shot dead on stage and could sympathize with his concern. As Jagger left his lawyers to keep up the pressure against the book's release he forced himself to face up to the other struggles going on around him.

On 19 July Keith Richard failed for the second time to appear as scheduled in the Toronto court. Absent because of in-patient treatment for heroin addiction at a New York clinic, the date of his hearing was this time postponed to 2 December. Asked about the threat to their songwriting partnership if Richard got a jail sentence, Jagger mused to journalists that as Richard would have little else to do in jail, he could easily continue to write songs there. If this attitude seemed cold-hearted, it was scarcely warmer than Richard's reaction to Jagger's new amour. Richard is said to have hated Jerry Hall. The tension between the old school friends had only worsened.

Unaware or uncaring of Richard's resentment Hall had decided she wanted to keep Jagger. Not a shy person, she made no secret that she had been brought up to know how to keep her man. 'There are three secrets that my mother told me,' she famously drawled. 'Be a maid in the living room, a cook in the kitchen and a whore in the bedroom. So long as I have a maid and a cook, I'll do the rest myself.'

In true Texan style she also proved an aggressive protector of her territory when other women attempted to encroach and was not afraid of literally kicking out along the way. Among the Stones' friends and entourage she split ranks. People either liked or loathed her. Some saw her as money-oriented and socially ambitious. Her supporters happily acknowledged then that Jagger had met his match.

Clearly Jagger wasn't convinced. Near the end of August he made what became a last-ditch effort to save his marriage by persuading Bianca to take a trip with him to the Greek island of Hydra. It was a sorry time, as was witnessed by locals at a disco when the couple were seen at separate tables, looking desperately unhappy. Jagger was thought to be particularly distressed, perhaps partly because he sensed a pending divorce settlement.

He could hardly complain. The six-foot Southern belle was hard not to notice. Bianca's friends later rallied round to reveal how, despite their very public mutual baiting, her feelings had run deep for Jagger. She tried to convince herself that Jerry Hall was just another passing fancy. Perhaps that is why she allowed Jagger back into her bed in October at Cheyne Walk, little knowing that the event would later be pinpointed by his lawyers during the divorce as the last time they had had sex.

Soon after the album *Love You Live* made number 3 in the UK charts, and *Get Stoned* was about to be released on the Arcade label, Jagger regrouped with the Stones at the Pathe Marconi Studios in Paris to begin cutting their new album. It was while he was there that the French press predicted that Jagger and Bianca were to divorce due to Jagger's adultery with Jerry Hall.

The recording sessions were interrupted late November when Richard travelled to Canada for his trial. The band's career, despite Jagger's attempts to steady it, hung in the balance. So deep was the rift between Jagger and Richard that when the guitarist appeared in court on 2 December, only to be remanded to a higher court the following February, Jagger could not mount a false show of support and stayed away. He preferred instead to take Hall to Morocco. When recording restarted in Paris the strain the band was under must have made it hard to concentrate. Especially when talk began of replacing Richard.

Jagger must have been glad of the excuse of the holiday period to make another getaway with Hall, this time to see out the year in Barbados. The timetable set for work on the new album meant that he couldn't lie in the sun for long. But if he breathed easier that his affair with Hall was now out in the open, when he stopped over in New York en route to Paris, he still felt needled by Bianca. She had fled Britain to escape the intense divorce speculation and had made a fine recovery to regain her throne at Studio 54. On something of a face-saving mission she now let it be known that she was physically repelled by her bag-of-bones husband. She would often be seen at this time in the company of the long-haired Swedish tennis star Björn Borg.

While she retained her poise, however, Jagger was rapidly losing his. He had begun drinking more heavily than usual and was easily riled. He had taken to lashing out indiscriminately at the pursuing paparazzi. One evening, on leaving a Paris nightclub with Hall, he suddenly punched a photographer. Much to his surprise, the man retaliated and knocked Jagger over on to his back on the pavement.

That blow was nothing to the one he felt he was dealt next. After announcing a Stones' summer American tour, despite a denial she had issued just weeks before, he learnt that Bianca had filed for divorce in a London court. She knew her husband well enough to believe him capable of trying to leave her high and dry. She had after all signed a prenuptial agreement under emotional duress an hour before their wedding, with which she effectively relinquished her rights.

But now Jagger's fortune, though a closely guarded secret, was thought to run into several million pounds. Having just passed their seventh wedding anniversary, Bianca felt entitled to a share. To assist her in this she hired New York lawyer Roy Cohn, who immediately brought on board his colleague Marvin Mitchelson. Mitchelson was one of America's most famous and feared palimony experts.

13

COSTLY AFFAIRS

AGGER WAS AGGRIEVED that Bianca had possessed the nerve to move first and that she was divorcing him for adultery. The nerve, however, was as much his. Though living with Jerry Hall at New York's Carlyle Hotel on Madison Avenue, on hearing the news he asked a friend if in all the years of his marriage he had ever been actually pictured in the newspapers with another woman? Maybe he had a point. But when a marriage breaks down there are always two people responsible. About to begin rehearsals with the Stones in Woodstock for their summer tour, Jagger took time out to retaliate.

First he had all Bianca's credit lines cancelled and their Chelsea home stripped bare. Marvin Mitchelson's natural habitat was California, and the lawyer was petitioning the London court to have the case heard in America. Jagger probably knew that under Californian law if a rock star makes a record while he is married, his wife is entitled to half the royalties, even as an ex-wife.

Jagger instructed his legal team to mount a rigorous challenge to keep the hearing in London. Three years before, Cher had purportedly settled for $25,000 a month from husband Sonny Bono. Jagger appeared to be getting off lightly when Bianca's lawyers filed a motion for temporary monthly alimony in the region of £7500. But Jagger was in no mood to roll over, and it quickly became clear to all concerned that a long campaign lay ahead.

The new tour also looked arduous, particularly with the precarious state of Keith Richard's health. The threat of a life sentence had undermined his battle to stay off heroin, and he was going through a rough time. Despite the tension between them Jagger allowed Richard to stay during rehearsals at his heavily guarded rented house in Woodstock. Jagger was said to be supporting him as he underwent heroin withdrawal with neuro-electric acupuncture.

'Mick was always trying to keep it together,' says Michael Lindsay-Hogg, 'but Keith was only into his stuff. It wasn't surprising that eventually Mick went one way and he the other. Mick said to me one night that he thinks so much of what a person goes through in life is chemical.

'He said, "For instance, I've taken every drug that Keith has ever taken, but my chemical balance allows me to dabble but not get hooked. Whereas Keith's chemicals don't. It's a lot to do with psychology." Keith was at his lowest point with the Canadian bust, and there was a lot of pressure building up on Mick at this time. Mick had also begun to drink a lot, or at least sometimes I felt that he pretended to be drunk to avoid dealing with any more.'

Band business, however, rolled on inexorably. Following release mid-May of the single 'Miss You'/'Far Away Eyes', on 9 June came the album *Some Girls*, considered an instant classic. It was an inspired blend of musical influences, including country, the current disco beat and punk, all built upon a bedrock of blues. The album sleeve provoked talk of lawsuits from actresses Raquel Welch and Lucille Ball, as their faces were among several superimposed on various old lingerie adverts. And once again some of the lyrics caused outrage at a perceived racial slur. Democrat Rev Jesse Jackson took offence at the words of the title track, which declared black girls just want to 'get fucked all night'.

'It is an insult to our race and degrading to our women,' he said, and campaigned to have the album withdrawn. *Some Girls* catapulted to America's number 1 and became the band's biggest selling album to date. This success provided the much-needed morale boost to kick off the tour due to commence next day at the Civic Center in Lakeland, Florida.

A hardness edged the entire North American tour. The casualty rate among fans reached new heights. One was shot and others, mixed up in a dispute over tickets, crashed through a plate glass window. Burying their personal differences as much as possible, Jagger and Richard rubbed along tolerably well. The Stones' repertoire, however, appeared to place greater emphasis on rhythm guitar, almost as if preparing for life without their lead guitarist. While recording *Some Girls* Richard had sometimes felt dismissed by Jagger, whom he thought determined to argue with him at every turn. On the road, they largely reverted to their professionalism, except for a reaction to a hoarding that announced WELCOME MICK JAGGER AND THE ROLLING STONES.

As they toured the country the Stones' cavalcade attracted groupies of both sexes. Too cute to trust Jagger loose on the road Jerry Hall travelled it with him. His performances varied. Sometimes he was subdued, other times only too ready to pull out all the stops. After watching Jagger in New York, John Lennon called him 'for ever the Charlie Chaplin of rock'. On the eve of the final gig, however, when they arrived in Los Angeles there was little of the comedian about Jagger. His past caught up with him there again.

Marsha Hunt had been living in LA for about a year, mostly staying with friends. By summer 1978, she still received just £9 a week towards Karis' care. Out of work, she discovered that she was not eligible for state aid unless she named her child's father so that he could be ordered to make support payments. Hunt was in turmoil at the thought of raising a second paternity suit. And she had another concern. This time Karis was nearly 8, old enough to be aware of and affected by any publicity. When she took legal advice she went to the top, to Marvin Mitchelson's Century City offices. His fees in those days were over $2 a minute. Once again Jagger's libido proved his downfall. In a hotel foyer Leslie Spiller, a rangy blonde, for whom the bodyguards had been waved aside, served him with a subpoena, probably the last thing that had been on Jagger's mind. He dropped the papers and took off for his limo, but Spiller pursued him and posted the court document through an open side window before it could snap shut. Mitchelson turned up the heat by a court order that froze Jagger's share of the two recent Anaheim gigs. This pended settlement of his client's claim to increase his weekly contributions for Karis.

The tour ended the next day with Jagger's 35th birthday party afterwards at the Oakland Coliseum. The celebration must have been tempered by the fact that he now had his wife and ex-lover after him. In Hunt's case, it launched him into a bitter attack, referring to her in the press as 'a hustler out for publicity', and on another occasion he declared, 'She's an idiot. She's a lazy bitch.'

Left in no doubt of Jagger's feelings, Mitchelson advised an out-of-court settlement, but this time Hunt was determined to proceed. She also wanted legal recognition of Jagger's paternity established. No matter how long it took, she later said, it was Karis's right to know that Mick Jagger was her father.

Throughout August while all this took its course, after a brief stay in San Francisco Jagger moved to LA. There he kept his head down at RCA Studios as the Stones were busy with new material. And there Jade, his daughter with Bianca, came to stay with her father and Jerry Hall. His precocious child, to whom he wrote often and on whom he lavished expensive gifts, had already shown signs of being difficult. Her teachers at London's Garden House School complained about her disruptive tendencies. So Jagger must have felt relieved therefore that when Jade and Hall had first met earlier in the year, they had instantly connected. Hall had assumed the role of elder sister, which was less threatening to the child who had been long aware of the hostility between her parents.

By mid-September a couple of further singles had been released, in America 'Beast of Burden'/'When The Whip Comes Down', and in Britain 'Respectable' with the same B-side. Then as Richard's D-Day loomed closer, Jagger left for London. It was around now that he became involved in the Sid Vicious defence fund.

The bass player with the Sex Pistols had been charged with girlfriend Nancy Spungen's murder, when Jagger stepped in.

'Mick offered to help when I went to New York struggling to appoint Sid's defence,' recalls Sex Pistol's manager Malcolm McLaren. 'The costs would have been enormous and Warners, the record company, refused to be associated and would not help. In fact they wished that Sid would just disappear. The Sex Pistols at that time were in total disarray. Mick Jagger sympathized in some way, and he said that record companies were notorious cowards when it came down to it.'

Whatever motive was behind Jagger's involvement in this case was irrelevant when four months later Vicious, facing trial in New York, took a fatal massive overdose of heroin.

On 23 October, Keith Richard finally stood trial in Toronto, at which he received a one-year suspended sentence largely thanks to the astuteness of his lawyer, and an order to play a charity concert at the Canadian National Institute for the Blind within the next six months. There was also a requirement that he continue with his therapy.

All in all it appeared lenient, and Richard was ecstatic. If Jagger shared in his delight, it was short-lived when 48 hours later at his London hotel suite he heard that Bianca's lawyers were about to attempt to serve him with divorce papers. He foiled them by leaving for Jamaica just hours ahead of the bailiff's arrival.

As the season of goodwill approached Jagger found no sign of it in the ever mounting pressure over their lyrics. On 29 November the single 'Shattered'/'Everything Is Turning to Gold' came out in America. The A-side came from *Some Girls*. The album itself was under such sustained fire from Rev Jesse Jackson that Ahmet Ertegun had grown nervous of a backlash, particularly against Jagger. He denied that there had been any intention to offend and got the Stones to issue an appropriate statement. Privately, though, Jagger was said to have responded that if people couldn't take a joke it was too fucking bad.

The one bright spot came when Japanese authorities announced that they were lifting their ban on the Stones entering their country. Though welcome, this breakthrough was diminished when Jagger and Jerry Hall were greeted by a hostile armed reception in Hong Kong. Denied permission to enter he went instead to Bali, where he rested before band work resumed in January in the Bahamas.

It was reported that on 23 January 1979, while Jagger was cutting new material at Compass Point Studios, Nassau, an LA court ordered him to pay $12,000 anually towards his daughter's maintenance with an additional payment in trust. His paternity was officially declared. The establishment of paternity was, of course, an embarrassment to all those who had accused her of fabricating her relationship with Jagger. Typically, those sections of the press who had called her honesty into question were clamouring now to buy the rights to her story. Considering the hurtful comments Jagger had contributed to past attacks on Hunt, he was lucky in that his ex-lover declined all offers. She says she wanted Karis to grow up thinking well of her father. She also didn't want to do anything that could preclude them from forging a close bond in the future.

Jagger found it hard to concentrate at Compass Point Studio when in February Bianca reiterated her terms for their divorce settlement. Calculating her requirements she anticipated interim monthly maintenance payments of around $13,400, which figure included a $2000 clothing allowance and $1000 for entertainment expenses. She also wanted half his fortune, which she estimated would bring her £5 million. Jagger felt squeezed and would soon claim that regardless of how much he might have earned over the years, he was lucky if he had £2 million left. It was another two months before her American lawyers finally served divorce papers on him in New York.

Much of May was taken up with attending or awaiting the outcome of court hearings. On the 4th Jagger was personally present at London's High Court for a three-hour session to determine whether or not the divorce be settled in Britain or the States. It was imperative for him to get it heard in the UK as the law there was advantageous to him.

Ten days later on the other side of the Atlantic Judge Harry Shafer listened to argument from Bianca's lawyers about her allowance, which Jagger had recently cut to £1000 a month. In her deposition to the court she revealed how he proudly boasted that he had 'never given any woman anything and never would, no matter what the circumstances'. Possibly this riled the judge because Shafer ordered him to increase his weekly payments by a further £500 pending the divorce settlement.

It was 6 July before another hearing was convened in London. When Jagger arrived for the four days of private deliberation fresh from the Pathe Marconi Studios where the Stones were now based, he had a full beard. There was no disguising the problems he faced, though. Bianca joined the proceedings from Nicaragua, where she had been on a rescue mission in the country torn apart by civil war. She revealed that Jagger had been defying Judge Shafer's order and had not paid her any money yet.

Finally Mr Justice Eastham arrived at his decision, and to Jagger's delight ruled that the divorce be heard in Britain. He left it open, however, for Bianca to proceed with her petition to the US courts, which seriously displeased Jagger. Court costs were already running high, and although he had won this important point, he felt things were still left up in the air.

But Jagger's marriage finally came to an end in November. With the Paris recording sessions over he was with Keith Richard mixing tracks at New York's Electric Lady Studio when he learned on the 2nd that a decree nisi had been granted. Bianca was awarded £750,000, later revised to £1.25 million, and she retained custody of Jade.

Jagger made a fresh start by purchasing a new New York house for himself and Jerry Hall. They moved into 135 Central Park West, even closer to John Lennon in the Dakota building. The never quite determined relationship between the ex-Beatle and the Stone would soon reveal all its flaws. Jagger wanted to stay associated with Lennon. It was Lennon who seemed tó shun him, ignoring the messages Jagger left with the security doorman that he had called. Irritated by this Jagger blamed Yoko Ono, maintaining that Lennon was under her control. When Lennon learnt of this he hit out with all the caustic wit for which he was famous. He went public in *Playboy* magazine when he attacked the Stones for rolling on as long as they had. More specifically he expressed the opinion that Jagger, whom he denigrated 'a little leader', hadn't the confidence to go solo. What was Jagger afraid of? he goaded.

It is not known what effect this had on Jagger, although he does seem to have heeded some of his remarks. With the 70s almost over, the signs were that the 80s would have a vastly different outlook on life. Jagger took the opportunity to reinvent himself again, this time quite radically. For a start he denounced drugs and, having witnessed Keith Richard's troubles at close quarters, was particularly outspoken about heroin. Young people, he insisted, ought to steer clear. When inevitably attacked over his past in this respect, Jagger announced, 'I very rarely take drugs. I think cocaine is very bad, a habit-forming bore. I don't understand the fashion for it.'

Such pronouncements pleased the newly health-conscious generation, but Jagger was saying one thing and doing another.

Friends, among others, claim to have witnessed his continued use of cocaine and marijuana, sometimes in extremely public places. He had, however, never taken heroin.

During this long period of inactivity, with the Stones scattered and involved in individual pursuits, Jagger remained in New York. He spent summer 1980 contentedly with Hall in a social whirl, where occasionally he bumped into his ex-wife. Surprisingly on these occasions they both managed to behave in a civilized fashion.

Perhaps spurred by Lennon's comments, Jagger confessed at that time to a desire to make a solo album. But, in a return to self-deprecating mode, he described himself as too lazy to do so. Not so indolent, though, that he didn't start to miss the band.

The only proof that the Stones were still professionally alive was the release on 23 June of the album *Emotional Rescue*. Jagger flew between Britain and America to promote it, and his efforts were rewarded when it became a dual chart topper. This, however, was a target missed by the accompanying title-track single. And possibly this wasn't quite enough any more for the rest of the band either, for by August there was dissension in the ranks.

Bill Wyman had told a music magazine that he would leave the Rolling Stones some time in the next couple of years. Swearing that he hated rock 'n' roll, Charlie Watts indicated that he found it hard keeping up with being a Stone. Jagger appeared unperturbed by all this, but there were contradictory comments from the band on almost every point at issue. Whether or not it was a sign of each Stone outgrowing the band, all five men clearly had differing needs.

In the face of this uncertainty Jagger decided to make the best of what he had achieved so far. On the day before 'She's So Cold'/'Send It To Me', the second single from *Emotional Rescue*, was released on 18 September he paid over £250,000 for La Fourchette, a 17th-century French chateau with its own vineyard near Amboise in the Loire Valley. He also bought an elegant apartment in Paris plus an estate on the exclusive Caribbean island of Mustique.

Jagger conducted his dealings from New York where he remained involved in the Stones' business affairs. Marshall Chess, the original head of the Rolling Stones label, had been replaced by Earl McGrath, himself now succeeded by Vice President Art Collins. Jagger still remained reluctant to sign new artists to the company. Reggae artist Peter Tosh was the only one so far, and he soon complained that he felt his interests were neglected by the Stones' management. Regardless of any backroom criticism, Jagger continued to chair regular meetings where he had gained the reputation for asking the right questions and expecting an immediate answer. Collins later remarked how obsessive Jagger was over who was doing what and earning what in the industry, with the secret of their success. About to embark on his third decade in rock it is clear that Jagger had lost none of his competitive edge.

He didn't, however, feel the need to take the Stones back on the road in the near future. On holiday in Morocco he let it be known that from his point of view it was a no-go. Richard was particularly annoyed about this. Especially by the way in which Jagger relayed his decision to him in a message sent via the band's office in New York's Rockefeller Centre. Richard later admitted, 'We almost came to blows or worse.'

Jagger's view was that Stones' tours should be set three years apart. At 37 he might have wondered how much longer he would have the stamina for them, but he seemed primarily concerned that there should not be overkill. He had also taken something of a personal battering in the past 12 months, although Jerry Hall's outspoken enthusiasm did wonders for him. In typically brash manner she had recently gained publicity for remarks made during an interview with the American magazine *Out*. Published in the British press under the headline HOW KINKY MICK TURNS ME ON she revealed how 'weird' and 'dirty' he was. Whenever she needed to be sexy during modelling assignments she said she only had to call to mind her athletic lover. Besides intimate personal details, such as how at 12 she experienced her first orgasm by rubbing against her horse, she gave an interview that provided Jagger with a huge ego-boost.

Asked about his roving eye, she gaily retorted, 'If a man didn't look at other girls he wouldn't be normal.' It was an opinion she would have cause to rethink in the future. And in fact within just a few weeks she would, in no uncertain terms, warn off Natasha Fraser, when rumours circulated that Jagger had taken an interest in her.

Jagger's ability to satisfy his lover sexually was no more than what it was intended to be, a piece of musicbiz gossip. Which was not true of something that happened to someone else with an equally high public profile in that world. On 8 December 1980 the unthinkable happened when John Lennon was gunned down at point-blank range outside his apartment building. It shocked the entire world, and particularly those in the music business. As far as Jagger was concerned his worst nightmare had come true, to someone else.

When asked officially to comment Jagger was too upset to do so. Later it was alleged that Jagger's name had been on a supposed hit list compiled by Lennon's murderer, Mark Chapman. Regardless of whether that were true, Jagger instantly tripled his security and was said once more to have begun to carry a loaded gun.

14

SEXUAL INDISCRETIONS

To Jagger's great relief the only shooting he was involved in during 1981 was on Werner Herzog's *Fitzcarraldo*, in which he took his first film role in 12 years. The true story of an eccentric Irishman obsessed with the idea of building an opera house on a Peruvian jungle mountaintop, it would be filmed in inaccessible terrain, miles from civilization.

'I had not seen Mick in either of his previous films,' says Herzog, 'but I had, of course, watched the Stones perform many times, and when it came to casting Fitzcarraldo's close ally Wilbur I had him in mind. I sent him the screenplay to read, and he liked the whole story.'

Jagger would be starring alongside Jason Robards and Claudia Cardinale, and from the safe haven of his New York house it must have seemed an exciting challenge. Reality proved something very different.

The location was the Amazonian jungle, on the Peru/Ecuador border.

'I had warned Mick that the jungle was no joke,' says Herzog,

'explained all the likely hazards, but he said, "Yes, OK. Let's go."'
There were so many problems that it is a testament to Herzog's tenacity that it came off at all.

'There were hardships galore,' he recalls. 'We had two plane crashes, and our camp was attacked and burned down during preproduction as we got caught up in an inter-tribal 11-day war, which meant we had to resettle 2000 kilometres away. In the film, Fitzcarraldo hauls a gigantic steamboat through the jungle, and it was a massive operation resettling this boat alone.

'In Iquitos, where we made our HQ, there were never-ending difficulties involving strikes which left us with a shortage of cars, making it awkward to move extras around. Much to my surprise Mick volunteered the use of his own car and acted as chauffeur into the bargain, ferrying people to location.'

Besides being grateful for Jagger's help, Herzog believes his instincts in casting the Stone were fully justified when filming began for his scenes.

'Mick has a presence and intensity. There is something crazy about him,' he says. 'It is a totally different thing performing for thousands of fans to performing at arm's length from a camera when you can't do grandiose gestures. But there is something looming inside of him. Wilbur is a deranged English actor who ends up in the jungle. He carries a big barber's chair on his back which weighed about 100 pounds. It's Wilbur's only safe seat, his throne, and Mick had to carry this thing about the whole time.'

Jagger's character catches the heart of Fitzcarraldo by playing Richard III, and, for Herzog, this particular scene captured the essence of his acting abilities.

'He was sensational,' he says. 'Mick Jagger acting Richard III in the middle of the Peruvian jungle was the wildest thing I had ever seen!'

Such cameo moments, however, were rare, outweighed, according to Jagger, by living in primitive conditions, terrified of the rats. After Robards came down with dysentery, everyone was scared even of eating. Herzog claims conditions were not really that desperate because Jagger always made sure that he had everything he needed. But he nevertheless complained to friends that he was constantly cold, wet, tired and scared. Robards dropping out of the film was followed not long after by Jagger's departure.

'When Jason's doctors forbade him to return to the jungle we eventually resumed filming with Klaus Kinski,' says Herzog, 'but by then there were only ten days left before Mick's stop date, which had been established at the outset. It was clear that even if we worked round the clock shooting around Mick we would never manage it, so I had to release him from his contract.'

Herzog was devastated.

'I had no option,' he says. 'I had to write his character out because I felt he had been so unique that he was irreplaceable in the role. It's probably the biggest loss in my professional life, losing the filming we did with Mick. I think he has big potential as an actor, and I consider him as a yet, great undiscovered talent. He was miscast in his past roles, and after *Fitzcarraldo* he ran into the wrong projects. Before the camera he has total discipline. He's intelligent and appreciates why a huge gesture is wrong when a whisper will do.'

Jagger has his own memories of the experience. To him it was weeks of toil in horrendous conditions, which was ultimately wasted. It didn't put him off trying to make it as a screen actor. There were other projects. He had a lucky escape in supposedly turning down £1 million to play Rooster in Ray Stark's film version of the stage musical *Annie*. He was said to have unsuccessfully screen tested for the role of Mozart in what became the Oscar-winning *Amadeus*. He also paid £600,000 for the rights to Gore Vidal's novel *Kalki*. Despite interest from Alec Guinness, Jagger decided not to pursue his plans to produce and star in a film version of it. But his absence filming in Peru had fuelled the strife within the Stones.

Bill Wyman appears to have felt particularly threatened by Jagger's acting ambitions. Perhaps he feared that had Jagger succeeded he might leave the band. It was this possibility the bass player was most open about when speaking in February to *Melody Maker*. Talking up their front man's unique image, Wyman nevertheless contended: 'We could go on stage without him, while he could not go on stage without us.'

Many would argue that he was deluded in seriously imagining that fans would accept the Rolling Stones without the anchor of the strutting, preening and pouting Mick Jagger. But though Wyman had already earmarked the following year as the one in which he himself would most likely leave the band, he now seemed to be saying that the Stones as a whole could implode in 12 months' time.

Certainly Jagger was reluctant to tour, which remained a sore point. He was recuperating from his jungle ordeal among the reassuring mod cons of Barbados' finest hotel with Jerry Hall, Keith Richard and his girlfriend Patti Hansen. Richard partially blamed Hall, but Hall maintained she was a big fan of the Rolling Stones.

'They make a lot of money,' she beamed. 'Why try to ruin a good thing?'

Jagger's resistance had understandably been increased following Lennon's murder, and Ian Stewart later attested to how Jagger's face would pale at the mention of gigging. While Richard and Ron Wood lived for the day they could go on the road again, Jagger was confiding to friends that it no longer held any lure for him. This could have put him permanently at odds with the others had they not opted to deal with it indirectly. It seems that everyone likely to make money from a tour threw their energies behind a campaign to encourage Jagger to reconsider. But although they couldn't know it, some help was about to come from elsewhere.

Recently a Stones' anthology album, *Sucking in the Seventies*, had been released. Several US stores refused to carry it, objecting to its title. The Stones were soon estimated to be losing over $250,000 in revenue. It can't be ruled out that it was this fact that might have brought Jagger round to their way of thinking. In any case when he returned with Hall from an Easter break in Mustique it was to give the go-ahead to preparations for a September tour.

In the intervening time the Stones had added the finishing touches to a new album at New York's Atlantic Studios and shot promo footage to promote it. Jagger spent the rest of his time travelling with Hall. She was lasting the course well, partly, she believed, because her influence on him was subtle.

'I never wanted to become a Yoko Ono,' she stated, knowing how Jagger had considered John Lennon harassed by her. She concentrated instead on fitting in with his world, while retaining the air of independence that had first so attracted him. But her goals were altering. She knew that he regularly cheated on her, something she could hardly call a crime having previously told the press, 'I don't believe in monogamy.'

But Hall had allowed herself to turn a blind eye provided Jagger was discreet. All the same she had no intention of letting him go. She longed for marriage and had let him know she wanted to have his child before the fifth anniversary of them being together. Not willing to look so far ahead Jagger gave no commitment and carried on as before.

They spent much of the early summer at their French chateau, where they watched videos of old movies and read a lot. Come weekends, when the house filled with guests, livelier entertainment was on offer. The books and boardgames were replaced by charades and cross-dressing.

From stories later leaked by guests, there were men in make-up, skirts and stilettos, chasing scantily dressed women. Risqué games usually incurred forfeiting an item of clothing. One in particular, devised, it is alleged, by the mistress of the house, involved a competition to see how far guests could carry a coin between their buttocks.

Fun and games ended when in late June Jagger returned to New York to film a couple of Stones videos for the singles 'Start Me Up' and 'Waiting On A Friend'. He was distinctly tetchy, as director Michael Lindsay-Hogg recalls.

'Mick was very ratty a lot of the time then. The Stones were nervous about the upcoming tour. They were fighting among themselves quite a bit and all were frayed at the edges.'

Six weeks later, the band had more than a month of rehearsals at Long View Farm in Brookfield, Massachusetts. While there, 'Start Me Up'/'No Use In Crying' was released. Soon after, Jagger made an official announcement at the JFK Stadium, Philadelphia, that the tour would kick off on 25 September and end mid-December. It had, for the first time in rock history, attracted sponsorship, on this occasion by the perfume giant Jovan Inc. On 31 August the album *Tattoo You* was released to colossal critical and commercial success, selling over a million copies in its first week alone. If this weren't enough to boost Jagger's confidence the response to what had been intended as an anonymous pre-tour warm-up gig ought to have done so. Using the pseudonym Blue Monday and the Cockroaches, the Stones had arranged to perform at Sir Morgan's Cave, a 350-capacity club in Worcester. When their cover was blown by a local radio station, however, over ten times that number of fans turned up. This caused a problem for the club's proprietor and resulted in the arrival of the riot police. Because of this a handful of other small venue warm-ups were cancelled.

As the starting date grew closer, Jagger concentrated on getting his nerves under control. He had got himself into shape physically with a rigorous daily workout, but mentally it wasn't so easy. He was in the front line in what had been proved to be a risky profession. Fear had entered the rock business because of Mark Chapman. Jagger rallied himself, 'You can't spend your life being paranoid. There'll always be nutters, and you have to watch out for them.' But he knew this was easier said than done.

To distract himself he had got involved in the publicity, finance and stage-set design of the tour, in fact with every aspect of its arrangements. The tension between Jagger and Richard grew worse. As far as Richard could see the consequence of leaving Jagger to oversee things was that everything seemed designed to put the spotlight on him. It is unlikely Richard got anywhere with his complaints. Jagger was still making it clear that he had begun as an unwilling party to this tour and to a certain extent remained so.

'The others pleaded with me until I said yes,' he said. 'I mean a tour is great fun for a while, but it's like sex, you don't want to do it all the time. I have to stay sober, in training for ten weeks, and it tears the life out of me.'

Their tenth assault on North America kicked off at JFK Stadium before 90,000 people. Jagger had recently claimed, 'Within three or four years I won't be able to do what I do now on stage.' But just days into the tour such was the enthusiastic audience feedback that he felt thoroughly rejuvenated.

'It's great to be back!' he announced as extra gigs were in constant demand.

There was an indefatigable attraction to this band now approaching the 20th anniversary of its formation. The success of the tour this time was phenomenal. But it came at a price. Routine door searches had at a single gig produced a frightening 30 handguns. For Jagger, facing his personal phobia each night, he confronted a couple of chilling reminders. During one performance, a fan penetrated the security ring and rushed him at the mike. Before he got too close, however, Richard sprang to Jagger's rescue and knocked over the man by clubbing him with his guitar. And in October outside the Kingdome venue in Seattle a woman armed with a gun was arrested and charged with menacing behaviour for circulating the crowd vowing that she was going to kill 'that son of a bitch Jagger'.

Two nights later at Candlestick Park in San Francisco the Stones played to 146,000 people; the biggest-ever crowd for an open-air show in that city. A new breed of reviewers appreciated Jagger's overtly healthy image. In step with the fitness culture he wore a vest, skintight leggings with knee pads and trainers. It wasn't a façade. Limbering up for each gig Jagger was pumping iron and running daily mini marathons. The result was that he was a powerhouse of energy, turning in some electrifying performances, hailed as raunchier than ever.

The band could still generate the old hysteria. By the time they reached New York the police were under such pressure that the security level was almost as high as that afforded to visiting heads of state. Jagger appreciated their achievement.

'He hadn't thought the tour would go well,' says Michael Lindsay-Hogg, 'but when they played New York he was so thrilled at the reception that suddenly he was cock of the walk again. The Stones had felt ripped off in the past and had also blown a lot of money, but Jerry said to me later, "This was the moment Mick at last felt secure money-wise."'

A second single from *Tattoo You* 'Waiting On A Friend'/'Little T&A' was released in America about a month before they hit the final stretch, and as the tour began to wind down they relaxed a little. At the Sun Devil Stadium in Phoenix, Jerry Hall made an unexpected entrance on stage during 'Honky Tonk Women'. 'We danced around and he hit me on the bottom. It was thrilling,' she said.

On the following night at Kansas' Kemper Arena ex-Stone Mick Taylor made a surprise guest appearance with the band. Taylor's fortunes had diminished since leaving the Stones. This must have been hard to accept when the tour ended in Virginia on 19 December to news that the band's estimated gross earnings for the 50-date tour were $50 million. As the group scattered, Jagger with Hall headed straight to France.

It was hard coming down from the sustained high and total self-absorption of touring, as Jagger soon found out. Hall's constant presence on tour had cramped his style, and now he was beginning to react against it. 'Hang Fire'/'Neighbours' was released as a single on 11 January 1982 in the USA. During the video shoot for the B-side in New York, Jagger, as Hall was quick to find out, had begun to trawl for women again. They were to him faceless, meaningless encounters, but Hall was on uncertain ground with regard to tackling him over his behaviour. Right then he was quick-tempered and unpredictable. Lindsay-Hogg who shot the 'Neighbours' video can vouch for this.

'Mick and I ended up having another falling out,' he says. 'He was very ragged anyway, and we had a clash of ideas about the composition of the video. When these were put to the others unfortunately for Mick they liked mine. By now Jagger was so powerful a figure in rock that the only people who could argue with him, or would dare argue with him, were those who had known him a very long time. He often had the attitude "I'm Mick Jagger, and you'll do as you are told," and really he prefers to have employees around him who won't oppose him.'

Being garlanded by awards at the *Rolling Stone Readers Awards* individually and as a band could only fuel this autocratic attitude. But Hall was determined not to be swamped. Her plan to have his child hadn't come to fruition, and friends of the couple marvelled at her patience in handling Jagger's mood swings. Still never his style to address emotional pressure head on and aware of Hall's hopes for a wedding, Jagger made his position clear when approached by *Woman's World* magazine for an interview. In it he implied that he had no intention of marrying again. 'If you're not successful at it,' he said, 'it isn't a case of try, try again.'

Despite his love for Hall, and attempts to deal with her restlessness, he also extolled the pleasure of pursuing a varied sex life. 'Sex,' he maintained, 'is important to me. For an artist it's another form of expression.' He talked about the importance of keeping a woman happy by ensuring she reaches orgasm. The bottom line was the same old story – he wanted to have his cake and eat it.

Having rediscovered his thirst for performing live Jagger also wanted to tour again. In London at the end of the month he announced that in spring the Stones would be going on the road around Britain and Europe. The first gig at the Capitol Theatre in Aberdeen on 26 May marked the Stones first UK gig for six years. When they played two other Scottish dates in Glasgow and Edinburgh it particularly pleased Jagger to note that they were now attracting a fan base among a generation too young to have been born when the band first emerged. It boded well for their longevity.

But not everything went smoothly. On 1 June their new live album *Still Life* was released together with the single 'Going To A Go Go'/'Beast of Burden', their first on the picture disc format. The album bombed with critics, who made the obvious comparison by complaining that it was as energetic as plastic fruit.

While Jagger had worked the previous year on putting the finishing touches to *Still Life*, yet another newsflash had announced that he had suffered a fatal heart attack in his sleep. At the time his reaction had been outwardly jovial.

'I've got to laugh,' he'd said. 'Already this year I've been shot twice, had an earlier heart attack, and now today I'm dead all over again.' Then it had been a front as he'd struggled against his fears. Now with the US tour safely under his belt Jagger seemed easier on that score. In fact the deadliest feeling for him was the rift between himself and Richard. It must have made life tense for the others when night after night each one's stage antics were designed purely to upstage and enrage the other.

On the eve of the first of two sell-out gigs at Wembley Stadium, Bill Wyman collected on the Stones' behalf the British Music Industry's Silver Clef Award for outstanding achievement in the world of British music. These gigs were considered the band's real homecoming, and as Jagger was anxious that nothing interfere with that, internal divisions had to be concealed. Film and music stars as well as royalty turned out to pay homage. Back stage, as wives, lovers and children arrived later, the celebration became a family affair. Feeling increasingly uncertain of her ground Jerry Hall lost no opportunity to point out that she was now in her fifth year as Mick's girlfriend. 'He's the greatest boyfriend in the world. He's so understanding,' she announced.

What some observers understood from this display was that she was insecure and beginning to panic. One might have expected the 14-year age gap between them to have worried Jagger. That Hall might have been tempted to look at younger men. But in fact the situation was the reverse. Hall had always been sensitive to Jagger's liking for young women, but now they seemed to be getting younger. As Jagger would be 40 the following year, some put it down to the male menopause. He still needed to prove he could attract women.

The tour ended around Jagger's birthday with a gig at Roundhay Park in Leeds. The next night Jagger and Hall hosted a party in London in a private room at Langan's Brasserie, Mayfair. Jagger waved off the last guest before attempting to negotiate his drunken way down the stairs. Hall was trying to help when a staff member came to her aid. The slightly-built figure recently praised for his erotic grace on stage seemed skeletal to the man supporting him, renewing speculation about Jagger's health. But it was also his wealth that seemed to bother Hall. Following behind, she joked 'Be careful. Don't drop him. You're carrying $40 million worth of pop star like a sack of potatoes.'

Jagger left for Paris soon after on business. Hall, as she had always done, looked to her own affairs, and over the coming months was often away on modelling assignments. Professionally she exuded all the required confidence and poise, but her trust in Jagger was being steadily eroded. Again she played up to him by stressing what a fantastic lover he was. Unfortunately it was becoming common knowledge that she was not alone in her judgement on this score. In September the single 'Time Is On My Side' came out in America, and, out to prove this, in Hall's absence Jagger's womanizing reached manic proportions.

His incurable infidelity, Hall had lived with. But there was a limit to how much humiliation she could handle. She tried to put it down to his realization of how close they had become. He was scared of commitment, she knew. But that did little to ease the hurt she felt every time she picked up a newspaper and saw Jagger pictured with a woman often much younger than her.

When Hall was away she rarely rang home without being greeted by an unfamiliar female voice on the line. On returning from her travels she found items of other women's jewellery abandoned carelessly beside the bed. Overpowered by her sense of betrayal, she moved out. She told Jagger to decide whether or not he wanted them to stay together. Perhaps he was happier having indiscriminate sex with an assortment of women. The tie wasn't totally severed. They agreed to go on seeing one another, but as Hall revealed Jagger even failed her there. 'We'd make a date. I'd get dressed up and wait for him, and he'd stand me up. Then he'd say,

I was out with some 18 year old debutante, rubbing it in,' she said.

It may not have been an idle boast. Among the many young women he was seen with that autumn was the Duke of Windsor's goddaughter Cornelia Guest, dubbed 'Deb of the Decade'. A press photographer followed Jagger at dawn from a New York club to the Carlyle Hotel, where he says he saw Guest, who appeared to be waiting for Jagger in the lobby. When Jagger spotted the photographer and other members of the press he became angry with them as he escorted Guest upstairs. There was so much gossip about so many affairs it was hard to keep count. This might have dragged on indefinitely had Hall not decided that she had suffered enough. She took the one step she knew was guaranteed to get his attention.

Earlier in the year Jagger had said, 'I think it's inevitable in a long relationship that one or both partner is unfaithful,' adding, 'I'm not saying you should do it every weekend. That wouldn't help things.' He thereby gave the impression that he would be sanguine about his girlfriend behaving as he did. In fact he was not. At the start of November in a mirror incident to the one years earlier with Marianne Faithfull and Mario Schifano, Jagger was at an airport, this time Paris-bound. There he was approached by a reporter who asked him for his reaction to the news that Jerry Hall had left him for multi-millionaire racehorse owner Robert Sangster.

Several years older and married, Sangster had consoled Hall in New York before flying to LA, where they took separate but adjoining suites in the Beverly Wilshire. There she honoured modelling commitments, and he attended the races. He was reputedly the most powerful man in British racing. Hall later disowned a comment attributed to her that Sangster could buy Mick ten times over, but with Sangster's personal fortune conservatively estimated at between £250 million and £500 million, she would not have been far out.

Jagger was angry, especially when her very public revenge was inevitably in all the papers. Sangster was no stranger to controversy, having left his first wife in 1975 for the woman to whom he was currently married. His only comment was a press release stating, 'I realize our current situation might set tongues wagging.' It did more than that. The gossip was moving into overdrive. While a few attacked Hall for being a gold-digger, many others predicted that Jagger was at last about to get his comeuppance.

Hall shrewdly displayed a no-hard-feelings resignation that gave it the hallmark of being truly over. In days Jagger had brought about a reunion. He knew what she wanted and had rung her from Paris tearfully begging her to come back to him. He promised to stop his womanizing and professed undying love. But it was when he proposed marriage that she agreed to meet him at the Charles de Gaulle airport. When Jerry Hall walked into the arrivals lounge Jagger suddenly sprang out from behind a pillar, asking, 'Where have you been then?' On cue, to the accompaniment of the paparazzi cameras, she rushed romantically into his arms.

The touching reunion was soon tarnished by stories of how the underlying tension between the couple, particularly in Jagger, found expression once he got her into the limo. Claims emerged that as Jagger started on at her in the back seat, he had been seen pressing his point home by gripping her wrist quite savagely. Certainly 24 hours after returning to their Paris apartment, Hall fled again. She later contended, 'I was having the closest to a nervous breakdown I've ever had. I just ran like a kid would run.' Friends declared that she couldn't stomach his abuse any longer.

Jagger abandoned work at Pathe Marconi Studios and systematically set about finding her. He sent trusted employees to search her every known haunt. Hotels were checked, and he spent hours on the phone ringing round her friends. It took a while, but eventually he located her. As if calming a skittish mare Jagger soothed, 'Come home. Everything will be OK.' He went on to promise this time that they would start a family. Hall joined him at La Fourchette, where soon they were photographed strolling hand in hand around the local market square.

For Hall it didn't seem an illusion. She believed his promise that they would marry and try for a baby. She also believed that she had now discovered how Jagger would react in a personal crisis. 'To have survived all that,' she maintained, 'really makes love stronger.'

Casting herself as a role model for women mistreated by their men, she advocated never standing for being shunted on to the fringe of someone's life. As the couple headed to Mustique Jagger, already bored by the continuing interest in the subject, more prosaically remarked, 'We broke up for a while, that's all.'

In New York outraged female fans had vandalized the outside of his house with attacks on Jerry Hall. But by the end of the year there was another kind of writing on the wall. Though he had won her back, she looked to have the upper hand. As Jagger never did like being powerless, it could only spell trouble ahead.

15

ROUGH RIDE

I T WASN'T THE future that concerned Jagger in the opening months of 1983 but rather the past. According to Michael Lindsay-Hogg, Jagger hates to look back over his life. However, London publishers Weidenfeld & Nicholson in paying him a reported £1 million advance for his auto-biography wanted him to do precisely that.

No sooner had work begun on the project than it became obvious that his notoriously poor memory was going to be a problem. To help the process along, in late February journalist John Ryle was hired for a fee of £50,000 to ghostwrite the book. A researcher undertook the task of speaking to family members, friends, ex-lovers and Bianca, after which all notes were passed to Ryle for checking through with Jagger. Believing that solitude might be beneficial to delving back in time, in spring Jagger headed with Hall for the seclusion of Mustique. But it wasn't just the extensive renovations to his house that distracted him from his task but more the awareness that he had accepted a huge advance and was already in trouble.

Around Easter Jagger contacted Marsha Hunt. The previous November on Karis's 12th birthday he had sent an array of gifts to her home in London. Jagger had also telephoned his daughter from New York. Hunt was relieved and hoped this was a sign that Jagger would now take a proper interest in his daughter's life. In the fullness of time he did, attending parent-teacher meetings for his eldest girl as he regularly did for Jade.

Feeling himself on better terms with Hunt, Jagger asked if she would be interviewed by Ryle. She agreed. When she got down to it, though, it was not easy working out what to say. All things considered it looked like becoming something that Jagger might soon regret having taken on. But at least he still had a life to reflect upon.

A few weeks before it was said that a contract had been taken out on Jagger, in a resurgence of trouble stemming from Altamont. There was a US Senate Judiciary Committee sitting that heard testimony from one ex-Hell's Angel, who had claimed that there had been a vow of revenge on the Stone.

Further stories emerged that two earlier attempts to kill him had failed. One had involved a gunman staking out the wrong hotel, and the other an attempt to reach Jagger's beachfront Montauk house by sea to plant explosives. This was scuppered when the dinghy sank on the way there. However inept the would-be hitmen sounded, it still chilled Jagger to the bone.

The biker's claims were swiftly denied by Hell's Angels' leaders, but Jagger was little reassured as he left Mustique for New York. There mixing work was required for the Stones' new album, but here again it seemed only tension awaited him. The division between himself and Richard looked to be out in the open when it was Wood he teamed up with at the Hit Factory. Although Richard did eventually join them, the rumours were that their difficulties were becoming irreconcilable.

What fanned the flames was Jagger's fervour to establish his new persona. He seemed determined to distance himself from the Rolling Stones' bad-boy image and took advantage of every opportunity to speak about how his fitness regime had become of utmost importance to him. Linking it to rock 'n' roll and his efforts to stay young he maintained, 'That's vital in a business that is as fast as this.'

Like a repentant sinner he also said, 'Once I led the typical dissipated life of a rock star, full of drugs, booze and chaos, but these days my health is my most treasured possession. When I am on tour, I never touch hard liquor.' He omitted to mention drugs.

Unlike the increasingly ravaged Richard, Jagger was in sound physical and mental shape. This could only have helped the giant record label CBS decide to sign the Stones in a $28 million deal, the biggest in rock history. Atlantic Records, not able to meet the sums demanded, had been sorry to lose them, but while Jagger prided himself that his firm hand in the band's business negotiations had paid off so well Richard was not so sure. 'Mick's not as good at business as people think,' he said. 'He's not as good as he thinks.'

The lucrative deal, however, pleased Jerry Hall too. It was a double delight. Two days later on 27 August, it was announced that she was three months' pregnant. The advent of the baby had stabilized their relationship. Now 40 Jagger had quipped about needing as much sleep as possible adding, 'I don't go to clubs or discos except to pick up girls.' But in fact he had been, and still was, toeing the line. The pregnancy had come about with the help of various fertility clinics, and he was thrilled.

Hall was triumphant, having achieved half of her long-awaited goal. Jagger's suggestion of a date for the marriage made it complete. He suggested a quick wedding before the baby arrived. But he was not so carried away that he was prepared to marry Hall without a prenuptial agreement. That's when their new-found harmony came unstuck. Though anxious to wear a wedding ring, Hall was equally too hard-headed to be prepared to sign away her rights.

Thwarted, Jagger assumed indifference, claiming publicly that wedlock wasn't for him. In private he pressured Hall to meet his lawyers to talk terms. They were still at odds over it two months later when Hall accompanied him to Mexico City where the band were to shoot sequences for a video to accompany their forthcoming single.

'Undercover Of The Night'/'All The Way Down' preceded by a week the new album *Undercover*, released on 7 November, simultaneously in the UK and USA. Jagger was disappointed though not surprised when BBC TV's *Top Of The Pops* banned the video of the single from being shown on the grounds of its excessively violent content. It was curious, considering Jagger's greatest fear, that the film should portray him being shot, his assassin played by Keith Richard. Not surprisingly Jagger had a hard time justifying the carnage.

The controversy only carried the album to number 3 in Britain and 4 in America just as Jagger returned to Cabo San Lucas. There, despite the increasing hostility, he was the only Stone to attend Richard's marriage to Patti Hansen on the day of the groom's 40th birthday. The remaining Stones joined them in Mexico in the coming weeks to film video footage for various numbers. While there, a second single from the new album came out. 'She Was Hot'/'Think I'm Going Mad' became one of their poorest sellers yet, barely cracking the Top 50.

Such considerations were forgotten when on 2 March 1984 Jerry Hall gave birth to Jagger's third daughter in Lennox Hill Hospital, New York. It was a complicated delivery, and Hall later revealed that Jagger, present at the birth, had been scared. The proud new mother could only coo, 'She has the cutest lips, just like her daddy's.'

A sinister cloud overshadowed the celebration when death threats resurfaced, this time against Jagger's family. The police cautioned Jagger to treat them seriously. Bodyguards therefore screened Hall and the infant days later as they avoided photographers and left by a side door for their newly fortified apartment at West 81st Street.

Any hopes that Hall might have had that the baby would bring out a domesticated side to Jagger were soon dashed. It became clear he was not a new man. Indeed his behaviour suggested the very common experience of feeling usurped in Hall's affections. When she took the baby into their bed to feed her, Jagger complained that he disliked the smell of breast milk.

None of this, however, would be on show at her summer christening. Held at St Mary Abbot's Church, Kensington, Jagger insisted it be traditional in every sense. With due solemnity family, close friends and godmother Shirley Watts watched as the baby was named Elizabeth Scarlett. The new arrival's two half sisters also looked on, and at the party held afterwards at a rented house in

Holland Park (48 Cheyne Walk having been sold after his divorce from Bianca) Jagger posed for photographs with his daughters by three different women.

Jagger had once been seen as the scourge of all parents, a man from whom all daughters should be protected. But he himself would become an exacting father as his girls grew up. About a decade earlier he had claimed that he would not object if Jade began having sex as young as 13. 'Just as long as she didn't turn into a tramp and was having it with anyone on the street,' he had said.

By this time Jade had been attending the exclusive Spence School in New York, and, worried about the scope for mischief in Manhattan, he took her away from there and enrolled her instead in St Mary's in the English country town of Calne. This was a girls' school that stressed academic excellence. At almost 100 miles from London Jagger thought it sufficient distance for his already worldly 13 year old not to get into trouble.

The only Stone invited to the latest child's christening had been Charlie Watts, which underlined the discord within the band. In late March when Wyman had made his remarks about Jagger having lost touch with himself, he was also quoted as saying, 'Mick is a very difficult person to know now,' adding, 'I'm not worried about saying what I think about Mick. He's not my boss.' He also called Ron Wood shallow and seemed to be moving more toward Keith Richard. Jagger he ultimately dubbed 'a business associate of 25 years'. How the band privately reacted to this was unknown, but a week later Wyman disowned the comments.

Within weeks the business associate was taking the stand on the band's behalf in a New York court as a witness in the Rolling Stones' law suit against ex-manager Allen Klein. They were petitioning to have nullified a contract giving Klein the rights to their sixties' material. Media reportage of the case told of an incident when Jagger, demanding ferociously of Klein the money he believed was owing to him, had chased the older man down through a hotel and out on to the street. The court correspondent also revealed how Jagger had stated in evidence that he initially intended to be reasonable about the issue, but at the mere sight of Klein he had yelled, 'Where's my $800,000?'

It has been claimed that Jagger had been obsessed with disliking their former manager for years. But it wasn't an all-consuming thing, according to Les Perrin's widow Janie.

'Allen was a client of my husband's too,' she says, 'and when the Stones and Klein parted company that put Les in a spot. He asked Mick, "What do you want? Will I let one go?" And Mick replied, "Hell, no. There's no problem that I can see."'

With so much money at stake this latest courtroom battle looked to be contested hotly. Yet a week later the suit was dropped on condition that Klein paid the Stones their royalties on time in future.

Just after this Jagger went into New York's A&R Studios to join Michael Jackson. Just as he was intrigued with the secret of Jackson's global success, so Jackson recognized the Stone's staying power and had related, too, to Jagger's earlier androgynous style. Surprisingly, although he liked to align himself with success, Jagger was initially reluctant when asked to record 'State of Shock' with Jackson. Perhaps because he knew he hadn't been first choice.

The previous year Freddie Mercury had recorded two numbers including 'State of Shock' at Jackson's Encino studio. But the Queen star's inability to conceal his cocaine abuse had cooled the working relationship. Jagger was to be the replacement. But Jagger was pragmatic about this. He had recently embarked on making a solo album. To separate from the Stones was always going to be a daunting prospect, and he possibly decided that this duet could act as a halfway house. With their combined fan base there was little risk of failure, and on its release in July it managed a creditable number 14 in the charts.

But it could not be said that either star cherished the experience. Maybe their collective egos collided, but each ended up speaking ill of the other. Jackson considered Jagger's singing to be off key and queried his right to superstar status. While Jagger resorted to condemning music's by then top-selling artist as lightweight.

What remained no light matter was the trouble surrounding Jagger's autobiography. In spring 1984 a partial manuscript was delivered to Weidenfeld & Nicholson and also submitted to a number of UK paperback companies, most of whom turned it down. On 10 May a Futura spokesman outlined their reasons to a daily newspaper. There was he said, 'No sex. No rock 'n' roll. Just boring stuff about his ordinary parents and ordinary upbringing.' He added his amazement at the poor standard.

For Weidenfeld, who had paid a record-breaking advance, the emotion ran deeper than surprise. A company executive said, 'It was a shambles. The excerpts we saw weren't publishable.'

The problem was thought to be a lack of cooperation between Jagger and John Ryle, who was said to have struggled to bring cohesion to the book. He had found it virtually impossible to pin Jagger down to work on the project. Perhaps Jagger preferred a sanitized version of his life story. Anything else would not sit well with his new health-conscious, at times even respectable, image. But feeling pressure from all sides he asked for help in remembering his past from Bill Wyman. The bass player's answer came back as a swift and succinct refusal.

Deciding to ignore the problem, Jagger headed to Mustique with his family, before carrying on alone to Compass Point Studios, Nassau, where he worked on his solo album. For all his complaints about Michael Jackson he was rejuvenated by the relative success of 'State of Shock'. He began to record diligently in Britain and America too, drafting in guest musicians who included Jeff Beck and Pete Townshend. He was totally absorbed in his solo début.

The first repercussions from this made themselves felt just prior to Atlantic Records' release of the anthology album *Rewind* on 29 June. The four original Stones had met at their London office, and Jagger let it be known there that he was going to devote almost the next six months to his own endeavours. Since this effectively grounded the Stones the others were not at all pleased.

According to Wyman resentment set in at Jagger's self-centred attitude. He was trying to finish and promote his own album at their expense. When anonymous sources suggested that Jagger saw his career changing direction, press speculation was inevitable. But Jagger did his best to quash rumours that the Stones were breaking up.

Jagger spent all summer in the recording studio. In the circumstances it was as well he was working with different musicians. He wanted the freedom to do as he desired. He also tirelessly insisted on a hands-on approach to all aspects of his album. He picked over the smallest detail with his co-producers Bill

Laswell and Nile Rodgers, displaying a unique perfectionism.

It was hard not to be conscious all the same of the increasing gulf between him and the Stones. Keith Richard refused to take his phone calls. And, by September, things had got worse when the band was forced to postpone recording their new album. Jagger refused to leave his solo work, now at the Power House Studio, New York.

The Rolling Stones were too huge an entity for Jagger to be reckless, however. By no means secure in his hopes of going solo, he could not afford to be overly arrogant. When he finally realized how deeply upset the rest of the band were, he convened another meeting in Amsterdam in late October. Unfortunately the others still felt that he believed he could have everything on his own terms. He was disabused of this by the usually placid Charlie Watts, who considered Jagger had crossed the line once too often. At some point during the meeting he punched him hard on the jaw, sending him sprawling. A third meeting the following month to discuss an early start date for work on the Stones' album also proved a rough ride.

His only tranquil environment was home. Jerry Hall was doing everything right as far as Jagger was concerned. She thrived on motherhood, played big sister to his other visiting daughters and turned a blind eye once again to his straying. Jagger, ever conradictory, commented, 'You can't have a stable relationship and go around and screw everything in sight,' nevertheless adding that it was unrealistic of Jerry Hall to expect him to ignore one half of the world's population.

He clearly wasn't ready for marriage and was relieved that Hall had stopped pressuring him on that score. But she had far from abandoned hope. Ever the optimist, wherever they travelled she packed a plastic wedding ring and suitable dress just in case. They went with her when she accompanied Jagger and director Julien Temple to Rio de Janeiro to shoot videos for his forthcoming solo album. And also thereafter to Mustique for Christmas and New Year. There they kept it secret that she was again pregnant.

For Stones' watchers irrefutable proof of Jagger's isolation came to light on 3 January 1985 when Ron Wood married Jo Howard in Denham. He was the only Stone not invited. Relations were no better when weeks later he rejoined the band at Pathe Marconi Studios to begin work on their album. The air was thick with unspoken resentment. Whether or not it was so, it seemed to the rest of the band that Jagger was not giving his best to the recording. Richard, quick to flare up, later revealed that his frustration became so intense that he came close to assaulting Jagger. However, he'd decided there was little pleasure from beating 'a wimp'.

The bad feeling was compounded when on 4 February Jagger's first solo single 'Just Another Night'/'Turn The Girl Loose' was released worldwide on CBS. The next day, instead of promoting his record, Jagger spent his time dismissing the notion that this solo venture heralded the demise of the Rolling Stones. When asked how it felt working without the others he replied, 'It is rather like having a wife and a mistress,' something he was qualified to know all about!

'Just Another Night', though sticking at 32 in the UK charts, rose to number 12 in America and thus fared respectably, though not coming up to Jagger's expectations. The album *She's The Boss* released exactly a month later did better. It was a ragbag of styles with no single thread running through it. As such it divided critics, but UK sales lifted it to number 6, seven places higher than in the States.

Inevitably interviewers pressed Jagger on the effect his branching out was having on the Stones. He pointed out that he was the last Stone to produce a solo effort and made it clear it was he who had grounds to resent all the accusations that were levelled at him over it.

'I was feeling very stultified within the Stones,' he said. 'It created a tremendous ruckus which was totally unnecessary. I think everyone made much too much of a fuss about it, and I think everyone should've been more supportive.'

It could have been viewed as an act of retaliation when on April Fools Day he made filming the video for his next solo single a priority before resuming work at the Paris studio. This absence had further delayed operations and taken the release date for the band's album back to September. He also returned to find a distinct change had taken place within the band's internal hierarchy as Keith Richard appeared to be the one to have more control now.

Mid-month Jagger's second solo single emerged. 'Lucky In Love'/'Running Out Of Luck' began to seem ominously appropriate when not only did it slump at number 38 but also coincided with Weidenfeld & Nicholson's attempt to recover their advance. As it had proved impossible to produce an acceptable manuscript the project had been abandoned. Ghost writer John Ryle was only paid for his services after having signed a confidentiality agreement that barred him from ever talking about Jagger in the future.

In the circumstances it came as no surprise when in June the Stones declined an invitation from Boomtown Rats vocalist Bob Geldof to take part in Live Aid. Equally unsurprisingly, Jagger agreed to take one of the 18-minute slots being allocated per act to perform as a solo artist. The event, televised around the world, would start at Wembley Stadium, then later at the JFK Stadium in Philadelphia. Initially word spread that Jagger planned a transatlantic duet with David Bowie, but the technical nightmare this entailed ruled it out. Instead at the end of the month they recorded a version of the Martha Reeves and the Vandellas 1969 hit 'Dancing In The Street'. They shot its impressive video in London's East End, which would also be shown during the Live Aid gig to be held on 13 July.

On the day Jagger performed backed by musicians Daryl Hall and John Oates, before Tina Turner joined him on stage for a medley including 'It's Only Rock 'n' Roll' and 'Honky Tonk Women'. Afterwards his supporters hailed his set a dazzling *tour de force*. And he did give it his all — during his duet with Turner, in a clearly rehearsed move, despite her shocked expression, he ripped her skirt off.

The video of 'Dancing In The Street', in which Jagger eclipsed Bowie, received its world première at Live Aid to great acclaim. This success reflected in its sales when the single was released on 23 August. The intensive publicity campaign behind it included screening in 5000 theatres across the States and four times as many advertising posters. Despite this, it peaked at number 7 in the USA, though the single went straight in at the top in Britain, giving Jagger his first taste of hitting the UK number 1 slot for 16 years. An offshoot of this success was that Jagger and Bowie were said to be considering a remake of *Some Like It Hot*.

At that moment Hall was expecting the imminent arrival of her second baby. At times during the past nine months she had understandably felt vulnerable. Not least when back in spring Jagger had been dining with Hunt and Karis in Paris. Hunt had also taken Karis to visit her father at his invitation to his hotel just off the Champs-Elysèes. He had asked her and Karis to spend a few days with him. Twice during Hunt's visit there Jerry Hall rang from America.

Hunt later stated that she disliked mistrusting his motives when he appeared cooperative but she enjoyed his company as a friend. Jagger took Hunt and Karis out on the town, and Jagger occasionally, casually held hands with Hunt. Once, a familiar flash alerted them to a photographer. The last thing Hunt wanted was for a newspaper to carry a photo of her and Jagger, aware that their stroll down a side street in Paris could be misinterpreted by the pregnant Hall.

If Jagger had considered rekindling dead embers, even to further his softening-up operation, at last Hunt had his measure. She had long been aware just how hot and cold he could run, so she was delighted to witness the rapport gradually building between Jagger and Karis. Jagger spoke to them too of his new family and told them he was hoping Jerry Hall would produce a boy this time.

On 28 August Hall didn't disappoint when she gave birth to a son at Lennox Hill Hospital in New York. Jagger, again present at the birth, found it at one point too much and turned away. He was further horrified when he was invited to cut the umbilical cord. Pushing the scissors away he told the doctor that that was what he was paying him to do. But he soon recovered to be the proud father.

'There's nothing like having a first son,' beamed Jagger. Hall was amused by his wish for a second traditional christening, at which the child was named James Leroy Augustine. Such was Jagger's joy that Hall's hopes of a wedding were stronger than ever.

With the arrival of his fourth child and the involvement he began to show in the lives of each of his children, Jagger was in danger of becoming seen as a real family man. His continued obsession with good health added to this, although it was in keeping with the times. Unlike the emaciated Richard and Wood who clung to the degenerate rocker life style, Jagger favoured the fitness culture.

But it wasn't only Jagger who had joined the bandwagon. At Live Aid Freddie Mercury too had looked vibrant and muscular, while David Bowie, distancing himself from his past, was at pains to reinvent himself in a far straighter vein. With the world waking up to the horror of HIV and Aids, Jagger was quick to come clean about his former self. He was heterosexual to the core, he wanted everyone to know. Anything to the contrary had all been part of the act.

Drugs got the treatment too. Jagger repeatedly talked down his past use of them and claimed that his current intake was all but non-existent. He denied ever having advocated their use, and expected people to accept that his lyrics had never been intended to be misogynistic.

In this new dawn of responsibility an announcement followed that he was to marry Jerry Hall. But in this respect she was to be again disappointed. Possibly feeling in a stronger position with the birth of their second child, she was apparently more pliable and had waived her earlier refusal to forsake any claim to Jagger's fortune. But she soon discovered he wasn't in a hurry to find the nearest church. Still she had the stamina and patience to wait.

Time, though had run out for another stalwart in the Stones' camp. On 12 December Ian Stewart suffered a fatal heart attack aged just 47. All the band found the time to turn up for his funeral; Jagger flew in specially from the Caribbean. With many stars from the rock world swelling the ranks of mourners, the Stones sang the 23rd Psalm. Later they played an invitation-only gig at London's 100 Club in his memory on 23 February 1986. But the apparent truce didn't last long.

In early March 'Harlem Shuffle'/'Had It With You', their new single, was released, followed three weeks later by *Dirty Work*. The album peaked on both sides of the Atlantic at number 4, considered a disappointment, and critics were quick to blame a lack of commitment on Jagger's part. It was enough to put Jagger and Richard at loggerheads again. This state only worsened when Jagger refused to back plans to go on tour to launch the album. To Richard this was tantamount to sabotage, especially with it being their first release with CBS. But Jagger remained intractable.

His obdurate stance was rooted ostensibly in his belief that the rest of the band were not in good enough physical shape for the rigours of touring. He also freely confessed to needing a change. There was more to life than leading the Rolling Stones. If all this was leading up to a solo tour, his old playmate had a message for him. 'If Mick tours without the band,' Keith said with a touch of menace, 'I'll slit his fucking throat.'

16

UNDER PRESSURE

KEITH RICHARD'S COMMENT was guaranteed to excite press interest. They had been poised to expose the Stones' internal feuds for a long time. The magazine *USA Today* devoted a three-day spread to the deadly rift between Jagger and Richard, which nobody had expected would cut so deep. When on 19 May the single 'One Hit To The Body'/'Fight' was released, its accompanying video seemed fully to corroborate the claims.

Shot at Elstree Studios in England the aggressive body language between Jagger and Richard, required to act out an on-screen fight, looked distinctly realistic. Richard later admitted that it almost mirrored the state of their relationship. No one could really argue that for the foreseeable future it was best for each to go his own way.

Despite Richard's anger, Jagger was contemplating his first solo tour. But not before he had released another solo album, and he didn't anticipate recording for that to commence until autumn. In the meantime he and David Bowie gave a special performance of

'Dancing In The Street' as part of the Princes Trust concert at the Empire Pool, Wembley. The fundraiser for Britain's rising number of unemployed was in the presence of the Prince and Princess of Wales. But the thrill of mingling with royalty escaped Jagger that night. He seemed dour and preoccupied.

On 21 July his single 'Ruthless People', the title track to a comedy starring Danny De Vito and Bette Midler, was released on Epic Records. It managed a meagre 51 in the charts before disappearing. Jagger seemed to put it behind him as with Jerry Hall he spent the remainder of the summer enjoying himself with the rest of the jet set.

In early August talk of his feud with Richard had at last died down when Jagger arrived at his French chateau for a few quiet weeks with his family. But just as he did so the Stones found themselves back in the spotlight, this time courtesy of a *News of the World* exposé of a relationship between teenager Mandy Smith and Bill Wyman. The crux of it was that their three-year long affair had begun when she was just 13. Because of that Scotland Yard were said to be taking an interest.

This worried Jagger. He was due to start work on his new album, the stepping stone to his first solo tour. For this entry visas had to be obtained for certain countries, and this kind of publicity was counter-productive to say the least. Jagger kept his head down but watched developments closely over the next few weeks. In the end no action was taken against Wyman as Smith (whom he later married) and her mother decided not to press charges. Mrs Smith, in fact, assured detectives that the affair had developed with her full knowledge and approval, which came as a huge relief, not only to Wyman.

Jagger wasn't noticeably at ease, however, when he arrived in LA in mid-September to begin work on his album. He had enlisted help from Dave Stewart of the Eurythmics, who was in demand as a producer/session man to the stars. While dining out with Stewart one night Jagger let his unease show when he took exception to a photographer trying to take his picture and lashed out at him.

His energies were put to better use when recording began two months later at the Dutch Wisseloord Studios in Hilversum. He was joined once again by Jeff Beck among others, and four weeks of hard work resulted in seven tracks, over half the album. A short break followed before work resumed on the other side of the world when Jagger switched production to the Blue Wave Studios in Barbados in early January 1987. Jerry Hall had accompanied him, herself en route ultimately to a modelling assignment in Paris. Some of her luggage was to follow, and it was when she went to collect this that the trouble started.

Hall had gone personally to Grantley Adams Airport to collect her things. There an airline official had brought to her attention a package said to have arrived for her, though not actually addressed to her. She didn't think it hers and said so. When pressed she suggested it be opened to resolve the matter. Unsuspectingly therefore, under the watchful eye of customs officers, she unwrapped 20lb of marijuana.

To her horror she was placed under arrest and taken to a cell for the night. She had been denied the chance to make a phone call, which meant that Jagger, busy recording, knew nothing of her arrest for a full six hours.

Next day before magistrate Frank King she denied that the drugs belonged to her or that she had any knowledge of them. The trial was set for 13 February, and £3000 bail was put up by Jagger. He had hired top Barbadian lawyer Elliott Mottley to represent her as well as flying in Hall's own US attorney Peter Partcher. Forced to surrender her passport and ordered to report twice weekly to Holetown police station Hall was trapped. Not only were her current assignment and her modelling career in jeopardy but also her freedom. The charge carried a potential custodial sentence.

To Jagger, it was clear his girlfriend had been set up. And from the start of the 16 February hearing it was obvious that the prosecution's case was slim. It fell apart when a customs supervisor admitted that he had previously lied to the court. But it nevertheless dragged on. For Jagger the suspense of waiting for the verdict exposed his real fears. He felt for Hall but was also worried about his own plans. 'It's a matter of guilt by association,' he commented. 'There will be countries that won't let me in to work. The attitude is that there is no smoke without fire.'

The verdict came after a laborious summing up, but King pronounced her not guilty. As the press corps enveloped the couple leaving court Hall reiterated her resistance to drugs adding, 'My only vice is Chanel.'

The crisis over, Jagger resumed work on his album, now at Right Track Studios. Hall, estimating her loss of revenue over the case at around £100,000, went on the chat-show circuit. The attention she received was never more so than when she broadcast on network TV that she and Jagger were to marry.

As talk grew that they would wed in Hall's home state of Texas, it was rumoured that Richard would be best man. This seemed unreliable information to judge from newspaper reports a week later. They told of a major row between Jagger and Richard over the former's plans for a solo tour.

'I'm not sure when it all started to go wrong,' Richard said, and blamed the loss of their former closeness on his friend having changed.

Wyman was more direct. 'Mick is the guilty one,' he stated unequivocally. 'He has decided to do his own thing and be famous in his own right.'

All of which made it clear that they saw this as the beginning of the end.

Jagger crisscrossed the Atlantic during July to shoot various videos, still anticipating October as the start of his tour. Just a month later this was postponed until the new year after a furious row had erupted in rehearsals between him and Jeff Beck. Jagger's office issued a statement that cited Beck's supposed reputation for being difficult, admitting mutual ill feeling.

'Jeff is a brilliant guitarist and will be very hard to replace,' it said. While not detracting from Jagger's strength as the Stones' anchor, cynics' suggestion that Jagger solo might need all the help he could get seemed supported by the reception to his new single. On 31 August 'Let's Work'/'Catch As Catch Can' was released, barely to breach the US or UK Top 40.

On the same late August day Jagger, with Hall, attended Dave Stewart's wedding. Amid the celebrations, there was no word of their own possible union. In any case Jagger's attention was focused on the emergence on 14 September of his second solo album *Primitive Cool*. Initial signs pleased CBS when it received universal critical acclaim across a broad spectrum of influential music publications.

Due to the well-documented background of hostility, people tended to interpret the lyrics of a couple of the songs as a jab at

Keith Richard. But overall the album was thought to set an optimistic, even virtuous, tone. There is little virtue in failure, however, especially for someone as ambitious as Jagger. When it struggled to reach number 26 in Britain and, worse, petered out at 41 in the American charts it was certainly no success.

This apparently left Jagger very bitter. He had tested his power without the Stones, only to find that it wasn't strong enough to allow him the freedom of a solo career. With his strong survival streak, if the Rolling Stones were a rock dinosaur he wanted out. 'I can't go on stage with them,' he said. 'They look like a bunch of pensioners. I don't need this bunch of old farts.' The trouble was that one look at how his second solo album had fared told him that he did.

It was hard too for him to accept the abandonment of his tour that autumn. The story behind Jeff Beck's departure began to emerge. Speaking to the press in early November the guitarist revealed that he had pulled out because of the low offer Jagger had made him to play in his backing band. He felt he was being valued no higher than any ordinary session man.

'Mick's problem is that he's a meanie. He is no better than a glorified accountant. I can't believe how tight he is,' Beck said.

He did hold out an olive branch by making it clear he could still be for hire for the right price. And he had agreed to appear on the video for Jagger's next single 'Throwaway'. The number released in America and Britain on 9 November was simultaneously matched with 'Say You Will'/'Shut Up Your Mouth' throughout the rest of Europe. But when Jagger's band was announced in February Beck was not in the line-up.

Beck had confidently challenged Jagger, 'If you want the best you have to pay for it.' Jagger's retaliation was to enlist Joe Satriani, presumably happy to accept the rates on offer. He would in a few years, be hailed as the greatest guitarist in the world. With two keyboard players, a drummer, bass player and second guitarist as well as a number of backing singers Jagger dug himself in at New York's SIR Studios for rehearsals. By the time these switched to Osaka in Japan, tickets for his first gig at the Tokyo Dome had sold out in one day. Estimates were that he would earn £1 million per night on his short Far East assault.

It began on 15 March 1988 at Osaka's Castle Hall before

11,000 fans. As it did so, Jagger appeared to be in a particularly reflective mood. Perhaps it was a combination of anxiety and nerves and a delayed response to all the preceding aggravation that had led up to this moment that made him talk as he did to Michael Lindsay-Hogg.

'I was there to film the tour as Mick had a lucrative deal with Fuji to produce eight shows, and I walked into his dressing room on opening night before he was due to go on stage. He was sitting in a barber's chair about to have his hair seen to, and I asked him how he was doing.

'He replied, "I'm fine. Really, I'm fine. I just didn't know that this would be my life. Years ago, it was fun, there were plenty of girls and stuff, but I didn't think that 25 years down the line I'd be doing the same thing."'

Lindsay-Hogg accompanied Jagger throughout that ten-day trip, during which his friend revealed more of his inner feelings.

'We realized that to fulfil Fuji's requirements we would need more footage, and so one day Mick and I with a handheld camera went out alone to do some filming. He relaxed as time went on and he said to me how much of a relief it was not to have the other Stones around. It was like it had been a big weight on him all these years, keeping it together. To me he saw himself as a middle-aged man secure within himself but recognizing that a certain amount of his life had gone already.'

Jagger's hopes of a solo career were perhaps both driven and compromised by this thought. At any rate some vague insecurity prevented him from allowing himself full rein on stage.

'In the sixties with the Stones he shot from the hip. By now, though his performances were good enough, they were fairly programmed. Each night it was like he pushed a button, and he'd be on this part of the stage doing this thing at this part of this song, and another at another. It was a step-by-step routine. It wasn't fresh or spontaneous any more.'

It could be argued that in Japan there was nothing wrong with this as Lindsay-Hogg concurs.

'The audiences were highly regimented and disciplined. Once in the halls they're instructed by loudspeaker which rows can take or leave their seats and so on.'

It was when this extreme order was suddenly challenged that the tour almost ended in tragedy.

'In each show there was a time when Jagger came off to change his clothes,' Lindsay-Hogg explains. 'This night his guitarist was playing away as usual, and Mick came up with the idea of returning to the stage from the mixing booth which stands in the centre of the auditorium. His security team were immediately worried, but Mick wasn't because he thought the Japanese were too orderly for there to be a problem. However, he took two bodyguards with him, Jim Callaghan and Rocky, a martial-arts expert, who flanked him either side. He got to the booth relatively unnoticed in the dark and then started to sing into his microphone as he walked towards the stage, some 200 feet away while the startled audience parted, in theory, to let him through.

'Well, it has to have been the shock, the fact that they'd never had a star literally in their midst before, because suddenly they completely lost all their inbred control and mobbed him in a very alarming way. I was shooting the video from the stage, and this wasn't artificial. He was in real trouble, and we in the crew all knew it and could do nothing about it. The situation was desperate, and through the camera I could see stark fear in Mick's eyes.

'However, Callaghan is a serious character in an emergency, and he finally got Mick to the stage. He was white-faced and in a sweat. When the Japanese released the video they had edited out the mob scene because they didn't think it politic to show Japanese kids breaking ranks. But for Mick and for me, it's a hairy moment we will never forget.'

By the time Jagger sang his last note at the Nagoya International Exhibition Centre on 25 March over 250,000 Japanese fans had flocked to see him. Flushed with this success, when he returned to New York he was gratified to be inundated with offers from US and Australian promoters to tour their countries. Around the same time he received another kind of offer, this time a tasteless one from an Australian businessman reportedly keen to part with $20 million for Jagger's ashes when he dies in order to make egg timers! Jagger would scarcely have had time to be appalled at such a sick suggestion before he found himself at odds with someone who, in contrast, wanted money from him.

His name was Patrick Alley, a Jamaican reggae singer from the Bronx, and he had raised an action accusing Jagger of copyright infringement over the début solo single 'Just Another Night'. The plagiarism charges were to be heard at White Plains Federal Court in New York State, and Jagger appeared personally when the case opened on 18 April. Alley, who claimed he wrote the song (featured on his own 1982 album *Just A Touch of Patrick Alley*) in 1979, accused Jagger of having copied both music and lyrics and had originally raised objections in January 1986. Now he was suing Jagger and CBS for around $7 million. Jagger strongly denied the charge.

It turned out to be an unusual hearing, during which, in order to demonstrate different techniques and to prove various points, instruments were set up and played in court. Jagger on occasions burst into song from the witness box, singing snatches of Stones' standards like 'Jumpin' Jack Flash' and 'Brown Sugar', which had fans in the public gallery joining in. He also played a series of tapes to take the six-member jury stage by stage through the development of the track. Even lawyers on both sides squeezed out a few lines to elucidate a point.

During the week-long trial, presided over by Judge Gerard L. Goettel, Jagger arrived daily ten deep in bodyguards. During the breaks in proceedings he managed to sign autographs and pose for photographs. The carnival atmosphere became inappropriate when fans broke through the courthouse door. And there was nothing lighthearted about what was at stake. Finally on 26 April, after two days of deliberation, the jury ruled in Jagger's favour. Outside the court he told reporters he thought the trial had been a waste of everybody's time and added, 'My reputation is really cleared.'

It was a different aspect of his reputation that preoccupied the media that spring. Just after the court case ended Jagger had to turn away from his rollercoaster professional life to face the turmoil brewing within his family. He had not been so involved in other things that he had not kept himself informed about his daughter Jade. Recently he had put his foot down to prevent his then 16-year-old daughter from appearing in a movie as a prostitute.

The British press fondly applauded this display of paternal outrage. Along with Bianca, Jagger also vetoed her plan to leave school for a lucrative modelling contract, which intervention was again viewed as the proper action of a protective father. When Jade, now 17, was expelled, however, from St Mary's School for a dawn assignation with Josh Astor, the 21-year-old son of Lord Kagan Astor, there was huge amusement value in the idea of a middle-aged rock star being given the runaround like that.

Jade pleaded misery at school and her love for Josh, but it hadn't taken Jagger long to discover that Astor, living on his inheritance, was attracted to celebrity offspring. Jade was only one of several. On top of this he had the measure, even if she had not yet, of fortune hunters and was automatically suspicious. Still he liked to shrug off as media invention the image of being a strict father who vetted his daughter's boyfriends, probably deeming it unStone-like. He later also maintained that he and Jade had joked about her expulsion from school. That he did no more than tick her off and tell her she was daft.

But when caught and brought before the school authorities Jade had reportedly cried, 'My dad will kill me! What shall I do?' It was also said that Jagger was in fact absolutely furious and had dragged her off to the Loire chateau to read his daughter the riot act.

The domestic turmoil continued. That summer Jerry Hall became the most restless she had been in years. She had delivered an ultimatum, either he marry her by their approaching tenth anniversary, or else. Jagger didn't react, but he became aware that she had then set about trying to strengthen her financial base so that if it came to a split from him she would have no worries. Independence, always so vital to Hall and appealing to Jagger, now took on a different hue. Jagger watched warily as she became involved in launching her own swimwear line and signed contracts for a range of TV advertising deals that in total brought her in close on £1 million.

To try to bring him into line she also played her trump card. Trading remorselessly on his well-known weak spot for being shown wanting she sought the company of other men, titled ones in particular, a double manipulation. Her amorous antics reportedly included flirtations with Lord James Neidpath and Count Adam Zamoyski. But it seems to have been her supposed association with Lord David Ogilvy, more her own age and extremely handsome, that riled Jagger most.

It has been privately alleged that Jagger's reaction to any

perceived flirtations could range from persuasive threats to looking the other way. The latter especially so if the aristocrat in question were someone with whom Jagger wanted to stay acquainted. Whether or not any of this has any foundation it is safe enough to guess that his pride might have been dented. It was no surprise then, after a few weeks, that he left for the Caribbean with Camilla Nickerson, a 23-year-old British model, in a tit-for-tat response.

Before the gossips could make too much of this, they came back together as quickly as they had separated. Like Jagger, Jerry Hall fancied a film career. Critics once described the extent of her talents as an ability to give an imitation of a teapot, and Hall, tired of being offered only sex scenes, ruefully christened herself 'the Bedroom Girl'. However, she had landed a small part in the Hollywood movie *Batman*, as well as the role of Cherie in a stage production of *Bus Stop*. By opening night for the latter, at Montclair College Theater, New Jersey on 26 July, Jagger was devotedly on hand to witness her stage début. The celebration afterwards doubled as a birthday party as Jagger turned 45. He had won her back in an appeal for unity for the sake of their children. But there was still no sign of a serious offer of marriage. This left them knowing they had only papered over the cracks in their relationship. It was something with which Jagger was familiar in other aspects of his life.

Although it must have been galling, Jagger had contacted the rest of the Stones to request a meeting. Months before, on May 18, for the first time in two years all five band members had met up in a suite at the Savoy Hotel in London. In an attempt to seize the initiative, Jagger had launched into a long speech, the essence of which was to renew his allegiance to the band. Something he now maintained had never really wavered. After initially giving him a hard time the others did not take long to follow suit, until they were all in danger of falling out again over who was the sorriest.

'We sat down, rowed like crazy for a day and stopped slagging each other,' Jagger revealed. Realizing their mutual dependency, the upshot was that they had tentatively discussed plans to work together again the following year, to release an album and possibly tour.

Bill Wyman, who had previously doubted that the band had any future, staunchly maintained that its revival hung on Jagger and Richard's reconciliation. And, although when Jagger had left Britain for America in mid-August he had happily announced to waiting press at Heathrow that the Stones were to get back together, that was still very much in the balance when the pair met up in New York to begin adding some detail to this overall game plan. The tenuous nature of the alliance, clear at that meeting, could only be made worse when Jagger had to leave the next day for San Francisco. There rehearsals were booked for his forthcoming solo tour of Australia, previously arranged, and something that had to be honoured.

His six-week trip kicked off on 22 September at the Boondall Entertainment Centre in Brisbane and ended on Guy Fawkes night at the Western Spring Stadium in Auckland, New Zealand. The stage sets were ever more elaborate with inventive stunts to match. But the fog of dry ice around Jagger, prancing and pumping his way through each night, couldn't conceal the reality behind it. As in Japan, his performance was a strictly programmed piece, its glitz and glamour something of a substitute for the old energized thrust. Though Jagger turned in a polished performance he appeared a rather remote, isolated figure in the centre of it all.

If the reason for this was that his mind had been on the bigger picture of what would come of the Stones' intended reunion, it was hardly surprising. Throughout the tour he had been preoccupied with what Keith Richard was doing on the other side of the world.

Talk is Cheap, Richard's début solo album, had been released on 4 October and performed substantially better than *Primitive Cool*. It had reached number 24 in the American charts by the time he was rehearsing in New York with backing band the X-Pensive Winos. More to the point, he had been doing the round of interviews to promote his new album, during the course of which his views on Jagger and their by now infamous rift were always in danger of becoming the main focus. No one was tuning in more closely to these remarks than Jagger himself.

The guitarist had come a long way from his former hostility towards Jagger. Instead he was now heaping praise on the friend he chose to remind all dated from childhood. But before Jagger could become too complacent there were other less complimentary remarks. To begin with Richard revealed how frustrating it had been suddenly to be picked up again just as he had embarked on creating his first solo album, expected to jump to attention simply because Jagger was ready. Sending a few home truths the singer's way via this medium Richard also described him as suffering from a Peter Pan complex and, in a roundabout way, accused him of believing he was semi-divine.

The essence of this public soul-baring was that Jagger's and Richard's problems were more complex than the wildest press speculation. Richard had no difficulty in pinpointing now the moment he believed it had all gone wrong. To him it was when he felt he had sorted out his drug problems and was ready to return to active service, prepared to participate fully in the running of the band. By then Jagger had come to consider this his domain.

A week before Jagger's Australian trip ended, and he returned to London, Richard announced his own solo tour with the X-Pensive Winos. He was tackling America first, and the first gig in Georgia was a sell-out the day it was announced. Knowing what his own hopes had been, it must have crossed Jagger's mind that Richard might by chance enjoy the kind of solo success he himself had wanted. That he might now discover what it was to have his career suspended by someone else's plans. It was not an eventuality Jagger had probably ever considered. And one that was distinctly undesirable. All he could do was helplessly watch and wait.

17

MARRIAGE OF CONVENIENCE

RICHARD'S RECENT MORE conciliatory tone made it easier for Jagger to face a meeting with him in Barbados in January 1989. There was a great deal riding on this two-man summit for the whole band. Richard had arrived at the recording studio none too hopeful. He had told his wife that he'd either be right back or would return in a few weeks. When within minutes of coming face to face they began yelling at each other, it looked to be the former. However, the storm blew over, and they managed to bury their differences. They consolidated their reunion by setting straight to work, writing three songs together in quick succession. If, with this hurdle jumped, Jagger imagined that everything was fine, he was wrong.

He already knew that the Rolling Stones were to be inducted into the coveted Rock 'n' Roll Hall of Fame. Its annual ceremony at the Waldorf Astoria in New York on 18 January seemed the perfect occasion to showcase the formal end of his hitherto much publicized rift with Richard. But then trouble in the band –

specifically, deep discontentment on Bill Wyman's part – spoilt things once again. His boycott of the ceremony would prevent them performing as the Stones and thus damage any hopes of showing a united front.

The bass player had dismissed the award as being too little, too late. But it was ironic that he craved such conventional recognition when their whole career had been sustained upon being anti-establishment. The new problem went deeper than this one issue, though, and even before Jagger, with Richard, left Barbados to travel to New York, word was out that the Stones were secretly looking for a new bass player.

Still, Jagger was in his glory at the star-studded event at the Waldorf Astoria, accepting the plaudits, while the rock world fêted their rebel leaders. Or at least three of them. Ron Wood was there, but Charlie Watts, like Wyman, stayed away. But even on such a night the latest upheaval that threatened to unsettle the Stones was never far from the surface. Especially when, at one point, Mick Taylor joined them on the podium. While some kept their eyes on how genuine the shared laughter was between Jagger and Richard, others considered the possibility of Taylor rejoining the group, shifting Wood on to bass and thereby ousting Wyman.

The band's future line-up could only be a matter of conjecture, with Jagger most preoccupied with the present, especially mending fences with Keith Richard. First there was an album to be cut, preferably backed by a major tour, and by early March all five Stones were cocooned in a Barbados recording studio. Backtracking from his earlier complaints Wyman now credited the band's long separation with having brought about a rejuvenation. But by any definition it was a five-way marriage of convenience, in which they individually had one very good reason for putting up with each other.

It was fortunate that common sense had replaced pride. It paid a handsome dividend when talks with promoters about a US/Canadian tour culminated on 15 March. With Toronto-based CPI, the Stones were to sign, once again, the most lucrative contract so far in rock-music history. The tour would embrace more than fifty dates and commence in September, but there was a lot to achieve before then.

Work on their first new album in three years moved from

Barbados to AIR Studios, Montserrat. After a month there 16 original tracks had been recorded. Whether it was the need to capitalize on their newfound rapport or fear that it could easily disintegrate again, the album was put together in the fastest time since the mid-sixties. For the mix they opted for Olympic Studios in Barnes, London, which they hadn't used for years. There was to be one further link with the past with the guest musicians invited to play on the track 'Continental Drift.'

It came about when Richard passed Jagger a letter received from Bachir el Attar, a Moroccan musician, who offered the services of his group of Master Musicians to contribute to the Stones' new album. Their link with the band was an old and tenuous one, via Brian Jones, who had heard and enjoyed the sufi music played by Bachir el Attar's father in the sixties.

Bachir el Attar, now in his mid-twenties, married to photographer Cherie Nutting and living in New York, had read about the Stones' new tour and had come up with an idea.

'I waited about two months before I got an answer from their manager saying that maybe we could do one song with them.' It was agreed eventually that they would like to have them play on one track, and Jagger, Richard and Wood went with a BBC *Arena* film crew to record the event in Morocco.

'We recorded "Continental Drift" with them for their new album, and it was fun,' recalls Bachir el Attar. The BBC also separately taped interview material with the three Stones for an *Arena* special, 'Stones in Morocco'.

Back in Britain Jagger talked in an off-guard moment to a journalist, admitting that individually the Stones had very little in common. When asked to answer the eternally provocative question of who was the group's leader, Jagger answered 'Me!'

If this annoyed the others it had to be hidden when on 11 July they staged an unusual press conference formally to announce their 'Steel Wheels' tour, also the title of their forthcoming album. On a flatcar of a train they pulled into New York's Grand Central Station to be greeted by hundreds of reporters and noisy fans held at bay by a cordon of police. Deflecting the now expected calls as to whether or not this was their farewell tour, Jagger played down any past remarks of his own or the other Stones about their differences. That done he left New York for Washington, Connecticut, where the band had turned a former girls' school into their rehearsal base.

Now that the ball was in play Jagger warmed to the no-risk venture ahead. It would rake in millions not only in ticket and record sales but also from merchandising. He even participated in a truly embarrassing promotional video for Rolling Stones Rockwear. This was a line of designer clothes and accessories to be available at concert venues and through a chain of Rolling Stones boutiques intended to be set up in US department stores countrywide. This latter seemed proof that the genuine rock rebels had finally sold out.

What Jagger had still never quite learnt to live with was the downside of his notoriety. The security measures implemented at their rehearsal base had converted the school into a virtual fortress. There was reinforced fencing and steel gates patrolled by armed guards, whose diligence had drawn complaints from nearby residents. Their oppressive presence was justified. In late August police insisted on affording Jagger extra round-the-clock protection after renewed Hells Angels' threats to kill him on stage.

Three nights later the Stones opened their first tour in seven years, appropriately enough at the Veteran Stadium in Philadelphia. Jagger stuck out his chest, jutted his jaw and wiggled his way through the performance with his much-loved trademark sneer an effective mask for all his anxiety. They went down a storm, which set the tone of the entire tour.

Prior to the tour commencing the single 'Mixed Emotions'/ 'Fancyman Blues' had trailered *Steel Wheels'* release. The album reached number 3 in America and 2 in Britain, their highest UK placing for eight years, although in contrast the single 'Rock And A Hard Place'/'Cook Cook Blues' failed to ignite. By the time they completed six gigs in New York's Shea Stadium in late October a slew of awards brought their total for album sales in America up to 15 platinum and 32 gold. But it was the live performances that earned the best accolades with the Stones comfortably retaining their 20-year-old crown as the world's greatest rock 'n' roll band. Jagger now was personally exalted as a major rock icon.

It was their most ambitious tour, staged with ostentatious set designs, giant video screens and rounded off by spectacular firework displays. Only the old-school Stones' fans, the die-hard faithfuls who had seen the Stones in the sixties, might have been disappointed. They were now faced with a combination show/variety act with some ten session musicians and backing singers who joined the band on stage. Still the fans came in their thousands. The compromises involved to coax the five Stones back together again had been more than worth it.

But if Jagger had entertained any notion of having his ego stoked by the countless attendant groupies, he was stifled by Jerry Hall's presence on tour with the children. The Stones' cavalcade had turned into a family affair with none of the band travelling solo. But even that didn't stop Jagger from flirting outrageously.

After almost four months the biggest grossing tour in rock history came to an end at Atlantic City's Convention Center on 20 December. It would revive in the new year with a Japanese leg, and when tickets went on sale for their ten Tokyo Dome dates, 500,000 of them sold out in 20 minutes.

Back in England, Jagger and Hall temporarily swopped roles as he supported her in her stage role in *Bus Stop*, which opened at the Palace Theatre, Watford, on 25 January 1990, later transferring to London's West End. She had recently reiterated her announcement that she and Jagger were to marry. While it could have been a ploy to hype interest in her appearance in the play, it was more likely to have been an act of desperation. She was well established as Jagger's girlfriend and as such attracted huge attention.

The previous year the press reported that Jagger and Hall had successfully sued a newspaper for damages. It had overstepped the mark by publishing photos of them naked in the bathroom of their home, taken by long-range lens. Admitting an invasion of the couple's right to privacy, the paper in question had apologized and paid up. But this was just one example of the obsessive media interest in the pair now hailed as rock's First Couple. But for Hall this kind of partnership wasn't enough. She had marriage as her goal. If Jagger sensed her restlessness, he wasn't saying as he forged ahead with his own pursuits and left Britain for Japan.

His return there this time with the Stones was a blistering success, from the first date on St Valentine's Day until the mini tour's end on 27 February. All ten gigs had been recorded for Japanese TV and radio and maintained their run of breaking all existing records. Jagger basked in the rash of nominations he, the band and their records attracted in the annual *Rolling Stone* magazine polls, though this wasn't his only source of satisfaction. Jerry Hall's stage commitments had meant that she couldn't travel with him now. It appeared Jagger had taken advantage of her absence when the tabloids reported him in the company of a mysterious blonde. Jagger, anxious that Hall shouldn't believe the gossip, bombarded her with flowers, long-distance phone calls and cards of reassurance.

It wasn't his liking for women, however, that kept him in the public eye after the phenomenal success of both the US and Japanese tours, with the inevitable European leg about to get under way. It was rather Angie Bowie's decision to tell US chat-show queen Joan Rivers on network TV about the time many years before when she had come home to catch her husband and Jagger naked in bed together. She did not, however, witness any impropriety.

In the midst of band rehearsals in Normandy, Jagger reacted with extreme anger. He had erased all trace of his once ambiguous sexuality, and many of the fans now coming to Stones' gigs were too young to remember that phase at all. The last thing he wanted was to risk alienating them. He is said immediately to have contacted David Bowie to issue a joint denial of his ex-wife's accusations. But Bowie allegedly declined.

One group of people not interested in this personal sideshow were Gun, the Scottish band chosen to support the Stones on their 'Urban Jungle' tour.

'We had just released our first album and were touring America,' lead singer Mark Rankin recalls, 'when half way through the six-month stint after we had played in this little bar in Texas, I got a call about 7 a.m. from Dante, our bass player, who just said, "We're supporting the Stones!" He'd got the news from the tour manager, and I asked "Which gig?" thinking it was maybe Hampden Park in Glasgow. Dante replied that he thought we were doing the whole lot, and I just couldn't take it in.'

It sounded like a wind-up, but as the morning progressed details unfolded, and Rankin like the rest of Gun discovered that they had been invited to join the Stones for two-thirds of their European tour starting on 18 May.

'I'll always remember seeing the 51 artic lorries with the Stones' equipment lined up and us rolling up in a small split van, front compartment for us and the back for the gear. A roadie ran up asking, "When's your gear arriving?" We thumbed behind us, "That's it!"'

To Gun the Rolling Stones were an institution.

'I'm too young to have been into them,' admits Rankin, 'but "Baby" Stafford, our guitarist was a huge fan.'

'That first evening we settled into our trailer as nervous as hell. Time seemed to drag suddenly, and when somebody looked out of the window and said, "Here's Mick Jagger coming," we all groaned, "Yeah! Sure!" But the door opened, and in he walked. He came up to each of us, offering his hand and saying, "I'm Mick."'

'By this time we're gaping at him muttering, "Well, yeah, we know!" He gets to our manager and says again, "I'm Mick," and he jokes, "Sorry. What's your name?" and Mick burst out laughing, which completely broke the ice.

'Mick told us, "Listen, I hope everything goes cool for you tonight. Don't worry, and it'll be fine." We really appreciated that because it's not, by any means, what normally happens when you support big names. We walked on that night in front of 55,000 people. At this point we'd only once played in a huge stadium when we had opened for Simple Minds at Wembley. I glanced to the right, and there was Jagger watching from the wings and Keith Richard stood over on the left-hand side. Just the thing to freak a guy completely out!'

Gun acquitted themselves well. Despite initial shyness over taking up the Stones' offer to mingle with them and their company back stage – an opportunity not always extended to support bands – they soon did so. Both Wood's and Richard's wives had joined the tour, but Jerry Hall with her *Bus Stop* commitments again left Jagger on the loose; something that would inevitably lead to trouble. On stage, however, he whipped up a storm each night.

'One evening in Hanover the Stones had to come through our dressing room to get to the stage,' recalls Rankin. 'Keith spotted a bottle of Jack Daniel's on top of the fridge. "The very chap," he said, grabbed it and took a huge slug of the stuff before going on. Keith plays any night with three-quarters of a bottle of something inside him, but I never saw the Stones play crap. They were rockin' every night.'

It was just how much Jagger was rockin' off stage that concerned Jerry Hall, and her fears seemed confirmed when he was pictured with a young beauty in a Munich club. What was worse was the girl claimed that the Stone had later gone home with her. Jagger's response, as it always was in a fix, was to send Hall flowers. The bigger the suspected damage, the bigger the bouquet. In this case he ordered £200 worth of orchids. He also went on record to deny more than talking to the woman, ending his press release, 'She is obviously making the most of this brief time with me.'

Following the release of 'Almost Hear You Sigh'/'Wish I'd Never Met You'/'Mixed Emotions' the tour passed through Switzerland before reaching Britain on 4 July for three gigs at Wembley Stadium. What had been intended to be their final date in Moscow, they were now informed, had been iced altogether. After the north of England they got back on track in Rome with a gig on 25 July, gigged through Italy and Scandinavia, paid their first visit to Czechoslovakia and honoured their Wembley dates with two performances finishing up a month later on 25 August.

Like the others Jagger was tired but exhilarated. The only disappointment was that this latest triumph hadn't been enough to float 'Terrifying'/'Rock And A Hard Place', the second single from *Steel Wheels*, released at the start of the month, higher than number 82 in the UK charts and that for only one week. Its failure paled into insignificance, however, against the fact that they had just completed over 100 shows spread over three continents, attracting a combined audience of over 6.25 million. US magazine *Entertainment Weekly* duly placed the Rolling Stones, for the first time, number 1 in the greatest rockers ever stakes, ahead of Elvis Presley, Bob Dylan and the Beatles.

As the tour ended everyone went their separate ways. Jagger, perhaps to assuage Hall, swept her off on a trek through Asia and the Far East, as if there had not been enough globetrotting in the last year. That summer his other idea of making up for almost eighteen months of lost time and countless rumours was to throw cash into house renovations. But Jerry still wanted only one thing. She had often joked to friends that she was always suspicious when Mick lashed out big on her but her mood had hardened and finally she issued her last ultimatum. Either he marry her and stop his womanizing or she and the children left.

Hall was a multi-millionaire in her own right and had no problem signing the kind of prenuptial agreement he'd insisted on, effectively intended to dissolve her rights to his estimated £100 million fortune. On 21 November 1990 they were married on the Indonesian island of Bali with only their children and Jagger's long time chauffeur Alan Dunn present. For years Hall had dreamt of a fairytale organza gown. Instead she wore a brightly coloured sarong that matched Jagger's own. They were married early evening in a Hindu ceremony in the grounds of a friend's hilltop house, after a number of traditional rituals had been observed. The ceremony was conducted by Banja, a holy man.

News of Jagger's sudden marriage quickly leaked out. His mother, Eva, rose to the occasion and pronounced Hall the ideal daughter-in-law, while Hall announced, 'I have never been so happy in my life.'

Two days later bride and groom were thousands of miles apart as she travelled to London, while Jagger flew to America. Before much more than a week had elapsed questions were being raised as to the legality of the wedding. The Hindu holy man had renounced the marriage, suddenly not convinced of the couple's genuine belief in the Hindu faith. The UK press reported that Jagger had inadvertently failed to register the marriage with the appropriate Balinese authorities within the stipulated period. When later asked whether or not his marriage was valid, Jagger's answer was vague.

To society columnists after a new dimension to the stories, Hall appeared anything but the blushing bride when she told them how Jagger had mended his ways.

'Now he doesn't drink,' she revealed, 'doesn't smoke and wants to go to bed early.' In the past the brash Texan would have been guaranteed to embellish on the latter, boasting about his prowess between the sheets. Now she said, possibly tongue in cheek, possibly not, 'It's a real bore.'

18

PLAYING AWAY

QUITE APART FROM the questions surrounding the legality of the Jaggers' marriage, by some standards he also failed to enter into the spirit of their union; certainly the pivotal part about forsaking all others. But Jerry Hall was not naive and already had a good idea of what she was letting herself in for.

As the Jaggers began 1991 on Mustique, photo journalists on a magazine assignment to the exclusive hideaway witnessed Hall at a beach barbeque hovering in the background, unconsciously fiddling with her wedding ring. She watched as her husband of barely six weeks flirted embarrassingly with several young women. One later remarked that it was insensitive, even by Jagger's standards, adding, 'but Jerry is obviously willing to put up with it.'

What Jagger had overlooked was that there was a limit to her patience. Especially when she began to harbour renewed fears over one particular woman about whom there had been on/off talk since the Urban Jungle tour. She was Carla Bruni, the blue-eyed Italian brunette whom Jagger had met through Eric Clapton. Born into a wealthy family, the exotic 21 year old was also a top model who had been romantically linked with a foreign royal prince and American magnate Donald Trump, all of which placed her in a different league to many of the other women Jagger had been associated with. Believing herself inured to his regular infidelities, and the discovery of unfamiliar telephone numbers on scraps of paper, Hall was confident she could handle all that. What worried her now was that, unlike past flings, rumours of an involvement with this woman had persisted for over a year.

The Stones' latest single had been 'Highwire', taken from the forthcoming album *Flashpoint*, both of which titles seemed appropriate now. While Jagger had walked a tightrope for a long time, somewhere in between these releases came the spark that lit the tinderbox. It was March when gossip suggested that Jagger was serious about Bruni, even though she apparently preferred Trump, and Hall exploded with jealous rage.

Such was the ferocity of her attack that Jagger packed his bags and stormed out. In the ensuing vacuum Hall began to panic. She panicked that by losing control she had given him the way out to trade her in for a younger model. And she immediately wrote him a frantic and apologetic letter begging his forgiveness; in one stroke demolishing the strong stand she had taken.

This letter was said to have been left carelessly on a bar table at a hotel in Barbados, where days later Jagger and Hall were dramatically reunited. A nearby guest claims to have seized the opportunity to read it as soon as the couple, engrossed only with each other, moved off for the privacy of a walk along the beach. The contents, according to the curious guest, are said to have included Hall's abject apology for being jealous and unsympathetic, pleas for him not to leave her and an assurance of his future freedom. So much so that she is alleged to have written, 'I won't mind if you fuck other girls. I'll do it with other girls and you too. I'll be good to you.' She ended, 'I don't want to change you at all,' thereby, if all true, making a rod for her own back.

After having been on the receiving end of Hall's wrath Jagger must have hardly been able to believe that she had capitulated so quickly and completely. She would live to regret the folly of making such a desperate offer, but for the moment they travelled together to America.

In Atlanta, Georgia, Jagger was due to start filming his scenes for the futuristic thriller *Freejack* with Emilio Estevez and Anthony Hopkins. It was an all-action part, and an experience he enjoyed. But the film was released later in the year to a tepid reception at the box office.

Shooting for *Freejack* had finished in the May, by which time Jerry Hall was pregnant again. She later admitted that trying for a third child was an attempt to rescue their rocky relationship. And, for the time being, they would try again at their marriage in the £2.5 million Downe House, an 18th-century Georgian mansion, overlooking the Thames from Richmond Hill.

But Jagger felt no compunction at putting into practice the licence that Hall had recently granted him. This was evident when the Stones regrouped at Twickenham Studios to shoot a video for 'Sex Drive', intended as the second single from *Flashpoint*. It involved Jagger lying on a couch attended by models wearing only cellophane dresses, and he apparently showed a transparent preference for one in particular, Lisa Barbuscia. Hyped as the Stones' raunchiest video, it went on an immediate collision course with TV censors. But it was the rumours that had begun of a romance between Jagger and Barbuscia that could have proved the most troublesome.

If Hall paid any heed to these rumours it didn't show as they spent the summer at La Fourchette. Surrounded by their celebrity friends they hosted elegant dinner parties and relaxing picnics beneath spreading chestnut trees. There were riotous cross-dressing parties too, when Jagger once imitated Madonna.

But with Stones' work currently in abeyance Jagger soon became restless, and his thoughts turned to starting work on a third solo album. In September Hall took the children to London, and Jagger headed to New York and the recording studio. What Hall didn't know was that that autumn he also apparently started seeing Carla Bruni again. He made every attempt at secrecy when it came to Bruni, but such is the media obsession with Jagger that it would not be long before it was made public.

Just as Jagger was heading for marital trouble again, professionally there were problems too. At the start of the year Bill

Wyman had been speaking his mind on US radio in generally unflattering terms about the Stones, and he had failed to turn up for 'Highwire's' video shoot. Although he did take part in the filming for 'Sex Drive', the speculation all year had been that he was ready to call it a day.

However, just as the Steel Wheels/Urban Jungle tour had silenced previous talk of leaving, so in mid-November a massive deal with Virgin Records temporarily quelled the rumours now. Richard Branson signed them up for three albums, and the package, to include the rights to their back catalogue post *Sticky Fingers*, was said to be worth £30 million. It was a tempting reason to stay. The music world took note that the Stones could still pull off one of the biggest deals in the industry's history. It also didn't pass unnoticed that when the band joined Branson for a celebration at a London restaurant, Wyman was not there.

Before long speculation would strengthen that the Stones were in line for another personnel change. Wyman's leaving would pose no risk to their lucrative Virgin deal, and it was likely that Jagger, with some justification, considered his own absence as being the only one ever capable of sinking the Stones. Inevitably he was asked to comment:

'If we have to get another bass player,' he declared, 'we will. I will even play bass if need be.'

As Hall entered the last weeks of her pregnancy, Jagger appeared a doting expectant father. In early December national newspapers devoted full-page coverage to a photograph of the couple strolling across Barnes Common together. On 11 January 1992 Jagger was photographed again, this time buying flowers from a stall to take to Hall, now in London's Portland Hospital. Next day at the private clinic Hall gave birth to a girl, Georgia May Ayeesha, but 24 hours later Jagger left mother and child and flew to Thailand. A curious press followed him to a rendezvous with Carla Bruni.

Reports broke that Jagger had booked them into a luxury villa at the Amanpuri Hotel in Phuket, where they were seen drinking by the pool and out on the town one night at a local club. Bruni denied that she was the dark-haired girl consorting with Jagger and insisted publicly that she scarcely knew him.

As humiliations go, this one took some beating, and Hall was devastated. 'I cried myself inside out when Mick went off with

Carla Bruni,' she later confessed. She also went into months of debilitating postnatal depression. In the immediate aftermath Jagger returned home and swore to Hall that there was nothing in the stories. He had not been with Bruni. She was unconvinced, however, and he was helpless to stop her ringing the model.

'I told her to leave my man alone,' said Hall, 'and she put the phone down on me.'

Issuing this kind of warning was not new. Just like Bianca before her, Hall seemed forever to blame the women for chasing her man. Still the hurt was too much, and she took the newborn baby and left him.

To date Jagger had thrived on his reputation as a womanizer, often emerging unscathed. But this time it was different, and, at Hall's insistence he agreed to seek marriage guidance.

Like the trouper she was by now recognized to be in her dealings with Jagger, Hall launched herself back into the old routine of speaking out publicly to bolster her lover and husband. But it was not long before Hall faced the fact that the marriage counselling wasn't enough. She later owned up, 'For a while I thought it was working, but Mick's never going to change. Both people have to be committed for these remedies to work. I don't know what the secret of keeping a man is,' she mourned. 'Maybe not being too possessive.'

No one could have accused her of that when she agreed to accompany Jagger in late May to New Haven to attend his eldest daughter Karis' graduation from America's Yale University. Jagger's friend Michael Lindsay-Hogg says that once Jagger recognizes that a child is his, he is a good father. His relationship over the years had indeed developed with his and Marsha Hunt's daughter. That summer too brought news of Jade, living with artist Piers Jackson on a Dorset farm. She had just given birth to a girl, Assisi, and Jagger rushed to her side.

A fortnight later, Jagger was back in the LA studio. Thousands of miles separated him and Hall, hardly improving their marriage. His every move was avidly reported by the press, Jagger's new status as a grandfather proving no deterrent to his womanizing. By the end of the month he was photographed with Kathy Latham, a stunning blonde, and other reports suggested that Carla Bruni was around again.

This latest betrayal was too much, and Hall opened her heart to reporters, 'It's unforgivable what's happened. I don't think there's any hope for us any more. I suppose we'll divorce. I'm in too much pain for this to go on any longer.'

That Hall was contemplating divorcing Jagger after only 20 months of marriage made front-page headlines around the world. Speaking out she admitted, 'I felt sick when I realized he was still seeing Carla Bruni. I honestly didn't know anything about it until it was in the newspapers.'

In interviews she reiterated that she didn't think that anything could save the situation but that did not stop her from squaring up to the woman she classed her most serious rival. As international supermodels it was inevitable that they would run into each other on assignment, and it was in Paris that they came face to face in a hotel lobby. Hall's temper snapped, and she's alleged to have called her fellow catwalk queen a tramp before hurling the usual edict about leaving her husband alone. To this Bruni countered by telling Hall to pass on a message to Jagger that he should leave *her* alone.

While all this was going on, far from adopting a low profile Jagger was still a man behaving badly. But as press speculation accelerated about a divorce and the likely cost to him financially there was little contest between Jerry Hall and any other woman.

Jagger is a master of brinkmanship, particularly in gauging how far to push a relationship. It surprised few who really knew him therefore that just before matters went too far Jagger telephoned Hall and begged her to have him back. Pride made her hold out at first, which induced a second frantic tearful call. This time she relented. She laid down the strict condition that she would stand no more infidelity, leaving him in no doubt that he ought to have outgrown all that.

When she agreed to join him in America towards the end of August the paparazzi were treated to the sight of husband and wife dining out together in one of Dallas's best restaurants; an exercise staged to show the world they were back together. Carla Bruni, still never having publicly admitted to an involvement with Mick, was said privately by friends to have been upset that Jagger chose Hall over her. She has been quoted as revealing she believed for a while that autumn that she would never recover from the pain of her broken heart and issued the fatalistic warning.

'As for sleeping with married men. Don't do it. It's a ticket to pain, and it leaves you very bitter,' she said.

As soon as work finished on his solo album at the end of September Jagger took Hall on a romantic second honeymoon to consolidate their fresh start. By mid-December, feeling matters had quietened down domestically, Jagger focused his energies once more on his musical future and that of the Stones. His solo album, which he had originally planned to have released before now, was scheduled for early in the new year.

Before that the announcement that had been expected for a long time that Bill Wyman was leaving the Stones came on 6 January 1993. Wyman called it quits live on the TV show *London Tonight*. He spoke of taking with him many special memories of wonderful times, but at 56 he confessed that he didn't want to do it any more. Displaying an assumed indifference Jagger said, 'I don't think it will faze us that much.'

He was indeed absorbed in other things, in particular in assessing the fortunes of his third attempt to go solo. On 25 January his single 'Sweet Thing'/'Wandering Spirit' was released on Atlantic Records. Although the number fared substantially better in Britain than it did in America, neither chart made sweet reading. Two weeks later it was a different story when his solo album *Wandering Spirit* followed. It reached number 12 in the UK, 11 in the States and was hailed his best yet. For it he would also collect a gold disc for sales in Germany.

After playing the Webster Hall in New York, his confidence riding high, Jagger left America with Hall to join their children in France. Spring would see him teaming up with Keith Richard at Blue Wave Studios in Barbados to commence work on a new Stones album, and the release of Jagger's second solo single from *Wandering Spirit* on 1 April, 'Don't Tear Me Up'/'Put Me In The Trash' could have mirrored Hall's still bruised sentiments when on a recent trip to America Jagger had been spotted in a crowded New York club talking to Australian supermodel Elle McPherson, nicknamed The Body. Jagger just being seen in the company of yet another world famous model was enough to make Jerry jittery that he was set to make a fool of her all over again.

19

ROUÉ OF ROCK

BY THE TIME Jagger threw a fancy dress party to mark his fiftieth birthday no Stones bass player had been named as Bill Wyman's replacement. However, when he, Keith Richard and Charlie Watts joined Wood at Ron's home studio in Ireland to begin work on the band's new album a variety of guest bassists came and went, among them Darryl Jones and Doug Wimbish. Because Wimbish had joined Jagger's 1988 solo tour, it seemed a fair bet that he was favourite to fill the slot. But after work ended in September, only to resume early November at Windmill Studios in Dublin, it was Darryl Jones who joined them for the five-week recording session.

It had been 24 years since a Jones had featured in the Stones' line-up, a fact that attracted comment just as nostalgia was heightened over the band's latest release. The new anthology album, *Jump Back,* included golden oldies from as far back as 1971. Maybe it was being temporarily touched by the past that took Jagger from mixing work in LA to record a version of 'Angie' in January 1994 for inclusion on a tribute album to Brian Jones. *The Symphonic*

Music of the Rolling Stones was released on RCA in spring.

Before that Jagger had headed to France to spend Easter with Jerry Hall and their children. It was difficult to gauge the true state of their relationship for he had spent much of the past twelve months in recording studios around the world and would soon be leaving her again as the band were due to begin preparation in April for a massive world tour. None of this was conducive to reinforcing marital harmony.

The Voodoo Lounge world tour was announced in New York on 3 May from on board a yacht at anchor on the Hudson River. As usual the media flocked to the press conference/photo call, where Jagger, in trenchcoat and dark glasses, escaped the accusation of looking like a bank manager. That was levelled instead at grey-haired Charlie Watts in his smart double-breasted suit. Sections of the press found it hard to resist remarks about their age, calling them 'the dinosaurs of rock'. What no one could deny was that the Stones still knew how to put on a show.

Retiring from the public gaze after the announcement, Jagger immersed himself in band rehearsals in Toronto until early July, when the single 'Love Is Strong' was released. Presumably waiting for the album, American fans held back, and it merely got to number 91 in the charts there, although it rose to 14 in Britain. When *Voodoo Lounge* followed a week later, however, it topped the UK charts and lodged at number 2 in the States, providing a healthy springboard for the North American leg of their world tour that kicked off on 1 August at the RFK Stadium in Washington, DC.

With Darryl Jones making his début stage appearance with the Stones, Jagger looked nothing like his age as he launched himself on an all-out offensive to shake off the veteran tag attached to him by the press. He succeeded so well that 'You Got Me Rocking', their next single, released on 26 September, could have been an audience anthem. In a crowded and competitive industry with a new generation of rock front men snapping at his heels, Jagger was determined to secure his domination and hold on to his crown. His best weapon in this battle he showed every sign of winning was his prodigiously high energy level. As the band gigged all over America and Canada critics repeatedly marvelled at his endless stamina and appetite for performing.

However, it was his zest for off-stage performances that worried

Jerry Hall, and her worst fears were confirmed ten days after another Stones single 'Out Of Tears' was released on 4 October. Touring gave Jagger the opportunity for sex with other women that he found too tempting to resist. Whether it was arrogance or just a risk he thought worth taking, everything fell apart in Las Vegas when the Stones arrived there for a gig at the MGM Hotel. Despite his vow in particular not to see Carla Bruni again, he was still in contact with the model. Judging, that was, by a fax message from her to Jagger urging a secret rendezvous, which Hall, on a visit, stumbled across at his hotel suite.

Hall went ballistic and for a second time walked out, incensed by what she called Jagger's infatuation with the Italian. They seemed once again to be on the verge of a divorce. This time sketchy details of possible terms were even revealed. Hall was said to want no money for herself, only to remain at Downe House with the children and to enjoy the use of their Mustique holiday home.

If this sounded horribly for real, there was not a lot Jagger could do about it in the immediate future. He was still committed to several weeks on the road. And now no lavish bouquets, customized pieces of jewellery or even sexy lingerie was likely to work. His friendship with Bruni was the focus of rampant showbiz gossip, and, speaking later of the hurt this caused her, Hall revealed, 'Sometimes I was absolutely heartbroken, but I was the loving wife.' Battle lines were drawn, as friends began to take sides.

When the Voodoo Lounge tour broke for Christmas Jagger rejoined his wife. But whatever he were to promise her by then Hall had made it clear that nothing short of fidelity would do for her now.

The tour resumed in 1995. After the handful of Mexico City dates, a short South American trip, then two gigs in South Africa at the end of February, the Stones hit Japan for seven concerts at the Tokyo Dome, followed by two in Fukuoka. It was in Tokyo that Jagger came across English model Nicole Kruk, who was on a six-month modelling assignment in Japan. On his arrival in the capital Jagger had ordered some designer clothes and asked the modelling agency for whom the designer worked to introduce him to some of the girls. Kruk was one of the volunteers eager to meet the infamous Stone at his £1000 a night penthouse suite at the Okura Hotel.

Skilled in the art of seduction Jagger set the scene to his liking and posted bodyguards outside. His years of experience in communicating with strangers, particularly women, meant that within minutes he had put Kruk at her ease, making her feel as if he were an old acquaintance and encouraging her to do most of the talking.

'He doesn't really talk about himself,' she recalled, but what he did often do over the next two hours was make physical contact, touching Kruk's knee or arm ostensibly to emphasize a point. He brought the evening to an end after supplying them – Kruk had gone there with a friend – with tickets to see the Stones the following night.

In the morning Jagger phoned the agency asking to see Kruk that night after the show. Once again she went along with a friend. At one point when she went into the bathroom suite he followed after her and roughly kissed her on the neck.

'It was quite exciting in a way,' she confessed, 'but I thought it best to go.' Jagger may have had other ideas, but they were curtailed as a minder burst into the room shouting, 'Quick! Jerry's on her way up in the lift!' The two women were unceremoniously shown the back way out down a flight of stairs. 'Mick looked very worried, and I was panicking too,' Kruk recalled.

But Jagger had no intention of giving up on his pursuit of Kruk, and again it had more to do with ego than a particular desire for her, as she soon discovered. Kruk's experience perhaps confirms it is the chase he enjoys as much as anything else. He finally managed to get her into bed on the first night she returned to the penthouse alone. When she arrived Jagger was still dining, and his first kiss came after he spoon-fed her some dessert. As the hours passed she relaxed, all his instincts telling him that she was prepared to succumb that night. As she later revealed, however, the atmosphere abruptly changed.

From sensitive to savage is how she described it. This it seems was ignited by a throwaway wisecrack from actor Robin Williams in the comedy *Mrs Doubtfire*, which video had been playing in the background, that his film character's skin was so loose he looked like Mick Jagger. As Nicole creased with laughter, Jagger went wild.

'He started biting me,' she claimed. 'He was pretty rough. It was like I was a piece of meat.' Although she cried out for him to stop she admits to being thrilled by his hungry passion. As Jagger got carried away and covered her body in bites it was hard to say next day who was the more dismayed.

'When I looked in the mirror, I was horrified.' But when she teased Jagger, hitherto unmoved by the results of his handiwork, that she just might show it off to reporters he turned pale. For all that, they met one more time before the Stones rolled out of town. It was only a year later when recalling this brief fling that Kruk's naivety showed when she mourned, 'After we made love he would talk, but he never once said he cared for me.'

The stark reality was that there were in all likelihood other such occasions before the tour's end. On leaving Japan the band played dates throughout Australia and New Zealand to the accompaniment of their latest single from *Voodoo Lounge*, 'I Go Wild'. A few weeks later it was the untamed sounds from his earliest days that concerned Jagger when a 35-year-old recording of him with Keith Richard and Dick Taylor went under the hammer at Christie's. It sold for over £50,000, and it soon leaked out that the buyer had been Jagger himself.

As the tour's European leg got under way, on stage during one of the three summer Wembley Stadium gigs Jagger told the crowd, 'I know you're all worried about our new bass player, but this time we've got one that dances and smiles!' Wyman, whom Jagger knew was present that night, didn't appreciate the joke and stormed out of the stadium, furious. In contrast British music critics, happy to have the Stones play on home soil for the first time in five years, had been giving them glowing reviews.

As in the USA there was acknowledgement that, while they would always have their detractors, the Stones had somehow vaulted the ridicule barrier of still being on the go at their age. And more, they had done so with style. Jagger personally was hailed 'the most carnal singer in history', and they continued to break records right up until the year-long tour came to an end in Rotterdam on 30 August, having grossed in the region of £400 million along the way.

Rumours emerged in October of a forthcoming Stones unplugged album of acoustic numbers recorded at various recent European gigs. Then there was further trouble for Jagger when Orsolya Dessy, a blonde Hungarian porn model in the *News of the World*, claimed an encounter with Jagger, recalling his 'delving tonguey kisses' all over her body. Appropriately enough *Stripped*, the Stones' new album, followed days later and held on to number 9 in the charts at the turn of the year.

David Bowie once called Jagger a mother hen, but not of the farmyard variety, more, as he put it, 'like a brothel-keeper or a madame'. In 1996 it was Jagger's interest in the more risqué side of life that was thought to stand him in good stead for some screenwork. It was announced in June that he was about to take on the substantial supporting role of 'Greta', an androgynous nightclub trapeze act, in *Bent*, a gay love story to be shot in British locations that summer with Channel 4 backing. Director Sean Mathias, producer Michael Solinger and actors Sir Ian McKellen and Clive Owen had already signed up for the screen adaptation of Martin Sherman's drama, predicted to be one of 1997's most compellingly explosive films.

Jagger's character by day is George, a married family man who by night turns into Greta, the hostess who performs her highflying act dressed in a slinky sequinned dress, kinky boots and top hat, twirling a silver cane. While the film deals with life in an horrific concentration camp Jagger was most drawn to the decadence of the role, particularly the nightlife scenes in a shady Berlin club. To prepare he studied the social history of Germany in the thirties and revealed about the film, in which he also sings a Sherman number 'Streets of Berlin', 'It's a very hard-hitting and thought-provoking script, and it's a great ensemble to be working with.'

Work for Jagger's scenes began amid much secrecy on 4 July in the disused Braehead power station in Renfrew, Scotland. His performances in the two night shoots there were guarded by tight security measures that included the station being cordoned off and the surrounding streets patrolled by a small army of minders on the lookout for the press. As a film company spokesman confirmed to journalists held at a distance, 'Mick isn't here to do the big superstar bit, so he won't be playing along for the media.'

While Jagger concentrated again on this dimension of his career, his home life had almost inevitably begun fragmenting behind the scenes. Earlier in the year Jerry Hall had appeared in *Vogue* magazine wearing only a pair of skimpy briefs saucily pulled down.

Publication sparked outrage, and Jagger was said not to have appreciated what he deemed to be his wife's brazen behaviour.

He had hardly been seen at his Richmond Hill home for weeks. He had apparently booked into a hotel for convenience while decorating work was carried out at Downe House, but neighbours were quick to reveal that from the few glimpses they had had of Hall she looked too unhappy to raise her usual letterbox smile of acknowledgement. Grapevine gossip had it that several of Hall's friends, on their own initiative, reportedly paid for a private investigator to sit on Jagger's tail.

The private detective began building a dossier on the Stone's activities, and before long he logged reports of Jagger in London hot spots with women less than half his age. He was also on hand to photograph him leaving the exclusive Halcyon Hotel in Holland Park after spending the night there with a mystery woman. Jagger had been at a party the night before, from where he is said to have placed a call to instruct that the woman be installed and waiting for him in the second suite of the two he had booked under a false name. Hotel reception was supposedly under strict instructions to put any calls from Hall through only to the main suite.

With or without her sanction, the news that there was proof of Jagger's fresh infidelity must have been a blow to Hall at a time when her confidence was already shaky. In the light of recent tension, plans to celebrate her 40th birthday had been aborted. Whispers that their marriage surely was foundering this time grew strong, and reflecting on this period Hall later confessed, 'We tried so very hard, although there's nothing more humiliating than loving him so much that you forget the infidelities.' There was no chance of that a couple of months later.

Jagger's recent involvement in *Bent* had whetted his appetite for a world he now had aspirations of breaching via film production. To this end he had headed to Hollywood. It was there in mid-October that his world blew apart, literally in the burst of a flashbulb. According to celebrity snapper Russell Einhorn he caught Jagger in a dark corner of the Viper Room with Uma Thurman, newly voted the world's sexiest woman. Einhorn claimed that Jagger had been all over the actress, but his thrill at catching the Stone thus was short-lived when someone from behind knocked him out cold.

He came to to find himself helpless in the grip of Jagger's minders, with the film ripped from his camera and the couple gone. Naturally the incident hit the papers immediately, especially as Einhorn had reportedly filed a lawsuit in California's Superior Court seeking damages from Jagger for alleged assault. Jagger moved swiftly to issue a statement denying a relationship with Thurman.

Recently Jerry Hall had returned to the international modelling circuits of Milan and Paris, only to invoke memories of old hurt. In one show, for designer Vivienne Westwood, at which she was the main model, she ended up on the same catwalk as Carla Bruni. It is said that when Bruni discovered that Hall held centre stage, she threatened to walk out. Although she was persuaded to stay, the glares between the women whenever they passed each other dropped the atmosphere several degrees.

Hall had been already raw from this experience when she had had to try to close her ears to talk that Jagger in LA had been seen socially in the company of Pauline Stephaich. Tall and blonde like herself but younger, Stephaich is a member of the Mellon family, one of America's richest oil dynasties. Reports of the Viper Room allegations barely had time to register with her, when just 24 hours later Jagger featured again in the world's press with yet another young model, this time having been caught spending the night with her.

She was Jana Rajlich, the 28-year-old Czech ex-girlfriend of actor Dolph Lundgren. After partying the night away Jagger had slipped her into bungalow 3a in the grounds of the Beverly Hills Hotel. The coverage linking Jagger to Thurman had been just the day before. Now the newspapers were filled again with the story of how one reporter had called the bungalow early the next morning, and Rajlich had answered, seconds before Jagger had snatched the receiver from her.

As soon as the journalist mentioned Jerry Hall, Jagger swore and slammed down the phone. Rajlich's only quote would be, 'I have absolutely no comment about my friendship with Mick Jagger. I am not confirming it, and I am not denying it.' If she intended playing it coy, it was not clever of her to open the door an hour after that call wearing only a towel.

As the papers had a field day, for Hall it was the last straw, and she made headlines of her own by immediately consulting lawyers for a divorce. Under banners like JAGGER SENSATION the fact that Jerry Hall was divorcing Mick Jagger made front-page news for a second time around the world. But this time mainstream TV news also reported on it, and the story became hastily scheduled for debate on daytime magazine shows. Her choice of legal adviser provoked almost as much comment. She had called on the services of Cambridge-educated Anthony Julius, nicknamed 'Mr Genius' at his London law firm of Mischon de Reya. He had recently represented Princess Diana in brokering her divorce from the Prince of Wales and was reputedly one of the legal world's toughest negotiators.

Touted as Britain's 149th richest man, Jagger saw himself warned far and wide to brace himself for a £120 million divorce battle. There seemed scant consolation in the knowledge that Hall had signed a prenuptial agreement, or even the past rumblings that their 1990 Hindu marriage in Bali had dubious legality in Britain. As the woman who had shared almost 20 years of his life and borne him three children she would, if the wedding failed to be recognized in court, be merely talking palimony instead of alimony. The difference was infinitesimal when he weighed up the sums at which he would be looking. His one ray of hope was the immediate counter-speculation that sprang up. Hall's shrewd choice of lawyer and the chosen battleground of Britain pointed to her move being more indicative of a major skirmish, than war; even just a warning shot across his bows.

Marital bust-ups involving multi-millionaires have become a growth industry in which lawyers make a fortune. Settlements have hiked since Bob Dylan allegedly paid £7 million to buy his wife's lifelong silence. Experts estimated that in the UK Hall could expect a seven-figure settlement, but that she stood to claw in one-third of Jagger's wealth if she fought her case in America, as she was fully entitled to do. The press embarked on a frenzy of reporting, almost every column of which was devoted to turning up the heat on Jagger.

Hall maintained a dignified silence. Friends were said to be shielding her, but she was also on set for a substantial cameo role in the movie *RPM*, being shot in the mountains above Nice. Her only comment was, 'It's a private matter. I'm very upset.' But with as chequered a past as Jagger's, others inevitably had plenty to say.

Miles of newsprint was devoted to dredging up his long and colourful lovelife, featuring a whole gallery of glamorous women. There were no signs there of him growing old other than disgracefully.

It was now that Nicole Kruk chose to go public. Her response to the recent revelations was to express pity for him, which could only have turned the knife for Jagger.

'I feel sorry for him,' said Kruk, 'he obviously does what he does for his own self confidence. God knows what his wife thinks of him, but I hope I'm not like him when I'm his age.' She added, 'The news that his marriage has broken up doesn't surprise me. But I don't feel guilty. Mick is incapable of being faithful.'

Statistically speaking, 70 per cent of all rock marriages fail. But the consensus that Jagger's marriage appeared to be truly over was offset by a few of Hall's friends. They stressed that although she had consulted lawyers to draw up details of a split, she had not actually yet filed for divorce. Jagger might never have paid closer attention to the daily coverage about himself than he did now. There were, however, crumbs of comfort that he might be talking trial separation only .

'When Jerry went to see Anthony Julius it put the fear of God into Mick,' a friend said. 'She had put her foot down about Mick's playing around. She won't be made a fool of, but at the same time she loves him and wants to be with him. She made him very aware of how badly she was being treated by him, and certainly in the short term he will be behaving like a puppy dog.'

It might have been hard for Jagger to have seen it all as merely a stern attempt to bring him to heel when Hall ordered him out of the house. But cries were raised in his support that his behaviour should be analysed as a last angst-ridden mid-life crisis. He ought, it was suggested, to follow the example of other celebrities, such as *X Files* heartthrob David Duchovny, and book himself into a sex addiction clinic. Instead he took the children and fled to Dublin after cancelling a host of social engagements.

Whether the fallout would be as major as threatened, the nights of passion that had sparked off the trouble were already taking their toll as Jagger looked as haggard as Hall was miserable. Common sense said that he was all out of excuses and had exhausted his chances. But, then again, in the past Hall had shown remarkable resilience. To emerge in one piece this time, though, she would require some deft and delicate handling.

In the face of a drama played out in the glare of unrelenting coverage in the world's press the first shoots of reconciliation came surprisingly quickly. At the end of October friends began claiming that Jagger and Hall were reunited. It looked premature, however, when days later they individually attended a gala dinner in aid of the Royal Court Theatre. Of the two Jagger arrived first, alone, then Hall appeared flanked by two friends. In contrast to him, she looked in good spirits as they were seated around the same table. With all eyes on them, their body language spoke volumes, and it appeared as if she had recovered her equilibrium enough to be confident of having the upper hand.

She already suspected she had him on the run. The week before he had sent her an extravagant gift of a diamond and ruby necklace, which Jagger had the consolation of seeing that she was wearing that night. The freeze between them though was as glacial as any diamond, and his hopes of her warming to him seemed slim when she would scarcely look his way or speak to him. Initially, the more Hall chatted and laughed with their group, the more Jagger sulked. One table guest later admitted that the atmosphere was very awkward. By the end of the evening, though, it had thawed enough for Jagger to risk making his first public overture to his wife. As Hall rose to leave, again with her friends, Jagger also stood and leant over to try to kiss her. At the last second she averted her face, and his unwanted lips were left barely to brush her cheek.

Pictures of this became the latest instalment in the rock soap opera that attracted as much interest as ever. The confusing signals must have made it hard for Jagger to navigate his way through the mess. With a mixture of humility and contrition he got to first base by mid-November, both then said to be thrashing out their difficulties. It is thought that Hall enjoyed putting Jagger through some hoops, laying down stipulations and redrawing the ground rules. She was confident that against the financial haemorrhage of a divorce he might agree to just about anything.

Almost immediately Jagger whisked Hall off to Bali for a third honeymoon. On their return to London the continued scrutiny of the tabloid press showed signs that he was on a short leash. An extension was being built to Downe House, and whenever Jagger left his home to walk the few yards of pavement outside to inspect developments huddled up against the winter chill and looking grim, Hall was often hovering at the window equally solemnly watching him.

As the uphill struggle to earn his wife's trust got under way Jagger filled the vacuum left by Stones' inactivity by picking up the business ideas that had originally taken him to Hollywood the previous autumn. Smothered under the scandal of his personal life had been press reports that Jagger, via his new film production company Jagged Films, had met with his friend playwright Tom Stoppard to discuss the prospect of a movie of Robert Harris's bestselling novel *Enigma*. Stoppard had agreed to write the screenplay. Subsequent reports confirmed that the film was planned for 1997, with Jagger, Stoppard and legendary producer Michael White at the helm.

For nearly 30 years Jagger had wanted to become an actor but, notwithstanding his performance in *Bent*, his prospects of succeeding had dimmed with each successive film. Now he had changed tack and was applying his financial sense to an industry that attracted him and was forever in need of sound investors. His involvement is currently said to include plans to produce a dozen big-budget movies over a five-year span.

Whatever success Jagged Films may achieve, forging on in a new direction can only be a smart move. Still, hanging up his mike was not on his agenda just yet. After the Voodoo Lounge tour Jagger had declared that it had been too much fun to say that the Stones would never go on the road again. Sure enough, in late December 1996 the band were rumoured to have regrouped in Ireland to kick around ideas for a new album. Through next spring into summer the speculation continued until news broke on 1 August of an upcoming album to be backed by a world tour, both to be called Bridges to Babylon. One month's rehearsal would take place in Canada but as Jagger made ready to fly out, his attention could not all be focused on work.

His absence on past tours had provided him scope for rampant infidelity and such an opportunity resurfacing at this time, it could be argued, stood a good chance of destabilizing his efforts to placate a wife who, not so long ago, had consulted a divorce lawyer. Their reconciliation had been given every appearance of a boost when, in summer, it had been revealed that Jerry Hall, at 41, was pregnant again. She had pronounced herself delighted, telling *OK!* magazine, 'Being a mother is the greatest thing by far I've ever done.'

Friends hailed this development as guaranteed to bring them closer and cement over the cracks in their rocky relationship. None of which had prevented the press, too fresh from the Jaggers' last domestic drama, from querying 'Will Jerry's baby save her marriage?' Psychiatrists, too, devoted whole columns to wondering whether Hall had fallen victim to what is referred to in their profession as 'the Elastoplast baby syndrome'. It was not such a far-out possibility. Six years before, pregnant with Georgia May immediately following a rough patch, Hall had admitted that trying for a third child had been a blatant attempt to salvage their marriage. This baby was due near Christmas, a period when the Stones' tour would be taking a festive break and Jagger planned to be home for the birth.

Rehearsals began in Toronto and were only interrupted in mid-August for a show-stopping press conference staged to announce officially the Bridges to Babylon tour. Images of the Brooklyn Bridge stunt were shown as TV news items around the world. In watery sunshine against the dramatic backdrop of New York's Manhattan skyline and with a police escort, Jagger drove the vintage red Cadillac convertible and the three other band members in grand style towards the waiting press corps.

Their first tour for two years would again be a year-long event and the 32-date US leg was due to kick off on 23 September 1997 at Soldier Field football stadium in Chicago. *Bridges to Babylon*, the new album, would be released one week later. This time they pledged to include some smaller clubs and theatres among the mainly outdoor stadiums. The stampeded began at once for tickets and turned so ferocious that though officially retailing at an average of $55 some were being touted on the black market for anything up to $1500 for front row seats for opening night.

Thirty-three years on from embarking on his first major

American tour, the 54-year-old Jagger was at last showing significant changes in lifestyle. Certainly, the tour had yet to commence, but so far there had been no hard-to-explain tabloid photographs of him with a beauty to distress the pregnant wife back home, helped, no doubt, by the sobering presence of his and Hall's teenage daughter Elizabeth Scarlett who had flown out to attend the opening night. If he wasn't indulging in his latest hobby of 'surfing the net', he spent hours in the gym at the plush Ritz-Carlton Hotel building up his body strength for the marathon string of energetic performances ahead.

He did not disappoint. Having previously played a secret warm-up gig at the Double Doors, a small Toronto club, the big night arrived and the 54,000 strong audience at Chicago's Soldier Field ranging in age from 15-50 were bowled over by the rip-roaring mix of classic hits and new numbers. The stage set had an African theme, the tour logo being the lion of Ethiopia and on either flank stood giant inflatable naked Babylonian female slaves. Criss-crossing this vast expanse was Jagger in an exotic tight-fitting gold lurex-backed suit, and proved himself as lithe and sinuous and dynamic as ever.

Rolling Stones fever had kicked in so hard that cynics attributed much of it to a collective desire to be there for the final curtain. Jagger, too, personally seemed to entertain a degree of doubt as Keith Richards revealed, 'After the fourth or fifth number, Mick turned around, looked at me and said, "It's all going too well!" I said, "Just shut up. Don't say another thing." Mick was in great form from the word go.' It was a view shared by the critics. 'Although the combined ages of Jagger and Richards is 107,' reported the *New York Post*, 'rock's original bad boys can still pull in the crowds.'

Morale was already high when *Bridges to Babylon*, earning many rave reviews, entered *Billboard* at number three, quickly going multi-platinum as the tour rapidly proved on course to becoming the most lucrative of the nineties, suffering no more than a hiccup when, three weeks in, Jagger's bad sore throat forced the Stones to cancel a special MTV gig in a downtown Port Chester theatre; the replacement act turned out to be David Bowie.

Another unscheduled event occurred just before the tour's Christmas break when, while Jagger was on stage at the Georgia

Dome in Atlanta on 9 December, Jerry Hall went into labour a week early in a private London hospital and delivered a baby boy. Jagger was reported to have been devastated at missing the birth of his second son (to be named Gabriel Luke Beauregard Jagger) and had to make do with spending the festive period with his wife and their now family of four. The tour resumed on 9 January 1998 in Canada at the Toronto Skydome whilst tickets for the UK leg went on sale in Britain. With stadium shows planned in more than a dozen European countries throughout the summer, the showcase Wembley Stadium London gig was set for mid-August.

Thirty-five years on in the business, Jagger's standing as a scandalous Stone has endured, defying the age barrier in having proved to be an irresistible magnet to a string of beautiful young women. Professionally his status as a major rock icon is undeniable and one of a handful of undisputed giants of rock who is endlessly imitated, he has influenced a new generation of front men.

He is someone who always provokes a strong reaction; love him or loathe him, the public remains fascinated by him the globe over. He has an elusive quality that is difficult to define, but amid all the high-tech production that creates and cushions today';s superstar bands, the raw sound of Jagger rasping out a Rolling Stones' classic still sends shivers down the spine as the Bridges to Babylon tour continues to bear out. Until the tour ends in September 1998, the rock star father of six and grandfather of two has no chance to slow down and has not, as yet, shown any particular desire to, either. As Jagger puts it, 'For a rock band, we are pushing the envelope as far as age is concerned. There is no mystery about that. There might be a time when I don't want to do quite so much. Right now, I can still sing the songs.'

INDEX

Aerosmith, 185
Aldred, Michael, 36
Allen, Richard, 5
Alley, Patrick, 233-4
Allman Brothers, 175
Altham, Keith, 39
Anderson, Ian, 102
Andrews, Pat, 20
Animals, The, 47
Arnold, P. P., 69, 136
Astor, Josh, 235
Atkins, Eileen, 91-2
Attar, Bachir el, 241
Avory, Mick, 18-19

Bailey, David, 32, 43, 61, 105
Baker, Ginger, 17, 24, 27
Barber, Chris, 13, 18, 26
Barbuscia, Lisa, 251
Barnet, Angie (Bowie), 148, 157-8, 244
Bath, the Lady Virginia, 48
Bath, the Marquess of, 47-8
Beach Boys, The, 50
Beatles, The, 28-30, 31, 43, 58, 63, 83, 84-5, 90, 91, 94, 97, 100, 106, 134, 143, 246
Beaton, Cecil, 77
Beatty, Warren, 149, 157, 184
Beck, Jeff, 14, 28, 165, 219, 228, 231
Beckwith, Bob, 7
Bennett, Estelle, 42
Bennett, Ronnie, 42
Bent, 262, 263, 268
Berger, Helmut, 166
Berry, Chuck, 11, 13, 14, 16, 17, 34
Berry, Dave, 42-3, 56-7

Blues By Five, 24
Blues Incorporated (Blues Inc), 12, 14, 16-17, 18, 24-6, 32
Bono, Sonny, 61-2, 190
Bowie, David, 143, 148, 156-9, 162, 222-4, 227, 244, 262, 270
Bradford, Geoff, 17
Branson, Richard, 252
Breton, Michèle, 97
Bridges to Babylon (album), 269, 270
Bridges to Babylon (tour), 268-71
Brown, James, 50
Browne, Tara, 147
Bruce, Jack, 14, 17, 27, 164
Bruni, Carla, 249-54, 259, 264
Buell, Bebe, 158-60, 178, 185

Caine, Michael, 129
Cammell, Donald, 94, 96, 97, 128, 134
Capote, Truman, 144, 146
Chapman, Mark, 198, 204
Chapman, Tony, 19, 23
Cher, 62, 189
Chess, Marshall, 146
Clapton, Eric, 14, 92, 94, 100, 133, 135, 158, 163-4, 249
Clarke, Allan, 43-4
Cliftons, the, 24
Cobbold, Lady Chryssie, 175-77
Cobbold, Lord David, 175-77
Cooke, Sam, 63
Cooper, Michael, 78, 82
Cream, 14
Curbishley, Father Thomas, 85-6

Daltrey, Roger, 162
D'Arbanville, Patti, 126

INDEX

Davies, Ray, 27, 28
Davis, Cyril, 13, 16, 26
Delon, Nathalie, 135
Dessy, Orsolya, 261
Diddley, Bo, 14, 28
Driberg, Tom, MP, 81, 89
Duchovny, David, 266
Dunbar, John, 44, 61, 69, 70, 94-5, 109, 113
Dunbar, Nicholas, 70, 74, 82, 86, 94, 109-10, 122
Dunn, Alan, 140, 247
Dylan, Bob, 63, 78, 146, 246, 265

Easton, Eric, 30-1, 35, 38, 41, 46, 63, 142
Einhorn, Russell, 263
Enigma, 268
Epstein, Brian, 30
Ertegun, Ahmet, 122-3, 127, 134, 156, 193
Etherington, Alan, 7

Faces, 133, 135, 154-5, 162, 168
Faithfull, Marianne, 44, 61, 69-71, 73-77, 79-80, 82, 83, 85, 86, 87, 90, 92, 94-9, 102-3, 105-6, 108-10, 112-5, 116-7, 122-7, 129, 134, 136, 148, 149, 162, 184, 209
Fensen, Ricky, 19
Ferry, Bryan, 173-4, 184
Fitzcarraldo, 199-201
Ford, Jack, 168
Fordyce, Keith, 36
Fox, James, 92, 96-7
Fraser, Natasha, 197
Fraser, Robert, 50, 76, 77, 80, 82-3, 86
Freejack, 251
Frost, David, 95

Geldof, Bob, 222

Gibbs, Christopher, 51, 76, 106
Glitter, Gary, 55
Godard, Jean-Luc, 93
Gomelsky, Giorgio, 25, 28, 29-31, 37
Greer, Dr Germaine, 64
Guest, Cornelia, 209
Gun, 244-5

Hall, Daryl, 222
Hall, Jerry, 173-4, 184, 186-7, 189, 191, 192-3, 195-6, 197, 202, 205-11, 213, 215-7, 220, 222-4, 228-30, 231, 235-6, 243-4, 245-7, 249-55, 258-9, 262-71
Hansen, Patti, 202, 216
Harris, Rolf, 36
Harris, Steve, 19
Harrison, George, 31, 76, 163
Havers, Michael, QC, 80, 82-3
Herzog, Werner, 199-201
Hollies, The 41, 56
Holly, Buddy, 7, 43
Howard, Jo, 220
Hunt, Karis, 131, 132, 133, 136, 140-1, 142, 150, 154, 191-2, 194
Hunt, Marsha, 105-6, 109, 111-4, 116-7, 122-3, 126-8, 130-3, 134, 136, 140-2, 148, 150, 154, 160-1, 191-2, 194, 213, 223, 253
Hunter, Meredith, 118, 145

Jackson, Rev Jesse, 190
Jackson, Michael, 218-9
Jackson, Piers, 253
Jacobs, David, 46-7
Jagged Films, 268
Jagger, Basil (Joe) (MJ'S father), 2-3, 5, 7, 126, 141

Jagger, Bianca, 128-30, 132, 133-7, 139, 140-2, 147-50, 153-7, 159-64, 166, 168, 171, 172, 174, 178-9, 182-4, 186-8, 189-90, 192, 194-5, 213, 215, 234, 253

Jagger, Christopher Edward (MJ's brother), 2

Jagger, Elizabeth Scarlett (MJ's daughter), 268

Jagger, Eva (MJ's mother), 2-3, 126, 141

Jagger, Gabriel Luke Beauregard (MJ's son), 269

Jagger, Georgia May Ayeesha (MJ's daughter), 252

Jagger, Jade Sheena Jezebel (MJ's daughter), 141-3, 154, 192, 195, 214, 234-5

Jagger, James Leroy Augustine (MJ's son), 223

Jagger, Mick (Michael Philip)
  acting ambitions/film career, 92-3, 94-9, 103, 112-4, 162, 165, 178, 199-201, 251, 262, 268
  childhood/adolescence, 1-8
  court appearances/law suits, 61, 76, 78-82, 121, 147, 150, 153-5, 161, 192-3, 217, 234
  death threats/rumours, 76, 116, 145, 164, 175, 204-5, 214, 216, 242
  drugs, use of and convictions, 53, 59, 66, 73-9, 81-2, 84, 86, 94, 96-7, 105, 121, 126, 144, 146, 148, 195, 213, 224
  early bands, 6-7, 15-17
  health problems, 68, 80, 109, 113, 172
  jealousy/trouble within the Stones, 27, 35, 37, 39, 51, 55, 68, 79, 87, 92, 98-104, 113, 137, 168, 180, 183, 186, 191,
  196, 201, 204, 214, 220, 221-3, 230, 236-8, 250
  marital strife/divorce, 137, 140, 142, 149-50, 155, 160-4, 166, 178, 180, 183-8, 189, 193-5, 249-55, 263-8, 269
  marriage, 135-6, 247
  musical influences, 5-7, 12, 13, 67
  relationships/casual sex, 5, 7-8, 12, 26, 32, 33-6, 40, 42, 43-5, 49, 57-61, 65-66, 69-72, 77, 79, 83, 85-6, 94-101, 102-3, 105-6, 109, 111-6, 130-33, 140, 147, 158-9, 173-5, 178, 184-5, 187, 197, 202-3, 206-11, 215, 220, 236, 246, 249, 251, 253, 259-61, 263
  sexual ambiguity, 24, 38, 45, 69, 75, 86, 116-7, 143, 157, 166, 203
  solo recordings/tours, 196, 218-23, 227-33, 237-8, 251-2
  songwriting, 39, 41, 45, 50, 54, 59, 62, 66-7, 84, 86, 90, 94, 156, 162

James, Catherine, 125

Johns, Glyn, 27-8

Jones, Darryl, 257-8

Jones, Lewis Brian Hopkin, 6, 14-21, 23-32, 34, 36-41, 43, 47, 50, 51, 54, 56, 57, 62, 64, 66-8, 70, 75-6, 79-80, 81, 82, 84, 86-7, 92-4, 98, 100, 101, 102, 103-4, 105-14, 124, 125, 127, 142, 147, 155, 164, 241, 257

Jones, Paul, 15-16

Julius, Anthony, 265

Kenner, Janice, 125

Keylock, Tom, 80, 90, 107

King, B. B., 143

INDEX
....

Klein, Allen, 63-4, 70, 87, 103, 109, 114, 127, 140, 217
Korner, Alexis, 13-14, 16, 17-19, 23, 24, 28
Kramer, Nicky, 76
Kruk, Nicole, 259-61, 266

LaBelle, Patti, 65
Laine, Denny, 111
Latham, Kathy, 253
Lawrence, Linda, 25, 38
Lear, Amanda, 147-8
Lennon, John, 39, 51, 84, 99, 101, 102, 134, 142, 162, 175, 178, 179, 191, 195-6, 198, 202
Lewis, Jerry Lee, 6
Lindsay-Hogg, Michael, 55-6, 59, 63, 68, 89, 91-2, 100, 101-2, 110, 112, 156, 160, 162, 164, 190, 203, 205-6, 213, 232-3
Little Boy Blue and the Blue Boys, 16
Little, Carlo, 19
Little Richard, 6
Loewenstein, Prince Rupert, 106-7, 108, 114, 127, 132

Mankowitz, Gered, 58
Mansfield, John, 32
Manuel, Vivienne, 145
Marriott, Steve, 82
Marsden, Gerry, 40
Mason, Dave, 28
May, Phil, 15, 19, 28, 45, 66, 110
Mayall, John, 102
McCartney, Paul, 39, 94, 135, 177
McGowan, Cathy, 36-7, 57-8, 62
McLagan, Ian, 155
McLaren, Malcolm, 192
McPherson, Elle, 255
Mercury, Freddie, 143, 169, 218, 224

Miller, Pamela (Pamela des Barres), 115-7, 122, 147
Mitchelson, Marvin, 189, 191-2
Moody Blues, The, 111
Moon, Keith, 135
Morrison, Jim, 94

Nash, Graham, 43
Ned Kelly (film), 112, 114, 125-6, 132
Neidpath, Lord James, 235
Nicholson, Jack, 144, 177
Nickerson, Camilla, 236
Nureyev, Rudolph, 142
Nutting, Cherie, 241

Oates, John, 222
Ogilvy, Lord David, 235
Oldham, Andrew Loog, 30-1, 33-4, 35, 38-9, 40, 41, 42, 44, 48, 49, 55, 56, 58, 62-3, 69, 70, 84, 86, 119, 142
One Plus One (film), 93
O'Neal, Ryan, 160, 180
Ono, Yoko, 99, 101, 142, 195, 202

Page, Jimmy, 115, 117, 165
Pallenberg, Anita, 67, 69, 75, 76, 79-80, 92, 96-9, 102, 114, 116, 130, 136, 140, 147, 150, 155, 161, 180
Parsons, Gram, 115
Peel, John, 133
Pendleton, Harold, 18, 19, 26
Performance (film), 92, 94-5, 98, 102-3, 125, 132
Perrin, Janie, 218
Perrin, Les, 104, 133, 135-6, 218
Peters, Mary, 53
Pink Floyd, 175
Pitney, Gene, 41, 43
Polanski, Roman, 178
Potier, Suki, 100, 126

Presley, Elvis, 6, 12, 146, 246
Preston, Billy, 173
Pretty Things, The, 15, 16, 19, 45, 110
Proby, P. J., 65

Queen, 140, 142, 169, 218

Rajlich, Jana, 264
Rankin, Mark, 244-5
Redding, Noel, 62-3, 85, 111
Rees-Mogg, Lord William, 83-4, 86, 89-90
Richard, Cliff, 41
Richard, Keith, 1, 3, 5, 11, 12, 13, 15-18, 20, 24-6, 31, 34, 38-40, 41-4, 48, 50, 54, 59, 62, 64, 66, 67-8, 70-1, 75, 76, 77, 78-80, 81-4, 87-91, 93-100, 102-4, 105-12, 124, 127, 130, 133, 135, 136, 139-42, 145-6, 150-1, 153, 154-5, 161, 163, 164, 165, 167-8, 171-4, 180-1, 183, 186-7, 190-1, 192-3, 195, 197, 202, 204, 207, 214-7, 220-1, 223-4, 227-8, 230-1, 236-8, 239-41, 245, 255, 257, 261, 270
Richardson, Tony, 103
Robinson, John, 85
Roeg, Nicolas, 94, 96
Rolling Stones (the Rollin' Stones/ the Stones), 1, 6, 16, 18, 20-1, 23, 24, 28, 30, 33-51, 81, 83, 85, 90-102, 105, 133, 134, 139-47, 150-52, 153-58, 160, 161-66, 168-9, 171-8, 179, 180-1, 183-8, 189, 191-7, 199, 201-7, 214-6, 217-8, 219-25, 227, 230-32, 234, 236-7, 239-46, 250-2, 255, 257-61, 268, 269-71

Ronettes, The, 42
Ronstadt, Linda, 180
Rossmore, Lord, 124
Rowe, Dick, 31
Ruggles-Brise, Col. Sir John, 85
Rundgren, Todd, 158, 176, 178, 185
Ryle, John, 213-4, 219, 222

Sangster, Robert, 209
Satriani, Joe, 231
Schifano, Mario, 116, 122, 209
Schneiderman, David, 76-8
Sex Pistols, The, 192
Shadows, The, 48
Sherman, Martin, 262
Shrimpton, Chrissie, 31-2, 33-8, 39, 40-4, 46, 47, 49, 53, 58-61, 64-6, 68-9, 71, 73, 74-5, 87, 107, 125, 127, 134, 149, 179-80
Shrimpton, Jean, 32
Simon, Carly, 146, 148, 160
Simple Minds, 245
Smith, Mandy, 228
Solinger, Michael, 262
Soskice, Frank, 85
Spector, Phil, 34, 42
Spiller, Leslie, 191
Starr, Ringo, 60, 135
Stephaich, Pauline, 264
Stewart, Dave, 228, 230
Stewart, Ian (Stu), 17, 24, 31, 144, 202, 224
Stewart, Rod, 167
Stigwood, Robert, 42
Stills, Stephen, 114, 136
Stoppard, Tom, 268
Sullivan, Ed, 58
Sylvestre, Cleo, 25-6, 32, 34, 35, 36, 42

Taylor, Dick, 4-8, 11, 14-19, 23, 65, 261
Taylor, James, 147
Taylor, Mick (Michael Kevin), 102, 105, 108, 110, 114, 127, 140, 149, 151, 161-2, 164-5, 205, 240
Temple, Julien, 220
Thurman, Uma, 263
Tosh, Peter, 197
Townshend, Pete, 219
Trudeau, Margaret, 181-2
Trudeau, Pierre, 181
Turner, Ike, 54, 69, 116, 144
Turner, Tina, 54, 69, 116, 144, 222
Tyler, Steve, 185

Vadim, Roger, 135
Vicious, Sid, 192-3
Vidal, Gore, 201

Warhol, Andy, 134, 146, 158, 168
Waters, Muddy, 11, 13, 15, 18
Watts, Charles Robert, 14, 16, 24, 40, 49, 64, 65, 75, 104, 112, 114, 127, 142, 151, 196, 217, 220, 240, 257-8
White, Michael, 268
Whitehouse, Mary, 95
Who, The, 63, 83, 101
Wickham, Vicki, 35, 37, 54-5, 57-8, 61-2
Williams, Robin, 260
Wilson, Brian, 56
Wimbish, Doug, 257
Winwood, Steve, 28, 101
Wood, Ron, 154, 163, 164-5, 167-8, 169, 172-3, 182, 202, 214, 217, 220, 240, 241, 245, 257
Woods, Robert, 117

Wyman, Bill, 24-5, 40, 41, 54, 56, 64, 65, 75, 90, 104, 109-10, 112, 114, 127, 142, 151, 153, 167, 196, 201, 207, 217, 219, 228, 230, 236, 239-40, 252, 255, 257, 261

Yardbirds, The, 28

Zamoyski, Count Adam, 235
Zeffirelli, Franco, 178

OTHER TITLES FROM BLAKE PUBLISHING

Up and Down with the Rolling Stones *by Tony Sanchez*
'The most famous rock 'n' roll book of all time!'

The People

The most exciting book ever written about the Rolling Stones.
Up and Down with the Rolling Stones has been a best-seller in the UK,
USA, Germany and Japan. Illustrated with more than 100 of the
author's original photographs.

Oasis — What's the Story? *by Ian Robertson*
'*What's the Story* deserves to stay on the best-selling list for a long time
to come.'

The Times

Ian Robertson, one-time Oasis tour manager, tells of life on the road
with the most exciting and outspoken rock band in the world today.

Sting: The Secret Life of Gordon Sumner *by Wensley Clarkson*
For more than twenty years, Sting has been rock's most complex and
intelligent star. He has sold more than 200 million records worldwide,
but is also a secretive man who reveals little of his true self to the world.
This first-ever full biography explodes the myths and creates a fresh
insight into this quintessential star.

Marc Bolan: The Legendary Years *by John and Shan Bramley*
Cult rock star Marc Bolan and T.Rexstacy live again in this official
biography from the Marc Bolan fan club. Bolan's friend, photographer
Keith Morris, contributes 50 cherished and unpublished images from his
personal collection.
This chronicle of Bolan's life details the golden years between 1970 and
1973. Supported by a complete discography and full listings of songs
and diary dates, this is the essential book for every Bolan fan.

Prices include post and packing in the UK.
Overseas and Eire, add £1.00 to the price of each book.

To order by credit card, telephone 0171 381 0666.

Alternatively, fill in the coupon below and send it, with your cheque or
postal order made payable to Blake Publishing Limited, to:

Blake Publishing Limited
Mail Order Department
3 Bramber Court, 2 Bramber Road,
London W14 9PB

Please send me a copy of each of the titles ticked below:

☐ **UP AND DOWN WITH THE ROLLING STONES** £6.99
☐ **OASIS — WHAT'S THE STORY?** £9.99
☐ **STING: THE SECRET LIFE OF GORDON SUMNER** £15.99
☐ **MARC BOLAN: THE LEGENDARY YEARS** £9.99

Name...

Address..

....

....

Postcode..

Please allow 14 days for delivery.